* * * * * * * * * * * * * * The Yamasee War

INDIANS OF THE SOUTHEAST
Series Editors

Michael D. Green
University of North Carolina

Theda Perdue
University of North Carolina

Advisory Editors

Leland Ferguson
University of South Carolina

Mary Young
University of Rochester

THE YAMASEE WAR

A Study of Culture, Economy, and Conflict
in the Colonial South   WILLIAM L. RAMSEY

University of Nebraska Press ⁕ Lincoln and London

Parts of chapters 1, 3, 4, and 6 originally appeared in "'Something Cloudy in Their Looks': The Origins of the Yamasee War Reconsidered," *Journal of American History* 90 (June 2003): 44–75. Copyright © Organization of American Historians http://www .oah.org/. Reprinted with permission.

Parts of chapters 2 and 7 originally appeared in the following articles: "A Coat for 'Indian Cuffy': Mapping the Boundary between Freedom and Slavery in Colonial South Carolina," *South Carolina Historical Magazine* 103 (January 2002): 48–66; "'All & Singular the Slaves': A Demographic Profile of Indian Slavery in Colonial South Carolina," *Money, Trade, and Power: The Evolution of a Planter Society in Colonial South Carolina,* ed. Jack P. Greene, Rosemary Brana-Shute, and Randy J. Sparks (Columbia: University of South Carolina Press, 2001), 170–90.

Library of Congress Cataloging-in-Publication Data
Ramsey, William L., 1961–
The Yamasee War : a study of culture, economy, and conflict in the colonial South / William L. Ramsey.
p. cm.—(Indians of the Southeast)
Includes bibliographical references and index.
ISBN 978-0-8032-3972-2 (cloth : alk. paper)
ISBN 978-0-8032-3280-8 (paper : alk. paper)
1. Yamasee War, 1715–1716. 2. Yamasee Indians—Wars.
3. Yamasee Indians—Commerce. 4. Indian slaves—South Carolina—History. 5. South Carolina—History—Colonial period, ca. 1600–1775. I. Title.
E83.713.R36 2008
973.2'5—dc22
2007040974

Set in Quadraat by Kim Essman.
Designed by Ashley Muehlbauer.

For Mei-Yee

Contents

Illustrations

Acknowledgments

Daniel Richter once referred to the writing of his classic book on the Iroquois as "the ordeal of *The Ordeal of the Longhouse*." Likewise, writing the history of the Yamasee War has been a war in its own right for me. That I have managed at long last to stop fighting my way through the numerous problems associated with this topic and stand up in polite society as if I had actually held my own is due mainly to a number of people who encouraged me in the effort or made it possible with their own work or guidance.

Academically, these include the handful of scholars who prepared the way for me by fighting their own battles against daunting odds: Peter H. Wood, Kathryn E. Holland Braund, J. Lietch Wright Jr., Charles Hudson, Daniel H. Usner Jr., Steven J. Oatis, Steven Hahn, James Merrell, Alan Gallay, Joshua Piker, Tom Hatley, Alex Moore, Theda Perdue, and Michael D. Green. Thanks also to my dissertation director at Tulane, Sylvia R. Frey, who taught me to see history from different perspectives. I am especially grateful to Ken Davis and the members of the Muscogee Red Stick Society who helped me understand Muscogee warrior traditions a little better. It was one of the great honors of my life to meet and speak on several occasions with John Yahola, a venerable elder and warrior in the Red Stick tradition. If I have misunderstood or misrepresented Creek history or culture, it is the fault of my own incompetence in spite of their generous and patient efforts to help me.

Funding for research and travel were provided by the American Philosophical Society's Phillips Fund for Native American Research, by the American Historical Association's Kraus research grant, and by the University of Idaho.

Both personally and professionally, I owe an enormous debt of gratitude to my parents, William and Lilly, who nourished my curiosity always and forestalled the consequences for me at key moments. Above all, I owe eternal thanks to my wife, Mei-Yee Kung. She listened to me talk about the Yamasee War on a daily basis for a dozen years. When I felt like giving up, she hugged me late at night or ordered me another cup of coffee as I gazed through the restaurant window in a depressed manner. She pounded on the door of the North Carolina State Archives to get a copy of a document after hours when I was too embarrassed. Last, my son Will lifted my spirits on many occasions by inviting me away from my embattled desk to play with him and his friend Thomas the Tank Engine on the imaginary Island of Sodor. It was there, really, that I learned how important it is to be reliable and patient.

Series Editors' Introduction

The Yamasee War was a watershed moment in the histories of Southern Indians as well as colonial Carolina. It reshaped economic and political relations between the tribes and Carolina, ended the Indian slave trade, and led to the collapse of proprietary government and the splitting of the colony into North and South. We have long known of its importance, but until now no one has developed a book-length study of the war and its causes and consequences. William Ramsey's work is not simply the first of its kind; it is remarkable in its breadth of research, sophistication of inquiry, and development of argument. Ramsey demonstrates that "trader abuses," the traditional explanation for the development of the largest and most threatening native coalition formed in the colonial South, fails to capture the story of the Yamasee War, either before or after the event, for either the Indians or the Carolinians. Trade is, of course, at the center of his story, and he sees it both in terms of the Atlantic market economy and as a central factor of Indian culture change. But he also sees it in terms of the development of plantation slavery in Carolina, the Indian slave trade, and the social and cultural impacts of these factors in both Indian and Anglo societies. Ramsey's argument captures the broader, more comprehensive and significant changes at work in South Carolina (as part of the Atlantic world) and in Indian country. We are most gratified to welcome Bill Ramsey's important book into our Indians of the Southeast series.

Michael D. Green
Theda Perdue

Introduction
The Problems

On April 14, 1715, the Yamasee Indians welcomed a group of South Carolinians in their principal town of Pocotaligo, south of Charles Town (now Charleston) by about sixty miles. Alarmed at reports of Yamasee unrest, the English had come to reassure the Indians of their friendship and alliance, and the talks appeared to have gone well. Everyone went to bed that evening amicably, "as if seeming well pleased." In the morning, however, Good Friday, the Yamasees killed the majority of the British negotiators. They spent the remainder of the day torturing those unfortunate enough to have survived the massacre at dawn. When the Carolinians cried out in agony, "My God," Yamasee warriors danced about repeating, "My God, my God." Thomas Nairne, as Indian agent for the colony, received special attention. He was "loaded" with wood and roasted for several days "before he was allowed to die." Clearly, the Carolinians had neglected an important step in the dialogue.[1]

In the weeks following, it became apparent that the English had neglected a great deal across the entire region. Warriors from virtually every nation in the South, from the Catawbas and their piedmont neighbors in the Carolinas to the Choctaws of Mississippi (see map 1), joined together in one of the most potent native coalitions ever to oppose the British in colonial North America. Southeastern Indians destroyed most of South Carolina's plantation districts and came within a few miles of Charles Town itself during the first year of the war. Shocked and bewildered, South Carolinians found themselves surrounded and under attack "on every side but the sea-side."[2]

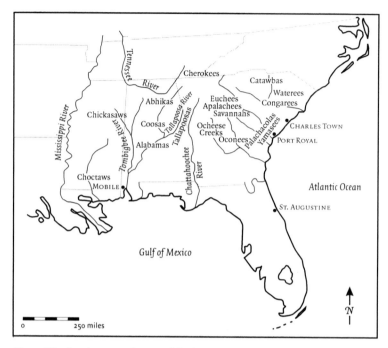

Map 1. The Southeast on the eve of the Yamasee War, 1715

The Yamasee War, as it has come to be known, has long been recognized as one of the most important events in southern colonial history. According to historian Gary B. Nash, Native American combatants came "as close to wiping out the European colonists as ever [they] came during the colonial period." By 1718 when peace returned to much of the region, over four hundred colonists and an untold number of Native American warriors had perished, making the conflict a serious candidate for America's bloodiest war in proportion to the populations involved. The war spurred extensive tribal migrations and alliance realignments that changed the diplomatic and cultural landscape of the region for the remainder of the eighteenth century, and it led directly to the collapse of South Carolina's proprietary government in 1719. British imperial responses to the war, moreover, prompted the first calls for a buffer colony to protect Carolina's southern border, culminating in the establishment of Georgia in 1733.[3]

The Yamasee War easily ranks with King Philip's War and Pontiac's rebellion as one of the major "Indian Wars" of the colonial era, yet it has not received the same level of scholarly attention. Pontiac's rebellion has been treated by Francis Parkman and, most recently, Gregory Evans Dowd, while King Philip's War has almost become a field unto itself, boasting at least five major studies in the last six years. For much of the twentieth century, by contrast, the only historical discussions of the Yamasee War were chapter-length treatments in Verner W. Crane's landmark study *The Southern Frontier* and Chapman J. Milling's *Red Carolinians*, both published more than sixty years ago. The conflict has traditionally been cast in moral terms as a righteous effort on the part of Native Americans to exact vengeance against unscrupulous and abusive Europeans. Verner Crane, for instance, viewed it as a "far reaching revolt against the Carolinian trading regime," in which Native Americans across the South rose up in anger over the "tyrannies of the Charles Town traders." John R. Swanton, writing in the same decade, also felt that the "misconduct of some traders" had been the "immediate cause" of the war but went on to add that fears of enslavement may have prompted the Yamasees to action as well. Elements of these versions were refined, interwoven, and reiterated for a generation and indeed continue to influence current scholarship in subtle ways.[4]

"Misconduct" and "abuse" as defined in European terms, however, do not necessarily add up to an explanation of war. Around the year 1711, for instance, a British trader named Alexander Longe became embroiled in a bitter feud with the Euchee Indians. Although the Euchees were considered allies of South Carolina, Longe got his revenge a few years later when a Euchee warrior unwisely came to his store to purchase gunpowder. According to a Cherokee leader named Partridge, the trader piled up the powder next to his unfortunate client and then "sett fier to itt and blew him up." Outraged over that and other affronts to their alliance network, Charles Town officials moved aggressively to prosecute him, and early twentieth-century historians such as Crane and Swanton followed suit. The Cherokee Indians, however, viewed matters very differently. They remained steadfast in their friendship and support for Alexander Longe even as Carolinians sought to bring him to justice. Indeed, as his fellow Englishmen suffered within their fever-ridden fortifications, he safely spent the entirety of the Yamasee War in Cherokee territory and continued trading there as an honored guest through the 1720s.[5]

"Misconduct" must obviously have meant different things to different people. For purposes of historical analysis, the term does more to obscure than to explain the Anglo-Indian trade relationship prior to the Yamasee War. As such, its use inevitably distorts any effort to assess the origins and root meaning of that seminal conflict. Alexander Longe may well deserve the bad reputation that historians have given him, and his actions undoubtedly did much to alienate the Euchees from the English interest. But there was clearly another facet to his career among the Cherokees that has not been adequately explored. If Longe was merely abusive, as traditional accounts assert, and Charles Town officials were merely attempting to protect their native allies and administer justice, why did the Cherokees embrace Longe and attack South Carolina? Surely, there are some problems here that demand rethinking.

METHODS

Modern studies of European-Indian exchange relations have moved far beyond the moralistic approach of the Crane and Swanton school. Recognizing that indigenous approaches to commodity exchange were embedded in complex social, political, economic, and cultural systems, scholars have sought to understand those systems and interpret the significance of intercultural trade for Native American participants. Such efforts have produced a more nuanced portrait of frontier relations in which profoundly different peoples encountered, accommodated, and influenced each other in pursuit of a shared objective: trade. Historian Richard White's study of French-Algonquian relations in the Great Lakes region, *The Middle Ground*, is perhaps the most notable achievement of this new approach. In his view, Indians and Europeans interested in trading with one another were forced to develop new, mutually intelligible ways of communicating that borrowed heavily from each culture. As a result, in certain places and times where the process reached its fullest development, the respective worlds of natives and newcomers sometimes "melted at the edges and merged" to create a new set of common understandings and practices specifically related to the trade.[6]

White termed this new, mutually created nexus the "middle ground," and the metaphor has been eagerly taken up, and occasionally debated, by a broad range of historians, anthropologists, and ethnohistorians. In fact the notoriety of the phrase itself almost seems to have overshadowed White's original methodology. The term is often used simplistically—for instance, as a geographical marker to designate the locus of intercultural relations; the place, that is, where cultures and cultural actors engage each other. As such, it sometimes functions as little more than a fashionable modern equivalent for the word *frontier*. White himself described the middle ground as the "place in between" peoples and cultures where cultural accommodation and change took place. Yet his model involved much more. The middle ground, he argued, was a new creation growing out of those accommodations, "a new set of common conventions" built by mutual innovation. Its creation, moreover, depended on a rough balance of power between participants that necessitated accommodation.[7]

In this respect the middle ground presents a challenge of sorts to scholars interested in analyzing specific cross-cultural conversations. Most ethnohistorical studies share White's interest in the ways that different groups engaged one another in a struggle to influence and determine the meanings, forms, and terms of the encounter. Cultures rarely seem to "melt at the edges and merge," however, even in discourse studies that employ the middle ground metaphor as a location for intercultural dialogue. Cultures and cultural actors remain distinct, driven by distinct objectives, as they creatively engage in cultural innovation to gain advantage in the relationship. New forms and tactics do emerge, as White points out, yet they are developed and deployed as the characteristic creations of one group or another for its own purposes. In many cases those new forms of discourse reflect or mimic the opposing culture in order to curry influence, yet they remain primarily the products of distinct voices pursuing objectives relevant to group identities. James Merrell's study of intercultural mediators on the colonial Pennsylvania frontier, *Into the American Woods*, for instance, focuses on what the English and Indians "had to say, and how they said it." Yet Merrell's search for "patterns in the tapestry of negotiation" nevertheless draws a clear line between participants. There was, for Merrell, no "debatable land between native and newcomer." Delaware Indians and Pennsylvania colonists were, instead, "firmly anchored on one side of the cultural divide or the other."[8]

Much serious thinking about approaches to Indian-white relations has thus made a new consideration of the Yamasee War especially timely, and several studies have begun this work. James Merrell's groundbreaking work on the Catawbas, *The Indians' New*

World, sought for the first time to demonstrate regional differences in the motivations of Indian participants, and Tom Hatley's The Dividing Paths offered unprecedented insight into the Cherokee experience. Alan Gallay's Bancroft prize–winning study The Indian Slave Trade provided the first detailed portrait of the traffic in Indian slaves that destabilized the South in the years prior to the Yamasee War. More recently Steven J. Oatis's A Colonial Complex challenged the traditional conception of the war as a preconceived conspiracy, arguing that it developed as a chain reaction of various alliance networks working independently. Finally, Steven Hahn's The Invention of the Creek Nation sought to assess the importance of the war in helping to shape Creek national identity and foreign policy.[9]

The present study seeks to build on these achievements to provide a new interpretation of the Yamasee War and its place in southern history. Although organized chronologically, the book does not seek to provide a narrative account of the war. Instead, it defines a number of problems associated with each phase of the conflict and pursues the most likely answers. By and large those problems involve the ways in which different peoples and their related cultures and economies—Indian, African, and European—influenced, understood, and interacted with one another before, during, and after the conflagration: phases identified here as tinder, spark, fire, and ash. In many cases, intercultural interactions in each phase were influenced heavily by South Carolina's growing involvement in the Atlantic economy, which spurred a series of complex changes that played a major role in both the origins of the war and the postwar settlement. The study is thus of necessity an attempt to come to grips with prevailing academic ideas about the nature of intercultural exchange and market involvement. In this context Richard White's middle ground metaphor figures less prominently than what historian Philip Deloria has called the "dialogic process" of White's methodology, his focus on the mechanics and import of cross-cultural interaction. The following chapters therefore focus wherever possible on recorded instances of conversation as windows into the competing identities and agendas at work in this history.[10]

FIRE AND ASH

The curious anomaly of Alexander Longe, a trader roundly reviled as abusive by colonial South Carolinians and modern historians, cries out for such a new perspective, for he was not regarded in that light by the Cherokees. Why not? Another narrative retelling of his crimes will not likely provide much additional insight to the problem. Somehow we must suspend the moral reflex when Longe blows up a Euchee warrior in his store with gunpowder. Instead we must ask questions. Why did the Cherokees like him in the first place? Was his store located in Euchee or Cherokee territory? Were observers of the event Euchees or Cherokees? How did the Cherokees feel about the Euchees? If we regard the episode as a form of dialogue, as a symbolic act, a form of communication intended for an audience, as it absolutely was, new problems of this sort emerge naturally. Even if the answers are sometimes fragmentary, the act of framing new questions goes a long way toward solving the paradox of Alexander Longe.

It also helps build a new foundation for discussing the origins and broader historical meaning of the Yamasee War. As it turns out, Longe blew up a Euchee Indian on Cherokee territory in front of a Cherokee audience who may have had reasons to resent the Euchees. Either he got lucky on this occasion or he knew what he was doing. The present study argues for the latter conclusion. Indeed, Longe's "Small Postscript on the Ways and Manners of the Indians Called

Cherokees" reveals him to be a shrewd and sympathetic observer of Cherokee culture, religion, and social practice. If he and other traders were in fact participating in a sophisticated way in local Indian politics prior to the Yamasee War, the nature of that local relationship must be examined. Moreover, if local participation and activism brought British traders like Longe into conflict with the government of South Carolina, as it often did, then it may also have played some part in bringing the native peoples of the South into conflict with the colony.

The violence of the conflict lends itself to scrutiny as a form of dialogue as well. When Native American warriors conspicuously spared English churches from the torch, collected armloads of red fabric, and waged a parallel war against domestic livestock, they communicated a complex set of priorities that need to be considered. By the same token, Governor Charles Craven's characterization of South Carolina's native enemies as "monsters of man kind" communicated more than simple anger. Because the low-country plantation regime relied heavily on Indian slave labor in 1715, efforts to dehumanize the external enemy inevitably entailed a reconsideration of the colony's internal human landscape. For Native Americans and English colonists alike, therefore, the rhetoric of violence expressed during the war was rooted in preexisting cultural, economic, and social realities.

Such voices expressed existing anxieties, but they also anticipated desired solutions in an era of chronic change and instability. The chapters that follow therefore trace an evolving, multifaceted series of discussions among Indians, Africans, and the English in an effort to understand the multitude of choices that transformed the South. Encoded in these colonial conversations, it is argued, are clues that can help refine and deepen some of the prevailing historiographical debates about southern history. The themes that became conspicuous in Peter Wood's classic book *Black Majority*, for instance, were clearly visible in the first year of the Yamasee War for reasons that Wood did not fully recognize. Scholarly debates about postwar Creek diplomacy, elucidated over the last thirty years by David Corkran, Michael Green, Kathryn Holland Braund, Steven Hahn, and Joshua Piker, can be cast in starker relief by restoring the dialogic tension of key negotiations. On an even broader level, Native American trade complaints prior to the Yamasee War, coupled with their postwar trade agreements with South Carolina and the internal economic adjustments made by the English, contain the germs of modern historical arguments about the capitalist or anticapitalist nature of the nineteenth-century southern slave economy, framed by historians Eugene Genovese, Robert William Fogel, James Oakes, and others.

In this sense the current work pursues the same ambition articulated by historian Daniel H. Usner Jr., who endeavored in *Indians, Settlers, and Slaves* to draw southern historical memory—so long mired in its obsession with the nineteenth century and the racial simplifications of the Civil War—farther back into its multiethnic colonial roots.[11] Students of history interested in the Old South simply cannot understand it adequately without reference to the older South that gave it birth. To state this more poetically, the nature of the tinder that fueled the fires of the Yamasee War determined the patterns of ash that followed it.

PART 1 Tinder

1. Carolinians in Indian Country

The fire kindled at the Yamasee town of Pocotaligo in April 1715 might be attributed to localized disaffection had it not spread in time to engulf the entire indigenous South. That it found ready fuel among neighboring nations in the early weeks of the war suggests the existence of a common set of grievances among certain nations. In this chapter I analyze the nature of the tinder that made possible the spread of the conflagration over such a broad region. I argue that participation in trade elicited a series of specific complaints from a distinct cluster of Indian Nations prior to the war, and in so doing, I challenge some of the prevailing assumptions about trader misconduct and abusiveness.

This is difficult, because Verner W. Crane and John R. Swanton have cast a long shadow over southern colonial historiography. Their explanation of the causes of the Yamasee War went unquestioned for more than fifty years. More recent studies have explored multicausal approaches to the war's origins, including environmental pressures and the consequences of dependency on Anglo-Indian relations. In addition to recognizing for the first time the need to consider geographical differences among Native American participants, James Merrell's work on the Catawbas broke new ground by assessing native perceptions and misperceptions of Europeans as filtered through the unreliable lens of trade. With few exceptions, however, even these studies routinely fall back upon the vocabulary of abuse and misconduct pioneered by Crane and Swanton in the 1920s.[1]

Efforts to apply dependency theory, in particular, have demonstrated a decidedly teleological tendency. Perhaps because Anglo-Indian trade relations had such a brief history prior to the Yamasee War, dating only to the 1680s, such studies tend to accelerate the advance of trade dependence excessively. At the same time, they often oversimplify the correlation between "abusive" English traders and the hegemonic power supposedly conferred on the English by advanced dependency. In short, they anticipate too much in too simple a manner in too little time. The present study invokes dependency theory sparingly and only to recalibrate scholarly assumptions about its rate of progress in the colonial South, on the one hand, and to urge, on the other, a more complex treatment of its local manifestations that includes not only the behavior of English traders but economic, cultural, and social changes as well.[2]

Southeastern Indians had their own ideas about proper and improper conduct and, for their own reasons, submitted a large number of trade-related complaints to Charles Town officials. Those complaints need to be analyzed as far as possible on their own terms as part of a complex, ongoing dialogue between southeastern Indians and Europeans. Yet in order to do so, native and European voices need to be untangled from each other to restore the basic outlines of the discourse. Some of the complaints traditionally cited as evidence of trader "misconduct," for example, were not submitted by Native Americans at all. In many cases they were submitted by British traders themselves and probably represent partisan rhetoric directed at opposing trade factions. In the *Journals of the Commissioners of the Indian Trade*, by far the richest and most systematic source of such complaints, roughly thirty-two of the sixty-five cases adjudicated between 1710 and 1715 involved internecine squabbles between British traders. The thirty cases that clearly emanated from Native American sources, however, contain a wealth of information about the sometimes subtle problems plaguing Anglo-Indian relations. The priorities framed in these complaints differed in several respects from those of British traders, and the well-founded frustrations of the peoples who submitted them deserve a more thorough analysis than mass categorization as complaints about "abuse." By plotting the Anglo-Indian dialogue and insisting on the importance of identity as a determinative element in the shaping of discourse, the present study seeks to build the foundation for a native interpretive perspective that revolves around specific, practical issues raised by Native Americans themselves, that recognizes geographical distinctions, and that acknowledges the asymmetrical distribution of power.[3]

GENDER

It may be best to begin where many historical accounts of British trade behavior prior to the Yamasee War have ended: with accusations of beatings and murders. These glaring incidents figure prominently in many characterizations of the Anglo-Indian trade relationship, yet they represented a distinct minority when compared with other categories of complaint. Only five English traders were ever accused of such crimes by Native Americans in the *Journals of the Commissioners*. At Altamaha, for instance, the principal town among the lower Yamasee settlements near Port Royal, South Carolina, a trader named Alexander Nicholas reportedly "beat a Woman that he kept for his Wife so that she dyed and the Child within her." He later beat up "another Woman being King Altimahaw's Sister." Nicholas then proceeded to a nearby Yamasee town and beat "the Chasee [probably Chechesee] King's

Wife." The headman of Altamaha finally sent word to the Commissioners of the Indian Trade in 1711 that if Nicholas were not removed and punished, the Indians "would quit the Town." A warrant was quickly issued for the trader's arrest. At Savano Town on the Savannah River, meanwhile, the Apalachee Indians had reason to resent the presence of Jess Crosley, who, "being jealous of a Whore of his, beat and abused an Apalachia Indian Man in a barbarous Manner." At another unidentified Apalachee village, Phillip Gilliard "took a young Indian against her Will for his Wife." He reportedly got her "drunk with Rum and locked her up" and then threatened to kill the girl's mother "becaus she would not leve her Daughter behind."[4]

There is no excuse, of course, for such behavior, but there is none either for historians who have taken it at face value, for it conceals a deeper set of issues that must be considered in assessing the nature of Anglo-Indian relations. Overwhelmingly, these incidents involved affronts to native women. Though prevalent in the patriarchal societies of western Europe, violence against women was virtually unheard of among many of the matrilineal societies of the indigenous South. Englishmen among the Cherokees, for instance, marveled that "the women Rules the Rostt and weres the brichess." On those occasions when domestic violence did erupt, moreover, it was invariably the women who "beat thire husbands within an Inch of thire life." Indeed, the typical Cherokee man would "not Resesst thire poure if the woman was to beate his breans out." Traders who raised their fists against native women therefore struck at more than a single victim. They attacked the social values of the community at large.[5]

Traders who married native women encountered a variety of sociocultural perils. Such unions offered immediate advantages for traders, such as kinship privileges and assistance in learning the language, but they also produced long-term problems for all concerned. The parties brought opposing expectations and presumptions to the marriage. Native women probably anticipated that they would rule the "rostt" and wear the "brichess," but English husbands viewed the roost and the britches as rightfully their own. Marriages that produced offspring may have been particularly prone to trouble. The typical English trader probably expected his children to take his surname and be subject to his authority as head of the household. His native wife, on the other hand, may have anticipated that her children would belong to her lineage, as was customary, and would fall primarily under the authority of herself, her mother, and her siblings. Indeed, in the typical Indian household, the dominant male figure in the lives of the children was the mother's brother, not the children's father. Such divergent agendas may have led to frequent episodes of domestic turmoil.[6]

Some traders may have responded to the dilemma by simply removing their children from the mother's influence and sending them to be raised in Charles Town. In March 1715, for instance, Reverend William Osborne of the Society for the Propagation of the Gospel in Foreign Parts reported the presence of five "molatto children being those of our Indian traders by Indian women" in St. Bartholomew's parish. Traders who resorted to this solution may have won a victory of sorts over their native wives, but they did so at the risk of offending many members of her kinship network, who may have considered their responsibilities and rights as much violated as hers.[7]

In such matters, private acts could carry very public consequences. Indian women who married English traders were often viewed by native societies as providing a valuable diplomatic service. They assisted in bringing outsiders into a familiar, understandable relationship with the community and, in doing so, secured the benefits of trade and the power that control over it conferred for themselves and their clan members. In practical terms, this meant that traders' wives were likely to be the relations of local dignitaries, thus adding a political dimension to seemingly private domestic problems. In the town of Tuckesaw in the winter of 1706, for instance, two English traders, John Musgrove and William Stead, became involved in a dispute with the leaders of the town. The nature of the domestic problems that precipitated the conflict are unknown, but according to the two traders involved, the situation came to a head when the *mico* of the town (a mico was the town leader) stepped in and took "away . . . [their] Indian wives." Musgrove was apparently so enraged by the intervention that he "threatned the lives of the Tuckesaw Indian king and another." He demanded, moreover, four slaves as compensation for the loss of his wife. Other reports gave a slightly different version of events, suggesting that in fact "the said Musgrove and Stead had turn'd away their said wives on purpose." It is also possible, perhaps even probable, that the women simply abandoned their husbands and sought protection with their family members. The traders eventually settled the matter "with the Tuckesaw King and the other Indian ffor three slaves in satisffac'on ffor their wives," but the basic problems that caused domestic turmoil in the first place went unresolved. Official relations with the "King" no doubt suffered in direct proportion.[8]

Violence against women may well have been the most corrosive form of "misconduct" perpetrated by Englishmen in Indian territory. Despicable in European circles, it must have been particularly jarring among Cherokee and Lower Creek towns, where female control of the agricultural and domestic sphere was rarely questioned. Amplified by the prestigious clan connections possessed by many of these women, private disputes sometimes broadened, as in the case of Musgrove and Stead, into political quarrels that threatened to disrupt trade relations. If English traders themselves, living and working among southeastern Indians, failed on many occasions to recognize and adjust to local patterns of gender relations, the Commissioners of the Indian Trade could hardly be expected to solve their cultural myopia from Charles Town. None of their regulatory instructions indicate that they ever considered the problem. Alexander Longe, however, a prime specimen of misconduct in European eyes for blowing up a Euchee Indian in his store, understood that different customs applied in Indian country. "Wee shold be well sett to worke," he warned his fellow Englishmen, "to take notice of womens actions." His sensitivity to such issues may explain why he was still welcome in Cherokee territory once the Yamasee War began.[9]

Yet gender-specific violence was not the only outcome of English-Indian marriages. In many cases, such unions fulfilled the diplomatic expectations of native communities and actually provided women with new avenues to power and influence. Indeed, the prevailing historiography suggests that the status of women within native societies tended to benefit from involvement in trade and, conversely, to decline as women were excluded from access to European trade. The corrosive effects of gender-specific violence on Anglo-Indian exchange relations thus did their damage selectively, depending on tribal affiliation and the specific clans or lineages involved, and always within the simultaneous context of positive influences for other native women and their kinship networks. Appalling as the behavior of some English traders may have been, their example cannot be applied as a formulaic constant among all southeastern nations or even, for that matter, among the towns of a single nation. It is even less pertinent when submerged with other problems as generalized "trade abuse" and swabbed liberally across the entire region.[10]

CREDIT

Other forms of trader "abuse" masked similarly complex issues. Seven of the thirty complaints levied against English traders by Native Americans in the *Journals of the Commissioners of the Indian Trade* involved incidents of "taking away" the Indians' personal belongings. A series of resolutions passed in the Commons House of Assembly on January 26, 1702, also indicates the prevalence of this activity. Of six resolutions concerning traders, five required them to give back or make restitution for what they had taken away from someone. William Greene was ordered to "pay ye vallue of ye cannooe he forceably tooke away from one of ye Indians belonging to Aratomaha [Altamaha], or return the same in good condition." Joshua Brinan (Bryan) and John Henry were likewise ordered to pay a Yamasee Indian named Assendo "for a cannoe taken from him," while Daniell Callahane was required to "give satisfaction to Hoos: Pau [the mico of Huspaw town] for two guns he forceably tooke from an Indjan widow of his towne, to be delivered to the said widow." Another Indian living in "Hoos Pau" town, named Old Ewhaw, was awarded compensation from William Page "for a gunn he forceably took from him," and finally Joshua Brinan was ordered to "pay Tho:ma:sa for . . . goods he forceably took from him."[11]

The expropriation of goods from Indians was practiced by many traders across much of the Southeast. Indeed, it appears to have been regarded more as an established and reputable order of business than as an act of burglary. In 1713, for instance, when Cornelius Meckarty was accused by two Indian leaders of "beating two of their people that came from North Carolina and taking some cloaths from them," he produced affidavits from eyewitnesses "to prove that he had not beaten" the Indians. He apparently considered it unnecessary to defend or deny the simple act of taking away their "cloaths."[12]

The key to understanding most of these incidents is probably linked to credit. Meckarty behaved as he did, for example, not necessarily because he was perverse or abusive, though he may have been, but because the Indians in question owed him an outstanding debt of eighty-three deerskins. He probably considered himself guilty of nothing more than repossession of merchandise for nonpayment. Similarly, when William Ford went before the Commissioners of the Indian Trade on June 27, 1712, to answer charges that he had taken away a slave belonging to a Yamasee Indian named Enaclega, he defended his action on the grounds that Enaclega "owed him 39 skins and that he toock the said slave for security of his debt." Far from condemning Ford, the commissioners ordered the Indian to pay the debt in exchange for the return of the slave.[13]

In its basic form, the practice of forcible confiscation did not overtly violate indigenous norms. Among the Creek Indians, whenever a particular individual contributed less than his or her quota of labor to the tilling of the communal fields or village improvements, the mico and his council routinely dispatched warriors to "pillage his house of such things as they [could] find." The confiscated goods were then sold and added "to the town stock." In cases involving personal debts between individuals, moreover, "if the debtor prove too negligent the creditor only goes to his house and takes the value of his debt in what he can find." These methods undoubtedly possessed a compelling logic among early historic period societies rooted in communal values, where property was generally held in common and private ownership was not yet pronounced, but English traders did not belong to the community. They did not share in the demands of communal labor, and they owned property exclusively as private individuals or, at best, as part of joint trading companies. As European markets increasingly cast their influence over the Southeast, moreover, the rate of such seizures rose at an alarming pace.[14]

Credit emerged as a point of concern in the first decade of the eighteenth century. Governor James Moore, certainly no friend to southeastern Indians, nevertheless advised his fellow Carolinians as early as 1702 that "care must be taken to prevent trade wth the Indjans on trust." "That alone," he cautioned, "in a short time will force the Indjans to apply them selves to the French for a trade, as well as protection from the severity of their creditors."

Troublesome enough in itself, credit introduced a number of unforeseen complications into Anglo-Indian relations. In May 1714, for instance, the Commissioners of the Indian Trade discussed a case of indebtedness that had become too complicated even for the English to untangle. A trader named Sheppy Allen, perhaps seeking to get out of the Indian trade, "made over his debts," as owed to him, to another trader named Glenhead. This transfer of debt from one trader to another no doubt puzzled Allen's native clients, who may not immediately have recognized their obligations to a man with whom they had never done business. Their confusion must have been multiplied when Glenhead again transferred the debt to Samuel Hilden. A fourth trader named Mackey then stepped forward to dispute Hilden's claim and demand payment of "his debts as assighne from Allen." Meanwhile, an Indian named Ingetange informed the commissioners that Allen was still indebted to him for the purchase of "severall slaves." Since other Indians still had outstanding debts owed to Allen, Ingetange argued, they should simply make their payments directly to him rather than to

Allen, or Glenhead, or Hilden, or Mackey. On another occasion, an Indian named Egabugga complained that the debt of "fower Hundred Skins" that he owed to "Capt. Mackey" had been purchased from Mackey by John Cochran for only eighty skins. If Mackey had accepted eighty skins as settlement of the debt from Cochran, Egabugga must have reasoned, why was he still required to pay Cochran four hundred?[15]

Sometimes the intermixture of native and European worlds produced hybrid concepts that created more problems than they solved. One such case involved the practice of collecting what traders termed "relations' debts," a fusion of European credit and native devotion to communal or clan responsibility. Many traders discovered that even if a particular Indian could not repay his debts, his family and friends, or even the leaders of the town, could often be counted on to fulfill his obligations. In one instance, a Chiaha Indian man named Tuskenehau, who had "gon to warr," returned home to find "that the Head Men of the Cussetau Town had taken away the said Tuskenehau's wife named Tooledeha, a free woman, and her mother, a slave belonging to the said Tooskenehau, . . . upon pretence of paying some town debts due from others of the said town to Mr. John Pight when the said Tuskenehau was no wais indebted to the said John Pight or any other person trading att the said town." The Commissioners of the Indian Trade recognized "relations' debts" as an unorthodox practice but refrained from banning it entirely. Instead, they attempted to refine it by insisting that traders first obtain the assent of all those who might be affected, after which "such relations or chief men of the town shall be liable and answerable for the payment of all such debts."[16]

Perhaps the clearest indication that issues related to credit played an important role in producing the Anglo-Indian rupture of 1715 comes from the close relationship between the outbreak of the Yamasee War in April and the seasonal nature of the credit cycle. Aside from the handful of traders who operated warehouses year-round, the majority of traders made only two trips into the interior during the course of the year: once in the fall and once in the spring. In the fall, traders laden with new merchandise arrived in villages across the Southeast and began selling their wares. Indians unable to purchase all the supplies they needed outright were extended credit. The traders then returned to South Carolina, and Indian men set out to gather as many deerskins as possible during the winter hunt, usually from about October until March. Then, as the weather improved the following spring, traders once again trekked into Indian territory, this time to collect deerskins in payment of outstanding debts. In the spring of 1715, however, they found an altogether different sort of payment waiting for them.[17]

There is reason to believe that several nations had run up heavy debts by the early eighteenth century. The Yamasees alone had amassed a collective trade debt of about one hundred thousand deerskins by 1711, a figure nearly twice the size of South Carolina's entire yearly export total. Historian Richard Haan has suggested that the Yamasees' plight resulted from environmental and de-mographic factors, primarily the depletion of white-tailed deer in coastal regions and difficulties in acquiring new Indian slaves. Yet they had access to extensive hunting grounds stretching along most of the coast of modern Georgia and possibly including por-tions of the Apalachee old fields in what is now northern Florida. It remains uncertain whether they could have denuded this whole region of game in such a short time, and Carolina's deerskin ex-ports continued rising dramatically for several decades after the Yamasee War. Some ethnohistorians have even begun to question whether deer populations were in decline by the mid- to late eighteenth century, well after the trade had reached its peak. Yamasee participation in the Tuscarora War, moreover, swelled the number of unfortunate captives brought in for sale on the Charles Town slave market.

While Haan's arguments deserve consideration, credit problems among the Yamasees and several more of Carolina's oldest trading partners probably had as much to do with a rapidly deteriorating exchange rate between English pounds sterling and Carolina currency, which must have increased the price of European trade goods dramatically, and with changing market demands that drastically restricted the range of permissible exchange commodities. Whatever the causes of the Yamasees' credit dilemma, such enormous sums meant that they and many other Indians were increasingly obliged "to goe to war and a'hunting to pay their debts," with very little to show for their exertions afterward.[18]

Yet here again, as with gender relations, indebtedness cannot be applied as a formulaic constant. Native Americans were not all debtors, and lines of credit did not extend solely from Carolina into Indian country. They sometimes ran in the other direction. The *Journals of the Commissioners of the Indian Trade* listed five separate occasions when Indian creditors sought the assistance of Carolina officials in forcing English traders to pay their debts. Several of these involved Yamasee Indians, including "King Lewis" of Pocotaligo Town, where the first shots of the war were ultimately fired. At about the same time, the "Coosata King" sought action against Theophilus Hastings for the sum of a thousand deerskins. The commissioners recognized the validity of his claim and persuaded Hastings to honor his commitment. Considered alongside incidents of "taking away" and "relations' debts," the prevalence of native creditors indicates that credit constituted a serious hot spot in the trade, producing tension on all sides.[19]

THE INDIAN SLAVE TRADE

Finally, incidents related to the Indian slave trade made up one of the most common categories of misconduct attributed to English traders. Six of the thirty complaints brought by Native Americans before the Commissioners of the Indian Trade in the five years preceding the Yamasee War had to do with slavery. English traders themselves appear to have been even more concerned about it, filing twelve complaints on this issue against rival English traders. With few exceptions, incidents of this type stemmed from legal ambiguities involved in the process of transforming human beings from a state of freedom into forms of property. While Native American complaints related to the slave trade certainly suggest widespread frustration, they also reveal a great deal more than the simple abusiveness that historians such as Verner Crane and John Swanton saw in them. Most if not all of these complaints were filed by the leaders and warriors of nations who were active participants in the trade as slave raiders, principally the Yamasees and Lower (or Ocheese) Creeks. As such, the complaints reflect the extent of Anglo-Indian partnership and cooperation as much as, or more than, reflecting English oppression of indigenous victims.

Because Native Americans did not arrive in the Carolinas as confirmed slaves, in European eyes at least, Carolinians found it necessary to improvise ways of legally dissolving their freedom. They justified their efforts theoretically, as the secretary of one of the Lords Proprietors did, in terms of conflict, stipulating that "no Indian shall be deemed a slave and purchased as such unless taken in war."[20] In practice, of course, South Carolinians "processed" a much broader range of humanity than was sanctioned by theory. In doing so, they often condescended to rival ideas about slavery and enslavement among their native business partners. In their regulatory efforts, for instance, the Commissioners of the Indian Trade warned traders against purchasing Indian war captives before the returning war parties had been "three dayes in there townes."[21] The commissioners thus hoped to allow native communities enough time to confer among themselves, usually the prerogative of native women, and to decide which of the captives should be sold to the English, which of them tortured to death, and which of them selected for eventual assimilation into the nation.[22]

The process of enslavement thus consisted of two distinct phases, with the first phase ostensibly controlled by Native Americans. This sometimes frustrated English traders anxious to maximize their profits, but the commissioners repeatedly warned them against attempting to influence or subvert native decisions concerning slave status, reminding them that "even those taken in war" if subsequently liberated "by their respective masters . . . shall be deemed free men and denizens of the said nation."[23] Far from the prying eyes of the Commissioners of the Indian Trade or the Commons House of Assembly, of course, English traders sometimes did interfere with or, more commonly, ignore this first step of the process, providing grounds for future complaints that could potentially delay or entirely forestall the enslavement of certain individuals. In April 1712, for instance, a trader named Samuell Hilden faced charges of having "intercepted and bought slaves from the Indians before they were brought into their townes," while three other traders, doing business that same year among the Yamasee Indians, allegedly "forst the slaves from the Indians the first day they brought them into their town."[24] Hilden pleaded "ignorance," but the prevalence of such behavior among English traders suggests that they knew very well what might happen to the prisoners if local deliberations were allowed to run their course.

Despite the efforts of Samuel Hilden and others to circumvent them, those deliberations carried much weight with the Commissioners of the Indian Trade. As they attempted to adjudicate the finalization of slave status, they sometimes referred back to those earlier decisions by seeking eyewitness reports and testimonials about what had happened. In September 1710, for example, the commissioners reviewed the case of an Apalachee Indian named Massony, whom John Musgrove claimed as his slave. In order to confirm Musgrove's ownership, they sought to verify that the "Toomela King" had in fact condoned Massony's slave status. The inquiry was complicated, however, by the headman's recent death. Without his authentication, the commissioners ruled that the Indian was "to be free till Capt. Musgrave can make it other wayes appeare." In the meantime, while Musgrove searched for someone who could testify under oath as to what the "Toomela king" had decided, Massony apparently returned to the Apalachee settlements "att the Savana Town."[25] Two years later, unfortunately, a trader named Cockett finally came forward and assured the commissioners "that the late Tumela king said that this Indian was a slave."[26]

There were numerous instances in which the commissioners demanded additional proof of slave status in this manner. On September 21, 1710, for example, they determined "that Ventusa, an Appalachia Indian, and his wife are to continew as free people till Philip Gilliard by a hearing before the board can prove the contrary." In another case reviewed the same day, the commissioners ruled that an Ellcombe (usually spelled Ilcombee) Indian named Wansella was "to be a free man till Mr. John Pight can prove him a slave."[27] That proof, the commissioners insisted, could only come from Indian country, and it must originate in choices made by Native Americans. In the case of Saluma, "a Slave Woman . . . taken by Paul, an Indian," no witnesses could recall whether Paul had given her to the leader of the Ilcombees. Ten years later in 1714, when she was owned by someone else, her status continued to stir debate. Yet the commissioners would not pass judgment on Paul's intentions without "all the evidences . . . being down." They finally delegated authority for handling the matter to the Indian agent "att his next going up."[28]

Although idiosyncratic and poorly regulated, the process of enslavement nevertheless proceeded according to a rudimentary protocol, recognized by Carolinians as well as their native trading partners. When English traders attempted to subvert that code, as they often did, they had to run a double gauntlet of complaint, beginning in native villages and ending in Charles Town. In 1706, for example, the cooperating traders John Pight, James Lucas, and Anthony Probert, probably headquartered among the Lower Creek towns in central Georgia, appear to have attempted to manipulate the enslavement process on a grand scale.[29] They had previously profited by capturing a number of victims from a small, powerless nation called the Ilcombees, making slaves at one time or another of two "Illcombee free people," a "free Illcombe woman & her sister," and another "free Illcombe woman" and her two children.[30] At length, however, the traders hit upon a labor-saving scheme to have the entire nation taken as slaves at once.

The traders undoubtedly knew that the process required some form of native consent, for they attempted to gain the support of neighboring tribes. A few Indians agreed to condone the plan, but most, including an enigmatic figure known only as "the Long Doctor," appear to have reacted angrily. Indeed, at one particularly tense "consultation" about the issue "in the Round House," Pight, Lucas, and Probert encountered such heated opposition that they became "afraid least the Indians would rise upon them." Perhaps fearing for their lives, they secretly gave orders to another of their associates, Theophilus Hastings, to slip away and "loade all his guns."[31]

News of the uproar apparently reached the Commons House of Assembly in late 1706, and they summoned all parties concerned to testify in Charles Town. As chance would have it, on their way to Carolina the Ilcombees encountered none other than Anthony Probert and a number of his Indian supporters. The Indians accompanying the trader tried to persuade the Ilcombees that "they had no occas'on to come to town ffor that they had done the buissiness already." But the Ilcombees, undeterred, responded by "telling them they had been to tell their story, and we will now go to tell ours." At that point Probert's allies apparently grew angry and revealed their true colors by announcing that "if the Illcombees were not declared slaves they would go home and kill them all." All the while, Probert stood quietly by and observed the encounter "but would not say a word."[32]

The Commons House ruled in the Ilcombees' favor in December 1706, and found Anthony Probert and his associate John Pight guilty of exercising "imprudence in the . . . trade." They were ordered to return to Charles Town for sentencing, but the judgment could not have been too harsh, for both men were still active in the Indian trade eight years later and still causing trouble.[33] The subsequent fate of the Ilcombee Indians, on the other hand, is a matter of pure speculation. Having doggedly told their own story, they set out for home, never again to appear as a people in the documentary record.[34]

South Carolina's official response to the Pight, Probert, and Lucas case followed an increasingly codified pattern. When it became clear that the partners had run afoul of local Indian leaders in their "round house" consultations about Ilcombee slave status, the Commons House of Assembly invited testimony from Indian country. The confrontation on the trade path on the way to Charles Town between the Ilcombees and the Indian allies of the English traders seeking their enslavement reflected the real heart of the debate. Even within the chambers of South Carolina government, the entire case ultimately revolved around the determination of various groups of Indians "to tell their story." When the Commons House found in favor of the Ilcombees, moreover, they merely ratified and defended the earlier decision of the "Long Doctor" and others in the round house. Carolina's action was not unilateral and arbitrary. It was, rather, responsive and deferential to indigenous decisions and testimony.[35]

On rare occasions, the commissioners questioned or even nullified decisions made in native villages during the first phase of the process. When the Chiaha warrior Tuskenehau's wife and her mother had been seized by the leaders of the Creek town of Kasita for repayment of relations' debts, he responded by sending two of his "slaves" to Charles Town to protest the action. Appearing before the assembled commissioners on June 12, Clugoffee and Pingoleachee explained that their master's wife, Tooledeha, and her mother (who was Tuskenehau's slave) had been "rongfully" confiscated by "the Head Men of the Cussetau town" and delivered to an English trader. The commissioners agreed and ordered that Tuskenehau's wife, Tooledeha, be returned to him. They also sent word for "Cussetau Town" to compensate the trader "for so much mony as he took the said Tooledeha for and no more." Their reasoning is hard to fathom, however, for Tooledeha's mother was not returned.

The response of the Cussetau town leaders at being contradicted in this manner is unknown, nor do the records indicate whether they complied with the judgment. If South Carolina officials lacked the ability to exert coercive pressure fully over British traders, they possessed even less power over Lower Creek Indian leaders. Indeed, the diplomatic repercussions of any effort to enforce punitive measures against Indian leaders could have been disastrous. For obvious reasons, the commissioners took such stands only in extraordinary circumstances. They appear to have attempted such a thing in only one other instance: the case of Alexander Longe.[36]

THEMES, PATTERNS, PROBLEMS

South Carolina officials either failed to recognize the underlying patterns of the cases that came before them or else considered these patterns unimportant. Incidents related to the slave trade, gender-specific violence, and credit matters inundated the Commissioners of the Indian Trade with personal anecdotes, affidavits, and details that undoubtedly obscured the larger picture. For many South Carolinians, moreover, it may have been difficult if not impossible to maintain the objectivity necessary to identify the various strands of the knotted mass confronting them. John Wright, for instance, who served as Indian agent from 1708 to 1712, considered the issues of credit and slavery to be integrally connected. His general practice in deciding whether an Indian ought to be enslaved or freed was, quite simply, "not . . . to declare any slave free where he had any notice that the owner was in debt to any white man." Nevertheless, these subcategories of trader misconduct suggest that Anglo-Indian relations were marred by much more than the personal failings and abuses of individual Englishmen, reprehensible though they often were. Anglo-Indian relations were riven by distinct lines of stress that formed in particularly troublesome areas. Native complaints and irritation clustered conspicuously around these cultural, economic, and social fault zones, not around individual traders. The nature of the exchange relationship itself thus appears to have concentrated tension along these lines, and few traders could wholly avoid contributing to the problem in one way or another.[37]

In addition to these fault zones, the complaints attributable to Native Americans prior to 1715 displayed a striking geographical pattern. Although Cherokee, Upper Creek, and Catawba voices occasionally found their way into the journals of the Commissioners of the Indian Trade or the Commons House of Assembly, the vast majority of voices belonged to Lower (or Ocheese) Creek, Euchee, Savannah, Apalachee, and Yamasee villages. These nations comprised a coherent zone of settlement along Carolina's oldest and most lucrative trade route, extending south and southwest from Charles Town into central Georgia. The volume of complaints from native communities in this region probably reflects their deeper involvement in trade more than it does any regional differences in the behavior of English traders.

At the same time, however, it is possible that these nations had fewer options open to them for European trade than others had, forcing them to rely entirely on Carolina. They had done much themselves, in fact, to limit their access to alternative sources of European goods between 1680 and 1704 by assisting in the destruction of the Spanish mission system in Florida. Having thus by the first decade of the eighteenth century entered into what economists term a monopsony relationship with Charles Town—one in which there is only a single supplier of goods or services—Yamasees, Euchees, Lower Creeks and others may have found it necessary to engage English officials more aggressively in order to affect the terms of exchange. Even so, their prominence in the historical record should not be read simply as evidence of greater victimization. In many cases, their protests suggest that they were active, intelligent participants in exchange, attempting purposefully to influence and direct the process for their own advantage.[38]

2. Indian Slaves in the Carolina Low Country

When John Norris wrote a promotional tract in 1712 encouraging British settlers to make their way to South Carolina, he emphasized the ease with which a profitable plantation could be established. All it would take, he assured his readers, was "fifteen Indian women to work in the field" and three more to work as cooks.[1] At the time, Carolina's slave population included a sizable percentage of Native American slaves, about 25 percent, far more than in any other mainland British colony, and Norris clearly expected that pattern to continue. It apparently mattered little to him whether white Carolinians victimized Indian or African laborers. Nor did he seem to consider the colony's multiracial slave population unusual.

South Carolina's example was, however, unique, and American Indians were not the interchangeable cogs in the plantation system that Norris advertised them to be. Although Africans and Indians worked side by side on low-country plantations for several decades, demographic factors set them apart in significant ways. Enslaved Indian populations, for instance, exhibited a profoundly different gender composition, skewed heavily toward women and children, while African slaves were predominantly male during early generations. The two groups also encountered different reproductive realities and may have faced very different processes of acculturation, involving for Native Americans the need to adapt not only to European culture but to African culture as well.[2]

In addition, the presence of Indian slaves sometimes forced colonial planters and officials to respond to a unique set of problems that did not present themselves with respect to African slavery in the lower South. As discussed in the previous chapter, Carolinians participated in the enslavement process of Native Americans to an extent they did not with African slaves, and they often found it a difficult and imperfect process, amenable to complaint and revision. In reversing slave status and restoring "wrongly" enslaved Indians to freedom, Carolinians responded to a range of motives and considerations that diverged in several ways from patterns of African slave emancipation. The resulting boundary between freedom and slavery for Indians followed a course of its own and became remarkably tangled in some cases. In this chapter I argue that Indian slavery as it existed in South Carolina prior to the Yamasee War posed specific problems for Carolinians. By analyzing the practical complexities of the prewar slave regime, I seek to establish a point of reference for understanding in turn the colony's wartime and postwar responses to those problems.

DEMOGRAPHIC PROFILE

The problem of quantifying Indian slavery in the Carolina low country is complicated by the scarcity of archival resources from Carolina's early years. Probate records from the proprietary period are too scanty to reconstruct a complete and precise portrait of the rise of Indian or even African slavery. Those records that do exist fall into two categories, which may be used to supplement each other: wills and postmortem inventories. The most numerous records for the years between 1690 and 1720 are the wills, which number about 170. By contrast, there are only about sixty postmortem inventories for the entire proprietary period.[3]

Despite this paucity of archival records, it is possible to make a few general observations about the composition of the enslaved population during the last decade of the seventeenth century. A survey of South Carolina wills indicates that between 1690 and 1694 about 13 percent of all households owned some number of African slaves. The number of households owning African slaves increased significantly between 1695 and 1699, however, to about 26 percent. On the other hand, the number of households owning Indian slaves fluctuated between 4 and 6 percent over the same period, suggesting that Indian slavery served only as an ancillary form of labor during Carolina's earliest years. These figures indicate that ownership of slaves was not as widespread during the 1690s as it would soon become. It should be stressed as well that the rates of household ownership of African and Indian slaves are not mutually exclusive figures. Most households that owned Indian slaves also owned African slaves.[4]

The twenty-seven surviving postmortem inventories from this decade tell a story similar to that in the wills. Although there is a significant wealth bias in this record series, as only those estates valuable enough to require systematic appraisal are included, Indians still appear to have been a minor component of the enslaved labor force prior to the turn of the century. Of the total of sixty-five slaves who appear in these inventories, only 6 percent were identified as Indians.[5]

As these numbers indicate, the trade in Native American slaves was still gaining momentum during the 1680s and '90s. Successful warriors could typically expect compensation well in excess of the usual profit from the deerskin trade, a single slave sometimes bringing the same price as two hundred deerskins. This amounted to a good deal more than most men could gather in an entire hunting season, so it is not surprising that many men from powerful tribes spent much of their time making "war" on weaker tribes, particularly those outside the Carolina trade system who had not yet acquired firearms. Of course, white Carolinians participated in the trade primarily for profit, but many also harbored more sinister motives. Thomas Nairne, for instance, the Indian agent for South Carolina, expressed hopes that the slave trade would "in som few years . . . reduce these barbarians to a farr less number."[6]

The first decade of the eighteenth century saw by far the greatest influx of Indian slaves, due in large part to the expeditions of Governor James Moore against St. Augustine in 1702 and the Apalachee missions in 1704. A census recorded by the governor and Upper House of Assembly (or Governor's Council) indicated that by 1703 the number of Indian slaves had risen to 350, or 10 percent of the enslaved labor force. It then exploded to 1,400 over the next five years, thus comprising slightly more than 25 percent of the slave population by the end of the decade. Probate records are almost nonexistent between 1700 and 1709, but the few wills available nevertheless suggest that the number of households owning Indian slaves rose dramatically. A more abundant supply of wills for the five-year period between 1710 and 1714 indicates that about 26 percent of all households owned some Indian slaves. These years, just prior to the outbreak of the Yamasee War in 1715, clearly represented the high-water mark of the Indian slave trade and of Indian slavery in South Carolina.[7]

Most enslaved Indians, both men and women, probably worked as field hands on plantations. Yet Indian slaves worked at specialized occupations as well. Slaves named Lawrence and Toney, for instance, sold by Peter Royere to William Rhett in 1716, worked as a cooper and a shoemaker respectively. Others, primarily women and children, appear to have worked as household servants. Judging from the prevalence of the name Nanny among Indian women bequeathed in wills by male testators to their wives and daughters, childrearing and care may have been one important function performed by enslaved Indian women.[8]

As with Nanny, slaves' names reveal a great deal about the world in which they lived. Although first-generation slaves were generally assigned names by their new masters, slave mothers exercised considerable liberty in naming their own offspring. As a result, African slaves in South Carolina succeeded over several generations in selecting a culturally distinctive set of names from the arbitrary collection originally assigned to the first generation. They even managed to retain a number of African names and many African traditions, such as naming a child for the day of the week when the baby was born.[9]

First-generation Indian slaves undoubtedly valued their own traditional names and naming practices as well, but they appear to have been far less successful in retaining those names than their African co-workers. Of the sixty-eight Indian slaves whose names are given in colonial South Carolina wills between 1690 and 1740, only one, a girl named Inotly, possessed a recognizably Indian name. The remainder were given common European names such as Lucy, Jack, and Hannah, or names from classical antiquity such as Nero or Pompey. Postmortem inventories from the 1720s reveal a similarly low rate of traditional Indian name retention. Only two of the 103 names listed for Indian slaves, or about 2 percent, appear to be of Indian origin: Tipa and Meggilla.[10]

Those numbers defy expectations based on African slave names. Admittedly, differences between Native American and African naming practices make a direct comparison between the two groups problematic. Among free Indian males, for example, birth names held little importance. Although Indian women generally possessed a single name throughout their lives, men typically had a sequence of names commemorating notable events, such as military achievements. Nevertheless, Indian slaves of this first generation clearly encountered intense pressure to relinquish the old trappings of their free lives in favor of new ones provided by their masters. African slaves endured similar pressures but still managed to retain African names at a rate of about 15 to 20 percent. The corresponding rate of only 1 to 2 percent for Indian slaves suggests that the two groups either responded differently to the experience of slavery or experienced slightly different forms of oppression. It may indicate, for instance, that white Carolinians considered Indian identity a greater potential threat than African identity, perhaps due to the large number of armed, independent nations poised just across the frontier. It is also possible that radically different gender compositions within the African and Indian slave populations, the former predominantly male and the latter female, may have conditioned their respective strategies for coping with the hardships of slavery.[11]

Finally, pressures acting to discourage the retention of Indian names may simply have arisen from the general demographic context within which Indian slavery existed. Many plantations prior to the Yamasee War possessed African laborers exclusively, but relatively few utilized Indian labor alone. Wherever Indian slaves worked in low-country Carolina, they generally worked amid mixed African-Indian populations, with Africans predominating. In 1720, for example, Robert Seabrooke's plantation in Colleton County listed a total of twenty slaves, 50 percent of whom were African, 35 percent Indian, and 15 percent mustee, the term for mixed Indian-African or Indian-European offspring. Meanwhile, John Goodby's plantation, probated the same year as Seabrooke's, was staffed by a labor force in which Africans comprised 79 percent and Indians 21 percent of the workers. Such cases, however, probably represented the upper ranges of the Native American presence. At the opposite extreme were plantations such as William Skipper's, where a single "Indian woman named Phebe" worked alongside sixteen African slaves in the mid-1720s. Similarly, John Whitmarsh recorded forty-eight slaves who worked on his plantation in 1718, one of whom was named "Indian Rose."[12]

It is not surprising that Indians, working alone or at best as part of a minority contingent within the "black majority," found it difficult to maintain overt vestiges of their heritage. Perhaps more curious is why more Indian appellations do not appear among second-generation offspring. Second-generation Indian mothers, like African mothers, probably exercised the liberty to choose the names of their own children. Yet Indian and mustee infants born into slavery continued to bear the names given by European masters to their parents' generation. The only movements away from this pattern were movements not toward a resumption of traditional Indian names but toward African names. An "Indian boy" slave, for instance, owned by John Royer in the early 1720s, bore the distinctly African name Cuffey. The tendency toward Africanization may have been especially strong among mustee children who had no personal memories of their Indian heritage, as suggested by the decision of a "mustee woman Phillis" to name her son Quacoo. Similarly, a mustee man owned by James Stanyarne in 1723 was named Sambo, while Nancy Gilbertson owned "a mustee boy" named Mingo. Such examples suggest that Native American slaves experienced a double-edged process of acculturation, requiring the accommodation of two foreign cultures in a demographic setting where both possessed more currency on a daily basis than did their own culture.[13]

Despite overwhelming pressures, however, certain aboriginal traditions did persist on low-country plantations, primarily through the efforts of Indian women. Throughout the colonial period, free Indian women appear to have clung more effectively to old customs and folkways than did their male partners, serving as "guardians of tradition" during an era of chaotic change. Archaeologically, their influence manifests itself in ceramic traditions, controlled exclusively by women, which remained vigorous and consistent even in direct competition with European trade goods. Native American women appear to have taken these skills with them to a number of South Carolina plantations, where they continued to make pottery characterized by recognizably Indian vessel types and decorative motifs. At Newington plantation near Charleston, for instance, excavations uncovered a fragment from an Indian-style earthenware vessel in the kitchen fireplace of the main house, suggesting that Indian slaves may have prepared foods using aboriginal utensils of their own making. Given the prevalence of ceramic artifacts, it is possible that other native crafts traditionally performed by women, such as the dressing of deerskins (much less likely to be preserved in the archaeological record), may also have found expression at some plantations.[14]

The presence of mustee slaves on many plantations testifies to the interrelation of Africans, Indians, and Europeans, but the extent of inter-racial unions is difficult to quantify. The first reference to a mixed-race slave dates only to 1716, when James Lawson bequeathed "a mastee girle called Dina" to his wife. By that time Indians, Africans, and Europeans had been working together for nearly two decades, and it is reasonable to assume that some degree of mixing had gone unrecorded prior to Dina's appearance. Women outnumbered men among Indian slaves during the first decade of the eighteenth century, the only decade for which there is reliable census information. Meanwhile, among African slaves during the same period, men outnumbered women by between six and nine hundred. For many Indian women and African men, therefore, it may have been easier to find suitable partners among members of the other race than among their own. This may also explain why slaves classified as mustees were the most common product of inter-racial unions for most of the eighteenth century, outnumbering mulattos by a considerable margin. The greatest number of mustees, most of them children, appeared in South Carolina wills during the 1720s. Between 1725 and 1729, approximately 6 percent of all households owned at least one mustee slave. Thereafter the number declined to about 3 percent, roughly the same number of households that owned Indian slaves. It is likely, however, that this decline represents changing habits of classification, and hence changing ideas about race, rather than actual population trends.[15]

Evidence of miscegenation involved Europeans as well. On several occasions plantation owners granted freedom to Indian women and acknowledged paternity of mixed-race children. In 1707, for instance, Richard Prize granted freedom to "an Indian woman of mine by whom I have two children Elizabeth and Sarah Prize." He went on to bequeath to his "Indian woman" two other Indian women, who unfortunately remained slaves. Prize may have feared, however, that the mother once free might attempt to raise his daughters as Indians, for he instructed his executors to "take my two said children and bring them up in ye fear of God." The eldest son of Governor Robert Johnson, named after his father, also developed strong feelings for his "Indian woman named Catharina, whom I design to marry." Robert accordingly made arrangements to "manumett and set free" his bride to be, and since Catharina was "with child" at the time, he stipulated in the same legal instrument that the baby once born should be entitled to a share of his estate equal to those of his other four children. Whether his "design" ever came to fruition is unknown.[16]

Indian slave manumissions that grew out of the master-slave relationship resembled African slave manumissions in one significant way. Virtually all of them involved women and their children, and in many cases a relationship of sorts with the planter was clearly the motivating factor. Other cases provided less detail than Prize's or Johnson's but nevertheless suggested the possibility of miscegenation. In 1714, for instance, John Burick drafted a will in which, while admitting nothing, he bequeathed to his "Indian woman Dido and her child their freedom." Even so, he attached the proviso that she "continue to stay with and serve my loving wife" for at least a year after his death. Unfortunately for Dido perhaps, his will was not recorded until 1725, suggesting that Burick may have recovered his health and thus postponed her freedom for another decade. Similarly, in 1721 Abraham Fleur de la Plaine bequeathed to his daughter the "use and service" of an Indian woman named Diana, but her term of service was strictly limited "until she [had] born another child and for two years then after and noe longer." At that time, he stipulated, Diana was at last to have "her freedom as I have promised her." Liberty may have seemed bittersweet for Diana, however, since de la Plaine evidently did not include her son Frank, listed as a "mustee boy," in his promise.[17]

THE BOUNDARY BETWEEN FREEDOM AND SLAVERY

Such examples suggest that Indian slaves had access to many of the internal, private avenues to freedom available to their African counterparts. In addition, however, issues and concerns originating outside the private relationship between master and slave sometimes reached into the plantation to fetch out particular Indians. Those concerns generally revolved around Carolina's diplomatic standing with powerful Indian nations on the colony's periphery, such as the Cherokees or Creeks, though the web of complications incurred by the enslavement of certain Indians could extend as far away as New York. If the external threat appeared too ominous, government officials moved to free the individual in question, occasionally in the face of bitter opposition and complaint from the slave's immediate owner, and to have him or her returned home safely. In this public, official capacity, Indian manumissions differed radically from the largely private character of African slave manumissions in the pre-revolutionary South.[18]

One of the earliest instances of a manumission prompted by concern for the public welfare occurred during Queen Anne's War. When Carolina officials discovered in April 1703 that Cherokee warriors had "taken some of our southern Indjans our frinds slaves and . . . sold them to our Indjan traders," the members of the Commons House ordered the captives to be "safely sent home." Their action, however, had more to do with the recent outbreak of hostilities with Spain and France than with any genuine humanitarian impulse or legal consideration, for they justified the release of these "frinds" on the grounds that their enslavement would be a "great disincouragement to such of ye nations that are in amity wth us to be any further assisting to this colony, now in this time of war."[19]

A similar situation arose ten years later during the waning phases of the Tuscarora Indian War in North Carolina. Unable to defend itself, the Albemarle government depended on a series of relief expeditions from South Carolina composed primarily of Yamasee, Lower Creek, and Carolina piedmont Indians. Most of those warriors participated in the campaigns in hopes of obtaining Tuscarora captives for sale in the Charles Town market, and they were not disappointed. Following a particularly successful venture under the command of former Carolina governor James Moore in 1713, the Carolinians netted a windfall of several hundred slaves. But among this cache of prisoners lay the seeds of future discord for both North and South Carolina. Upon closer inspection, a captive named Anethae "turned out to be Iroquois." A further inquiry into the matter revealed that he had been "sent by ye Senecas pursuant to an order from ye goverm't of New Yorke to caution ye Tuscaroras agst going to warr wth ye English."[20]

Confronted with the prospect of offending the powerful Iroquois League and perhaps even the governor of New York, North Carolina Governor Thomas Pollock and his council "thought fitt" to step in and save the South Carolinians (and themselves) from their own success. They suggested "that ye said Indyan be purchased . . . by ye publick and sent back to his owne nation." Yet the situation was not so easily solved. Having determined to act, Pollock now had to find a way of freeing Anethae without offending the "South Carolina Indyan" who claimed him as a just reward of war. The unidentified warrior must have surmised the unusual bargaining power that his Iroquois captive gave him, for he agreed to release Anethae only in exchange for "three Tuscaroro men & one Mattecumska." In order to prevent any unforeseen misfortunes on the long voyage home, Pollock arranged passage for the young man aboard a ship sailing directly to New York.[21]

In addition to prompting government action, free Indians also influenced individual planters and their slaves directly. Most of South Carolina's plantation districts prior to the Yamasee War were bordered by Indian settlements or hunting grounds, and virtually all plantations shared common waterways with native groups upstream. Indian slaves thus worked under the conspicuous shadow of a large free Indian population and, in some areas, regularly interacted with its members. On the fringes of the Yamasee Indian settlements, for instance, Alexander Mackey owned plantations on Port Royal and St. Helena islands. His labor force, as of 1714, included at least five Indian men and six Indian women. How the immediate presence of more than a thousand free Yamasee Indians affected respective patterns of resistance (and, conversely, planter discipline) among Indian and African slaves can only be inferred.[22]

It is clear, at any rate, that planters in the Port Royal region failed to keep free and enslaved Indians away from each other. In 1707, for example, a free "St. Helena Indian" named Shamdedee found himself in a precarious situation as a result of "his brother being killed by an Apalachy slave." Principles of clan justice required that he reciprocate by killing the offending slave or one of that man's kinsmen, but such an act might bring down upon Shamdedee the wrath of the slave's English owner or even the Carolina government. The Commons House of Assembly, perhaps seeking to salve Shamdedee's honor without further bloodshed, awarded him a "gratuity" of five pounds. Five years later the situation was reversed when a planter named John Jackson complained to the Assembly that "an Indian man of his [had been] killed by the Yamasee Indians." Rather than confronting the Yamasees about the matter, Jackson evidently hoped to receive compensation from the government and forget the affair.[23]

No case better illustrates the uniqueness of the boundary between freedom and bondage for many southeastern Indians than that of Cuffy, who received the commendation of the Commons House of Assembly on August 12, 1715. He had endeared himself to South Carolinians four months earlier by "bringing the first intelligence of the Yamasee Indians' design to massacre the English." As a reward, the Assembly ordered that he receive "out of the publick treasury" the rather chintzy sum of ten pounds Carolina currency and a "coat."[24]

He did not receive his freedom for the simple reason that he was apparently not a slave. The Commons House Journal identified him as "an Euhaw Indian," while another source referred to him as "Indian Cuffy Yamesa." Both designations were probably correct, since Euhaw was one of the Lower Towns of the Yamasee confederacy, located near Port Royal, South Carolina. But this is only a beginning at unraveling the mystery of Cuffy's identity, and it is a mystery worth exploring, because even a tentative and speculative profile of his predicament sheds light on the problem of Indian slavery at a time and place of crucial importance for southern colonial history.[25]

While no information about his birth or chronological age exists, he probably entered the world on a Monday, the son of a slave. Cuffy was an African day-name often given as a personal name to babies born on that day, according to African custom. Common among African slaves on South Carolina plantations, the name simply did not exist naturally among the free Indian peoples of the region. Among the enslaved Indian population, however, African names did in fact begin to appear in the second generation among children born to Indian mothers in slavery.[26]

At some point, Cuffy appears to have shed his slave status by means that are not apparent in the records and to have resumed his status as "an Euhaw Indian." Evidence of his freedom is entirely circumstantial, based mainly on the manner in which the Commons House addressed him (slaves discussed by the Assembly, whether African or Indian, were almost always identified in association with their owners and rarely by their own names alone) and on later developments involving his wife. If he was free, his retention of the name Cuffy indicates either that he had only recently been emancipated or, as seems more likely, that he was only partially incorporated into the social life of the Yamasee Indians.

Most southeastern Indians considered a male child's birth-name temporary, to be exchanged as soon as possible for another one that more precisely matched his personality and exploits. In adulthood, young men routinely changed names to commemorate noteworthy accomplishments (a phenomenon that frustrated Europeans). It is possible, of course, that among the Yamasees Cuffy had other names not known to Carolinians. But if he had not in fact outgrown his birth-name, this may indicate that in spite of the European perception of him as a Yamasee Indian from Euhaw Town, he did not participate in a meaningful way in Yamasee politics, diplomacy, or military efforts.[27]

Marginalized though he may have been, there is reason to suspect that he was sufficiently aware of (and trusted with) internal Yamasee affairs to acquire sensitive knowledge of diplomatic matters in April of 1715. A few days before the outbreak of hostilities, an English trader named William Bray reported that during his absence "a Yamasee Indian came to his wife and told her he had a great matter to tell her, which was that the Creek Indians had a design to cut of[f] the traders first and then to fall on the settlement, and that itt was very neare." In his landmark study *The Southern Frontier*, Verner Crane felt certain that the anonymous Indian who alerted the wife of William Bray in April was the same man rewarded by the Commons House of Assembly in August for "bringing the first intelligence of the Yamasee Indians' design to massacre the English." Crane was a canny historian; his insight remains persuasive seventy-five years after the publication of his work.[28]

Even so, his terse characterization of Cuffy's action as a "friendly warning" overlooked a number of ethnographic possibilities. The Yamasee Indian who brought early warning of the war to Mrs. Bray, whether it was Cuffy or not, reportedly did so because of his "great love for her and her two sisters," not necessarily because he was "friendly" toward her husband or whites in general. He may even have waited intentionally until William Bray was "gon towards St. Augustine after some of his slaves" before making his visit. It is impossible to determine whether he expected or intended to disrupt the impending conflict, but he promised to make a second visit just prior to the zero hour, at which point "they must goe immediately to their town." Several questions arise here: first, what and where was "their town"? Second, why would they have been safe there? And third, was William Bray supposed to go with them?[29]

The answers to these questions and the real meaning of the incident depend of course on the identities of Mrs. Bray and her sisters. If they were Englishwomen, a retreat to "their town" would have put them directly in harm's way. It is difficult to imagine, moreover, in a colony with such a radically skewed sex ratio, that three English sisters would have lived together at a Yamasee Indian trading post. If, however, Mrs. Bray and her sisters were Yamasee Indians, then Cuffy's "great love" for them becomes a good deal clearer. The Yamasees, like other southeastern Indians, practiced a matrilineal system of descent reckoning, in which a man's first order of obligation was not to his own wife or children but to his sister and her offspring. The safest place for them would logically have been "their town" (perhaps Euhaw), where they could find refuge with other Yamasee women and children far away from the fighting. Marriages between English traders and Native American women were not uncommon. Indeed, they were considered a standard order of business by many traders, providing them with instant clan privileges that extended far beyond a woman's home village.[30]

In addition to "bringing the first intelligence," Cuffy appeared "friendly" because he chose to remain with the English rather than to fight for the Yamasees. Yet here again, other motives may have been at work. Although Cuffy appears to have been free in 1715, his wife Phillis and her daughter Hannah (she may or may not have been Cuffy's daughter as well) were still very much the property of an English planter named Edmund Bellinger.[31] Although he satisfied his obligations toward his immediate female relatives, Cuffy's affection for his wife may have outweighed his loyalty to the Yamasee Nation, into which he was as yet only partially incorporated, and this factor may have drawn him to the English side of the skirmish lines.

When the Commons House of Assembly awarded him ten pounds and a coat in August 1715, it entirely ignored the obvious issue of manumission for Phillis and Hannah. Edmund Bellinger, for his part, does not appear to have been highly motivated on the issue either, postponing action for more than a year after the Assembly's gift. Not until December of 1716 did he find time to "acquit, exonerate, & discharge" them from slavery. He did so, moreover, only after "having rec'd full satisfaction from the publick, in the lieu of her & child," thus suggesting that the real impetus for freeing the two originated in official channels, though this is unrecorded.[32]

THEMES, PATTERNS, PROBLEMS

The ambiguities and uncertainties of the aforegoing profile, I submit, are more than the symptoms of spotty archival holdings or an overactive imagination. They reflect the actual confusion and fluidity inherent in the practical operation of Indian slavery in certain regions of South Carolina, in this case Port Royal. That such a portrait stands as even a remotely plausible construction suggests the level of complexity that Indian slaves could potentially bring to low-country plantations. In many ways, Indian slavery as it existed in South Carolina exhibited the characteristics ascribed by scholars to "slave-owning" societies; that is, societies in which slaves are present but not yet the dominant feature of the economy. Indian slavery existed within a web of legal ambiguity, offered significant prospects for the restoration of freedom, and functioned amid a highly flexible range of Anglo-Indian relationships.[33]

The same may be said of African slavery during South Carolina's "charter generation," but with respect to Indian slavery, these characteristics did not necessarily result from the economic marginality of slavery that typified slave-owning societies. By the first decade of the eighteenth century, the high-water mark of Indian slavery, South Carolina had come to depend heavily on slave labor. Indeed, Russell R. Menard has argued that South Carolina "became a slave society before it developed a plantation regime" with the advent of intensive rice production in the 1690s. The complications attending the use of Indian slaves thus appear to have had their origins, rather, in the structural dynamics of Indian slavery itself, principally in the bipartite process of enslavement discussed in the previous chapter and the external influence of free Indian populations.[34]

Problems associated with Indian slavery were encountered elsewhere in the New World as well. Brazilian planters, for instance, experimented with a multiracial labor force during the sixteenth and seventeenth centuries, and historical studies of the Brazilian plantation regime have identified a number of comparative disadvantages to Indian slavery that led planters to rely increasingly on African laborers. Historian Stuart Schwartz has cited higher "management costs" for Indian slaves as a major factor in the transition to African labor. Such costs included supposedly higher mortality rates for Indian slaves, greater ease of escape, and perhaps lower overall productivity as reflected in lower prices for Indian slaves. Coupled with management costs, the capacity and volume of the

Atlantic slave trade also offered considerable advantages over a localized, smaller-scale indigenous slave trade.[35]

The nature of the documentary record for South Carolina makes it impossible at present to say whether the same disadvantages at work in Brazil were also characteristic of Indian slavery in Carolina. While Indian slaves working on low-country plantations may have suffered a higher mortality rate than did African slaves, probate records are silent on the issue. Similarly, there is little basis for comparative studies of the frequency of African or Indian runaways, since the South Carolina Gazette did not begin publication until the 1730s, long after Indian slaves had become a rarity. Nevertheless, by the 1720s Indian slaves in South Carolina were clearly considered less valuable than Africans, suggesting that white planters had begun to factor two different sets of variables into their equations when evaluating Indians and Africans, just as the Portuguese had done a century earlier.

The differences elaborated here between Indian and African slavery in South Carolina constituted a form of what Schwartz has termed "management costs." The idiosyncrasies of the enslavement process, resulting in frequent reversals of slave status, coupled with public manumissions coerced by the state and the subversive influence of local free populations, made Indian slaves a more complicated labor pool than Africans and undoubtedly influenced white perceptions of their value. While broadly compatible with Brazilian "management costs," however, these issues differed profoundly in type and significance. Brazilian planters judged Indians and Africans by shared criteria common to both, such as mortality rates and resistance; South Carolinians may in addition have included in their evaluations institutional considerations that were different for the two groups. Hence, very different mechanisms may underlie the apparently comparable price differences in Brazil and the Carolinas.

Regardless of the complications inherent in Indian slavery, South Carolinians showed no signs of backing away from it prior to the Yamasee War in 1715. Had that early line of development continued, the colony would almost certainly have been forced to respond more effectively to the challenges of a multiracial slave labor force. The idiosyncratic boundary between freedom and slavery for Native Americans may eventually have led to a greater sophistication and fluidity of racial categorization than existed elsewhere in British America. It may even have blurred the line for African slaves as well and produced an unusually flexible and creative plantation regime in South Carolina. Ultimately, of course, the abrupt and total destruction of the Indian slave trade during the Yamasee War and the consequent decline of the Indian slave population from 1715 onward spared Carolinians from coming to grips with such challenges. Indian slavery, at any rate, cannot be dismissed as a mere curiosity along the inevitable road to more familiar forms of eighteenth-century bondage. It posed distinct institutional and social problems that must be addressed on their own terms rather than as parallel extensions of African slavery.

PART 2 **Spark**

3. Market Influence

Prior to the war, Cuffy undoubtedly walked the dozen or so miles separating the Yamasee settlements and the slave quarters of Edmund Bellinger's plantation on a regular basis to visit his wife, Phillis. Accompanied along the way perhaps by the chatter of Carolina parakeets, he navigated a troubled landscape that could lead from freedom to slavery and back again. It was a landscape, moreover, distressed in several distinctive ways by the growing trade that traveled across it. As evidenced by episodes of gendered violence, complications related to the trade in Indian slaves, and problems involving credit, it might even be said that the region was fast becoming a tinderbox, lacking only a spark to set it aflame.

The stress fractures plaguing Anglo-Indian trade in the South were not unique, however, and need not necessarily have resulted in warfare. They appeared at various points in other regions of North America as well. In the normal course of business in 1684, for instance, cultural, economic, and social friction led to the deaths of thirty-nine French traders in the hinterlands of New France. Yet cordial relations between Quebec and its native clients did not break down, because the two groups, meeting on what historian Richard White has termed the "Middle Ground" between cultures, managed to resolve their differences and arrive at mutually agreeable ways of interacting, observing, and accommodating each other's cultural values. Indeed, as complaints about English "misconduct" poured into Charles Town, the French in Louisiana and New France were engaged in some of the most adept and creative frontier diplomacy of the age. If English "abusiveness" no longer functions as an analytical tool, it is not immediately apparent why Carolinians and their native clients could not arrive at a similar accommodation. Why did the English and Indians in the colonial South move farther apart when other groups experiencing similar difficulties managed to establish a sustainable, responsive dialogue?[1]

NEW ENGLISH TRADE BEHAVIOR

In the aftermath of the Yamasee War, a number of Native American voices found their way into the records on this topic, and they tell a complicated story. Many accounts denied that there was a problem at all. Cherekeileigie (Cherokeeleechee) of the Lower Creeks, recalling "the Yamasee Wars," insisted in 1735 that he was "not the occasion of breaking the peace at that time." He was "averse unto it because [he] lived as happily as any white man in those days in my own house . . . [and] wore as good apparel and rode as good a horse as most of them." Nevertheless, once "engaged in the wars, [he] did the English all the harm he could." Such statements make it clear that many southeastern Indians made war on South Carolina for reasons that had nothing to do with traders or the trade.

Other comments do cite English trade relations as a source of irritation, and at first glance they seem to reinforce arguments about trader misconduct. In 1747, for instance, Malatchi of the Lower Creeks recalled that "we lived as brothers for some time till the traders began to use us very ill and wanted to enslave us which occasioned a war." The Cherokees also reported in 1716 that English traders "had ben very abusefull to them of latte, and not as whitte men used to be to them formerly." Such accounts do more than raise the specter of trader misconduct. They generally dismiss it at some earlier period. According to these sources, relations between Englishmen and Indians were not always troubled. Native accusations of generalized abuse were almost always framed in comparison to earlier periods of supposed harmony. What these documents really say, therefore, is that traders and the trade, and therefore their relationship with Native America, had changed in a way that did not please Native Americans.[2]

If a mature "middle ground" had not yet emerged in the early eighteenth-century South, Malatchi and others had nevertheless developed a clear set of ideas about the protocols of intercultural exchange that allowed them to assess the adequacy of French, English, and Spanish behavior. Although ideas about exchange were grounded in traditional notions of reciprocity, gift giving, and alliance, by 1715 such ideas had undergone decades of contact with and adaptation to European approaches. According to ethnohistorian Gregory Waselkov, a low-level but significant Spanish-Indian trade in the early to mid-seventeenth century prepared aboriginal cultures in the region for more intensive trade relations in the eighteenth century, primarily by introducing them to a broad range of material goods. The lessons learned in that trade served southeastern Indians well during the early phases of trade with Carolina and, beginning in 1699, with the French of Louisiana. In the first decade of the eighteenth century, however, trade relations with South Carolina began to accelerate and take on new dimensions, adding tension to the inherently delicate process of intercultural trade. Measured against previous exchange patterns, the Cherokees had no trouble recognizing that English traders were not behaving "as whitte men used to be to them formerly."[3]

MARKET DRIVEN CHANGE

The observations of Jean-Baptiste Lemoyne, Sieur de Bienville, the principal architect of French Louisiana's frontier policy, may provide some insight into the nature of this new behavior. He conceded in 1715 that the English of Carolina had a natural economic advantage in that they "sold . . . merchandise very cheap and . . . took the peltries at a high price and here [in French Louisiana] it is quite the contrary." But he understood that southeastern Indians factored more into the bargain. Unable to offer a better deal, he chose to focus French efforts instead on "*good faith in trading*" (italics mine). This meant a good deal more in practice than equitable treatment and honesty. For the first half of the eighteenth century, French Louisiana remained very much at the margins of the emerging Atlantic economy. Historian Daniel H. Usner has aptly described the colony as being involved in a "frontier exchange economy," dominated by indigenous, regional patterns of exchange rather than the demands of external markets. The informal nature of this "exchange economy" allowed Indians greater freedom to control and adapt the volume and terms of trade with Europeans to serve their own needs. As a result, French trade was conducted not only in "good faith" but in closer accordance with traditional forms of ceremonial gift exchange and tribute.[4]

Bienville believed that the Indians noticed and appreciated the differences between the English and French approaches to trade. Those differences, he felt, were most evident in relation to the trade in Indian slaves. According to Bienville, the majority of southeastern Indians had come to "despise" the English "because of the little scruple that they have against buying slaves of the nations with which they are not at war, which we do not do at all." On those rare occasions when overzealous French traders took slaves from allied nations, Bienville invariably had them returned. "Barbarians as they are," he wrote in 1711, "they do not fail to make the distinction between our sentiments and those of the English."[5]

The difference in French and English sentiments regarding Indian slaves, as with other aspects of trade, was not the result of French moral superiority or English deficiency but of the contrasting economic imperatives at work in Louisiana and South Carolina. Whereas Louisiana remained an insular and economically backward region, allowing Bienville to cultivate "good faith," the Carolina economy by the end of the first decade of the eighteenth century had come to depend on a continuous flow of unfree labor, both for use within the colony on rice plantations and for export as trade credit to other plantation colonies. That demand increasingly encouraged English traders to take risks they might not previously have taken. The deerskin trade accelerated as well, transforming the trade, in the words of historian Converse D. Clowse, from "haphazard bartering . . . to a business carried on by professionals." Although English traders were able to offer goods at competitive prices, by the early eighteenth century their attention was more attuned to the demands of the Carolina and Atlantic economies than to the complaints of their native clients. In short, they had less power to shape the basic contours of trade or fashion it to fit local conditions than did their French rivals.[6]

DEMISE OF THE FUR TRADE

In the decade preceding the Yamasee War, the market effected a sweeping reconfiguration of the Carolina Indian trade. It is a phenomenon that has entirely escaped scholarly notice thus far, perhaps because export totals for deerskins—the most obvious barometer of Anglo-Indian exchange for most of the eighteenth century—do not reflect this early transformation. Although deer-skins became the primary staple of the trade, and had predominated from the beginning, there was initially a trade in other types of pelts that more closely resembled the northern fur trade. During the 1690s, black bear, panther or wildcat (listed as "cat"), fox, muskrat, woodchuck, otter, raccoon, and beaver pelts were traded in meaningful volumes. From 1699 to 1701, southeastern Indians received European goods in exchange for 3,373 beaver pelts, 3,675 fox furs, 1,228 otter pelts, 529 cat skins, and 2,460 raccoon skins. By the end of the first decade of the eighteenth century, however, the trade in beaver had declined to insignificance, while the rest had virtually disappeared as viable items of exchange. From 1713 to 1715, English traders accepted only seven raccoon skins, twelve otter pelts, thirty-nine fox furs, and not a single cat skin.[7]

The market clearly lay behind this transformation. English traders obeyed economic imperatives and purchased from their native clients only those items they could expect to sell most profitably abroad. For other items they likely offered such unappealing compensation that the skill and labor involved in acquiring panther skins, for instance, made the trade unattractive. Although this has hitherto been invisible to modern historians, Carolina officials were painfully aware of the process at the time. As early as 1708, the Indian agent Thomas Nairne was already reminiscing about the days "when beavor was a comodity." Observing "multitudes of beavor dams" in Chicasaw country, he lamented not only the loss of revenue but also the diplomatic leverage the trade conferred. "We can easily ruin Mobile," he argued, "meerly by purchasing beavor skins." He urged the Commissioners of the Indian Trade to "study all means" by which the beaver trade might be revived, suggesting ultimately that "if it's no comodity in England" it might "be sent else where."[8]

South Carolinians were not alone in their concerns. In New York, where the economy relied even more heavily on the beaver trade, its decline became a major point of concern on both sides of the frontier. According to Governor Bellomont, the beaver trade in his colony as well as in Boston had "sunk to little or nothing" by the turn of the century. Whereas New York had formerly exported in excess of 60,000 pelts annually, it cleared only 15,241 between June 1699 and June of 1700. Like Nairne, he blamed the collapse on the English market, where beaver skins had "grown almost quite out of use." As a result, the price had dropped from fourteen shillings per pound to a discouraging five shillings per pound by 1700, making the pelts "scare worth the transporting."[9]

While no records have come to light concerning the responses of southeastern Indians to this state of affairs, the Iroquois discussed it at considerable length with New York officials. At a conference at Albany in the summer of 1701, Iroquois delegates demanded that New Yorkers "lett the beavers come to their old price again." They even sought to diagnose the problem and suggest a possible solution for the English. The Iroquois negotiators offered to send ten beaver skins to King William so that a hat could be made for him. They hoped that once his loyal subjects saw him wearing it, they would "follow his example and were beaver hatts again as the fashion was formerly." Despite their kind advice, however, the Iroquois were not prepared to wait for the market mechanism of supply and demand to reach a natural equilibrium in the beaver trade. "Wee believe," they insisted, that "as you are governour you have the command and that the traders must obey if you order itt." Thus, if the English of New York wished to remain on good terms with the Five Nations, the traders were expected to "begin to day to sell good pennyworths."[10]

The Iroquois analysis of the root causes of the beaver trade's demise was astute. The trade depended heavily on the fortunes of the English hat industry, which utilized the beaver's dense undercoat to produce waterproof felt. That industry had gone into a steady decline in 1697 after King William's War, and the demand for beaver pelts declined with it. Falling hat sales, moreover, affected the market for otter, fox, and other pelts that hat makers often worked into the felt along with beaver to reduce costs. In part the decline resulted, as the Iroquois surmised, from changing fashions in London, where a new type of broad-brimmed leather hat was becoming popular. The "Carolina hat," as it was known, required deerskins rather than beaver pelts. Combined with the numerous other uses for raw leather, the popularity of Carolina hats helped make deerskins a hot commodity on the London market in the first years of the eighteenth century. Not surprisingly, deerskin exports from South Carolina increased dramatically between 1699 and 1715, even as other fur trade staples fell into catastrophic decline.[11]

The economics of the beaver trade crisis went deeper, of course, than fickle London fashions. Falling prices in the metropole resulted not only from reduced consumer demand but also from colonial overproduction of raw materials. New York, New England, Pennsylvania, and "Rupert's Land" of the Hudson's Bay Company continued pumping pelts into the market faster than it could accommodate them throughout the first decade of the 1700s. Dutch commerce managed to siphon some of the surplus into the Russian fur market, but London suffered from a chronic glut of beaver skins throughout this period. It is perhaps understandable that colonies such as New York and Rupert's Land that were deeply invested in the fur trade persisted in it even in the face of such discouraging prospects. In South Carolina, however, where merchants and traders could rely on a profitable alternative, it made good economic sense for them to turn their backs on the local beaver trade and encourage the harvesting of deerskins.[12]

South Carolinians appear to have made that choice abruptly in the span of only two trading seasons. Rather than declining gradually, as one might expect, beaver skin exports from Charles Town dropped from 2,724 in 1702 to only 489 the following year and remained at that level or lower through 1715. Indeed, in three of those subsequent seasons, beaver exports did not rise above 100 pelts. Other traditional commodities of the old fur trade displayed similar patterns. They were not phased out. They simply stopped. During the same trading seasons of 1702 and 1703, fox exports fell from 1,748 to 632 furs. After a brief rebound to 992 in 1704, fox fur exports collapsed utterly to 186 in 1705 and never revived. By 1714, South Carolina was reduced to shipping the embarrassing yearly cargo of five fox furs to the home market. Even minor staples such as otter and raccoon conformed to the 1702–3 collapse curve. Otter skins fell by two-thirds during those seasons, while raccoon skins fell from 571 to 140. Alongside the five fox furs exported in 1714, British ships carried just one otter skin and seven raccoon skins.[13]

Most striking of all is the completeness and uniformity with which all of these commodities disappeared. A more gradual decline might be explainable in terms of rational, economic choices made independently over time by indigenous hunters, Carolina traders, or English merchants in response to the steady nudging of the market. For all of these commodities to disappear suddenly at the same time, however, suggests that the Carolina beaver and fur trades, already burdened by a failing market, encountered additional, insurmountable problems between 1702 and 1704 that made continued participation in them untenable.

Although additional studies of transatlantic shipping and trade need to be done, it seems likely that the disruption of shipping routes resulting from the outbreak of Queen Anne's War in 1702 played a major role in the phenomenon. In order to protect British merchant shipping from the depredations of French naval vessels and privateers, the Board of Trade devised a system of convoys to sail under escort of armed frigates. In theory, the convoys would make regular, scheduled runs to all quarters of the far-flung British empire and ensure the uninterrupted flow of trade. In practice, however, they often created havoc. The elaborate system of sailing dates and destinations drafted by the board did not accommodate the diversity of regional needs and economic rhythms adequately. As a result, convoys sometimes arrived at the wrong time of year to transport perishable seasonal harvests. Prices, moreover, were destabilized in some places by the arrival of multiple convoys in rapid succession. Such was the case in Virginia, where the chaos of the 1703 convoy season reportedly dealt "a fatall blow to trade." According to Robert Quarry, the convoy system had "done more damage to trade and the intrist of these provinces than all that were concern'd in it were worth."[14]

The prospects of sending beaver pelts "else where" than the English market, as Thomas Nairne suggested, became unlikely during this period as well. Of course, the convoy system intentionally channeled colonial goods into the mother country, but the exigencies of war and new imperial trade legislation also functioned to restrict access to alternative markets more effectively than ever before. For instance, the Dutch, who had formerly connected English mainland colonies with French and Spanish consumers, reluctantly cut off trade with hostile nations in 1703. The prohibition lasted only a year, but it had profound economic consequences while in effect. Even if Carolinians had managed to make sense of the dislocated shipping industry, they faced another problem: the British government placed the colony's most lucrative export, rice, on a list of "enumerated" commodities in 1704. Henceforward, South Carolina's rice planters were required to ship their rice harvests directly to England. The legislation eliminated a number of Iberian markets for Carolina's rice planters because their fall harvests could not be transshipped from English ports in time to satisfy seasonal needs. As a result, much of the colony's rice was diverted into the coastwise trade to other North American colonies. Fur shipments dependent on those pre-1704 routes may have been curtailed as a consequence. A profitable reexport system capable of serving northern as well as southern European markets did not emerge in Great Britain until the 1720s, by which time furs had disappeared from Carolina shipping lists.[15]

Similar transatlantic economic pressures touched New France. In the first decade of the eighteenth century beaver was "no commodity," as Thomas Nairne phrased it, anywhere. Plagued by a declining European market, interrupted shipping routes, and runaway local overproduction, the Canadian beaver trade failed spectacularly between 1696 and 1713. The collapse was so complete that the French ministry proposed at one point a total cessation of the Indian trade. It continued only because Canadian officials explained to the ministry how catastrophic the diplomatic repercussions of such a move might be. Unprofitable as it had become, they argued, the beaver trade nevertheless kept valuable Indian allies in the French interest. For that reason alone, while taking a loss, New France continued to exchange European goods for beaver pelts, consciously sublimating the demands of the market to the greater good of friendship and alliance. Much has been written on the subject of "administered" or "treaty" trade; that is, trade conducted predominantly for political purposes rather than for profit. If the Canadian trade was not generally "administered," it nevertheless displayed on this occasion the wisdom to shield its native allies from the harshness of the market.[16]

Although a minor part of the imperial scheme, Louisiana also experienced its share of hardships with respect to the declining beaver trade. The French ministry apparently sought to bolster the sagging Canadian trade by reducing the number of beaver pelts that were exported southward down the Mississippi River to Louisiana. This policy affected the Illinois region, and the link between economic hardship and diplomacy became a major point of concern for Bienville in 1706 and 1707. French missionaries informed him "of the distress in which their Indians are who have beaver skins and other peltries in abundance and [state] that if the French will no longer give them assistance, they will kill, they say, the Frenchmen whom they meet." Bienville could do little on his own to solve the systemic economic problems creating that distress, but he sought to forestall a formal diplomatic rupture by sending gifts of powder and shot. He hoped that the gifts would be enough at least "to make them hope for a more happy future."[17]

MARKET INFLUENCE ON ANGLO-INDIAN RELATIONS

The French examples in Louisiana and New France suggest some obvious, if costly, ways of countering the negative impacts of market-driven change on European-Indian relations. New York responded to Iroquois complaints with diplomatic finesse and increased gift giving. Indeed, New York's relations with the Iroquois carried such importance during Queen Anne's War that all English colonies, including South Carolina, contributed financial assistance for frontier diplomacy and defense. Aside from the comments of Thomas Nairne, however, Carolina officials spent little time considering the problem in their own neighborhood. They certainly made no effort during the same period to assist their native client/allies in making the transition from a mixed skin and fur trade to one based solely on deerskins. From the perspective of Charles Town merchants, the continuing profitability of the deerskin and slave trades undoubtedly argued for a laissez-faire approach. Yet involvement in the Atlantic economy created unsettling new hardships for key participants in the trade, both Indian and English. Without even the token encouragement offered by Bienville, some may have begun to despair of "a more happy future."

It is difficult to determine precisely where the economic burden of the fur trade's sudden collapse hit hardest; all parties were losers in the disastrous trading seasons of 1702–3, but some may have been more adept at passing on the hardship to others through higher prices or harsher trade practices. Interestingly, the demise of a diversified fur trade coincided exactly with the rise of large-scale, English-led slave raids on the Spanish missions. Most historians have assumed that Governor James Moore's attacks on the Apalachee mission Indians of northern Florida were spurred by imperialist objectives related to the beginning of Queen Anne's War, but there may have been economic motives at work as well. Given Moore's intimate involvement and interest in the Indian trade, it may well be asked whether his actions in 1702 and especially 1704 were intended in part to make up for the loss in furs by increasing the supply of Indian slaves.

The 1702–3 collapse appears to have created a wave of credit stress, the progress of which can be traced through the rest of the decade. The suicidal behavior of the Pight, Probert, and Lucas trading partnership in 1706, for instance, may have been linked to this rolling credit vacuum. The reckless persistence of the traders even in the face of angry native opposition, discussed previously, had much to do with economic forces beyond their control. At the time of their tense confrontation with the "Long Doctor" in the "round house," members of the partnership faced legal actions in the South Carolina Court of Common Pleas for collection of debts.

Both Pight and Probert were in desperate financial trouble in late 1706, with Probert being sued in November 1706 by the merchant William Smith for the enormous sum of fifteen hundred pounds Carolina currency. He was forced to put up bail in order to continue trading. His troubles in the round house grew directly out of his troubles in Charles Town.[18]

The same may be said for most of the traders discussed in chapter 1 with respect to issues of credit and the forcible confiscation of goods. Their aggressive pursuit of debts in Indian country was linked in all probability to the aggressiveness of their own creditors in Charles Town. Most of those traders were in the process of being sued for debts themselves, including Joseph Bryan (Brynon), Philip Gilliard, Shippy Allen, Richard Gower, Samuel Hilden, and John Wright. Wright was in such desperate financial trouble in 1713 and 1714 that he mortgaged most of his slaves and his entire plantation. The lump sum payment was to come due, ominously enough, in the spring of 1715, just as he was making his ill-fated trip to Pocotaligo to negotiate with the Yamasees.[19]

In addition to the distressed behavior of some Carolina traders, Native American participants in the trade experienced internal changes as a result of the market's changing desires. It may be argued that increased deerskin production smoothed the transformation of the trade for Native Americans by offsetting the decline in the fur trade commodities, but this net equivalency in economic terms concealed a drastic redeployment of labor on the part of native hunters and trappers. Such a process demanded the curtailment of diversified activities, probably predating the era of market involvement, that drew on a variety of species and habitats in favor of a single, seasonal pursuit targeting a single species. The practical difficulties of this transformation, involving issues of hunting territory, technique, and technology must have been immense. If the distress created by market influence was not extreme enough to prompt southeastern Indians to issue death threats against South Carolina traders, as the Illinois Indians did against French traders, it nevertheless contributed to the growing tensions created by the trade.

Archaeological excavations at Upper and Lower Creek town sites in Alabama and Georgia corroborate the date of the transformation and suggest how profoundly it altered traditional lifeways. Before 1700, the Muskhogee- and Hitchiti-speaking towns that later comprised the Creek Confederacy routinely constructed "winter houses," built with a sunken floor, circular walls, and wattle-and-daub construction techniques. Sturdier than rectangular "summer houses," these structures provided additional warmth and protection during cold winter months. As the commercial deerskin trade came to dominate native economic life, however, hunters were forced to extend their winter hunting expeditions for months on end. Labor formerly devoted to the construction of winter housing may have been devoted increasingly to the hunt, and the extended absence of hunters and their families may have rendered such housing unnecessary. Not surprisingly, winter houses uniformly disappeared from villages across the region. More than a simple architectural loss, the demise of winter housing altered the actual and social landscape of proto-Creek villages. The appearance and spatial structure of southeastern towns changed, and seasonal patterns of family life and gender relations must have shifted to fit the new order as well.[20]

In the first decade of the eighteenth century, deer hunting drew Native American men farther into the Atlantic economy than ever before, and their mothers, wives, sisters, and daughters followed them. As raccoons, panthers, foxes, muskrats, otters, and beavers disappeared from Carolina shipping lists between 1699 and 1715, the entries for deerskins displayed a pronounced shift toward a certain method of preparation in addition to an increase in volume. Whereas exports had previously included large numbers of "undrest" deerskins, comprising about 30 percent of the total number exported at the start of this pivotal decade, that percentage had withered to only 10 percent between 1713 and 1715. In place of those undressed skins, roughly 90 percent of all deerskins exported from Charles Town between 1713 and 1715 were "half-drest," a process of partial preparation specifically geared toward trade. Because women were generally responsible for the preparation of deerskins, this may indicate their growing involvement in at least one aspect of the trade. We may never know whether it was a voluntary strategy to maximize exchange rates or a grudging concession to market demands. Since half-dressed skins generally commanded higher prices, however, the shift benefited native consumers and may thus have represented an effort on their part to counter the largely negative developments under way at the time. Such a strategy would have been particularly useful in offsetting the deteriorating exchange rate between Carolina currency and British pounds sterling. Kathryn Holland Braund has identified a reverse process at work in the 1760s, when the trade shifted back toward undressed skins. She viewed this as a market-driven transformation that carried with it a built-in price rise for Creek consumers. It may be that this initial shift away from undressed skins just prior to the Yamasee War marked the adoption of a defensive economic posture that southeastern Indians could no longer maintain after the 1760s.[21]

Whatever the mercurial demands of the market may have been, it is clear at least that English officials in Charles Town and London recognized the dressing of deerskins as a matter of imperial significance. According to mercantile economic theory, raw materials ideally flowed from the colonies to the mother country, where they were subsequently crafted into finished products. The British Parliament sought to ensure this model in 1710 by granting a "draw-back" on undressed "Hides and Skins" exported from the American colonies. A few years later, in 1714, the South Carolina Commons House of Assembly passed complementary legislation placing "a duty on all tanned leather exported." Unexciting as the laws may seem, they once pulsed with human aspiration and drama. In essence, members of Parliament hoped to entice Native American deerskin producers to move voluntarily into the proper colonial relationship, while South Carolinians actively sought to restrain them from usurping the finishing trades of the home market.[22]

English leather workers in London, who had as much to gain or lose in this struggle as southeastern Indians had, followed its progress intently. If the proper balance of taxes, duties, and draw-backs was not struck, they warned the House of Commons in 1711, "the Natives abroad" might grow frustrated with the trade and simply choose to "Wear the Skins which are the product of their own country." They knew full well that such a decision, favoring self-sufficiency over market involvement, would in turn cost them "a great part of their Livlyhoods."[23]

As profitable and stable as the southeastern deerskin trade appears in unadorned customs reports, therefore, its entry into the imperial economic system in the years just prior to the Yamasee War involved comprehensive efforts to restrict and manipulate indigenous behavior. While mandated at the highest levels of British government, those efforts ultimately found effective expression in the business conducted by South Carolina traders in Indian country. For Creek, Cherokee, or Catawba producers seeking to add value to their product by seasoning the leather themselves, the obstacle was not the House of Commons in London, or even the Commons House of Assembly in Charles Town, but the man on the ground who stopped buying it from them. In this context, the emergence of half-dressed skins as the dominant export staple in the years prior to the Yamasee War may represent a tense compromise between English traders who, as representatives of the market, desired undressed skins and Native American producers who sought to exchange dressed skins in spite of imperial restrictions. Half-dressed skins may thus have satisfied neither side entirely. The result of these divergent agendas, it should be stressed, was yet another occasion for disharmony between Englishmen and Indians.

A FINAL TWIST

In the three years immediately preceding the outbreak of the Yamasee War in 1715, market involvement once again brought sweeping changes to the fabric of the Carolina-Indian exchange relationship, this time with respect to the Indian slave trade. The historian Richard L. Haan has argued persuasively that Yamasee and Lower (Ocheese) Creek slave raiders may have begun to experience difficulties prior to the war. Their principal slaving targets, Apalachee and Guale in Spanish Florida, had probably been denuded of victims well before 1715.[24] Thomas Nairne observed in 1708 that English-allied Indians endeavoring to capture slaves "are now obliged to goe down as farr on the point of Florida as the firm land will permitt," having "drove the Floridians to the islands of the cape." As a result, the center of gravity of the slave trade appears to have shifted west, where Upper Creek and Chickasaw warriors stepped up the brutal business in pursuit of Choctaw and other French-allied Indian victims.[25]

Nevertheless, all participants in the internal southeastern slave trade, regardless of their access to "resources," experienced a sudden contraction of external markets for Indian slaves between 1712 and 1715. Alarmed at reports of Indian atrocities during the Tuscarora War in North Carolina, which erupted in 1711, as well as by the behavior of its own Indian slaves, Massachusetts passed an act in 1712 to prohibit further Indian slave imports:

> Whereas divers conspiracies, outrages, barbarities, murders, burglaries, thefts, and other notorious crimes, at sundry times, and especially of late, have been perpetrated by Indians and other slaves, within several of his Majesties plantations in America, being of a malitious and revengeful spirit, rude and insolent in their behaviour, and very ungovernable; the over-great number of which, considering the different circumstances of this colony from the plantations in the islands, and our having considerable numbers of the Indian Indians of the country within and about us, may be of pernicious consequence to his Majesties subjects and interests here, unless speedily remedied.[26]

Pennsylvania and Rhode Island followed suit the same year by enacting prohibitive import duties on "Carolina Indians," as they were known in the northern colonies. In 1713 and 1714 respectively, New Jersey and New Hampshire also took measures to curtail Indian slave imports by levying a duty of ten pounds on every slave brought into port. The loss of these markets left Carolinians with only two major buyers for their slaves: Carolina rice planters and the West Indies (principally Jamaica, Barbados, and Bermuda). In each case, the insatiable demand for slave labor probably took any surplus off the market. Yet the local consequences for Carolina slave traders included at the very least a significant decline in prices as more "Carolina Indians" were funneled into fewer and fewer markets. It is impossible to quantify the diminished profitability of the Indian slave trade, but traders must have begun passing it along to Native American suppliers by 1714.[27]

The probability of increased sales of Indian slaves to South Carolina rice planters after 1712 raises another difficult but inescapable problem. Because the colony was chronically short of coin, planters had little with which to purchase slaves aside from their own rice and the paper currency or "current money" printed for local circulation by the South Carolina government. This local currency had remained relatively stable in comparison to British pounds sterling since its first issue in 1703, mainly because the colony redeemed each cycle of notes in a timely fashion. In 1712, by contrast, the Commons House of Assembly voted to issue a new supply of paper currency on a semi-permanent basis. The economics of what happened next are still a matter of scholarly debate, but the consequences are clear. South Carolina's paper currency immediately began depreciating. The exchange rate in terms of pounds Carolina currency per 100 pounds sterling jumped from 150 in 1712 to 200 in 1713 and then to 300 in 1714. For planters who had contracted debts, this was good news. It meant that by 1714 they could pay off debts at less than their original value. But for the traders and merchants who sold them goods, it meant financial ruin and another wave of credit stress to be transferred to their native business partners.[28]

Lower Creek and Yamasee observers noted the growing Carolina obsession with credit. Significantly, they remembered that "rumors" about the meaning of the new English stridency began to circulate in Indian country about three years before the war: that is, about 1712. In early 1715, the principal "cacique of the town of Caveta" traveled to Pocotaligo to discuss the situation with the Yamasee "without the English watching." He proposed that they offer to pay the English with a variety of goods, including otter and beaver pelts. Here then was the heart of the Indian conspiracy against South Carolina: a proposal to broaden the range of acceptable commodities. In essence, it was a call to restore the trade to its earlier diversity and flexibility. The records do not indicate whether the Yamasees and Lower Creeks presented the plan to local English traders as a proposal or, as seems more likely, an ultimatum. There can be no doubt, however, about the market's answer.[29]

THEMES, PATTERNS, PROBLEMS

Scholars of the southern deerskin trade (often working from a more abundant mid- to late-eighteenth-century document base) typically take for granted the wholesale transformation of Native Americans into full-fledged participants in the Atlantic economy without scrutinizing the process by which it supposedly occurred. The result is a sometimes glib generalization of their transformation into a "forest proletariat" as "rapid and easy," made "with minimal adjustments." As I seek to demonstrate in this chapter, however, it was a more complex, culturally demanding, and extended process than is generally supposed. Gregory Waselkov's suggestion that the seventeenth-century Spanish-Indian trade prepared southeastern Indians for more intensive trade relations with Carolina was limited mainly to the integration of European goods into indigenous material cultures. The limited nature of that early trade did not require native participants to depart radically from preexisting economic pursuits. It had hardly reduced them to a "forest proletariat." Developments in the Carolina trade during the first decade of the eighteenth century represented a marked departure from prevailing seventeenth-century patterns of exchange and from continuing French and Spanish models.

Southeastern Indians were forced to alter their habits in order to meet the increasingly ardent and specific demands of the market. The process was coerced, moreover, by the credit power of English traders, and their behavior in turn was often a credit-generated reflex.[30]

Although an integral part of the phenomenon, Carolina traders were in part the unwitting personification of larger economic forces over which they had little control. In contrast to the scattered effects of gender-specific violence or the localized hardship of indebtedness among the Yamasees, the new economic imperatives communicated by English traders touched all native communities involved in trade relations with South Carolina. The torque thus exerted on Anglo-Indian relations further strained the inherently delicate mechanisms of intercultural exchange, already critically stressed in key areas, and placed Carolina's extensive alliance network on a tenuous footing. By the end of the decade, South Carolina's relationship with its native clients and allies had come to depend more than ever on official acts of diplomacy from Charles Town, carried to the frontier by the Indian agent.

4. Trade Regulation and the Breakdown of Diplomacy

✳ ✳ ✳ ✳ ✳ ✳ ✳ ✳ ✳ ✳ ✳ ✳ ✳ ✳ ✳

In the early years of the eighteenth-century South, Anglo-Indian trade drew many new voices into it, not all of them harmonious. Southeastern Indians who purchased goods from Carolina traders increasingly haggled with Englishmen beyond the horizon. As a result, English traders carried the voices of London felters, hat makers, leather workers, and members of Parliament with them up the Savannah River and inland across the Ocmulgee. As the trade extended its reach and influence, they frequently carried the colony's diplomatic voice far abroad and were pressured to serve its imperial ambitions in Indian country. Most troublesome of all, however, traders spoke for themselves and pursued their own economic advantage.

In the midst of that choir of voices, southeastern Indians listened for the official voice of South Carolina. They listened for it because traditional approaches to trade, predating the arrival of Europeans, led them to value the diplomatic meaning of exchange as much as the commodities it provided. Deerskins destined for Charles Town and muskets destined for Coweta could only travel along paths that had been purified and made "white" by the rituals of peace and alliance. That whiteness required diligent maintenance, for peaceable paths between allies could become obstructed through misunderstandings, insults, mismanagement, or simple neglect; should one party or another subsequently "stain the path with blood," peaceful commerce could no longer move along it. Trade could only travel on paths that were kept "streight and white." The arrival of English trade goods meant a great deal more, therefore, than material gain for Yamasees, Apalachees, Euchees, Cherokees, etc. They announced the continued whiteness of the path and served to keep it clean. As such, the various intrigues and individual interests of English traders, embodying the voices of Parliament, London leather workers, and distant fur markets, nevertheless spoke for the purity of the path that united Indians and the English.[1]

If Charles Town officials did not entirely grasp the political complexities that guided Native American participation in commodity exchange, they nevertheless understood the power of the informal diplomacy performed by English traders in the normal course of business. In fact, as the Indian trade accelerated in the first decade of the eighteenth century, officials came to regard the voices and actions of "the multitude of traders" as a dangerous threat to the colony's safety and diplomatic agenda. According to members of the Commons House of Assembly, the traders sought "their own Advantage" regardless of the consequences for the colony. The outbreak of the War of the Spanish Succession in 1702 added a new urgency to the need for greater control over traders as Carolina competed against Spanish Florida and French Louisiana for Indian allies. As a result, the Commons House of Assembly, after much rancor, passed an "Act for Regulating the Indian Trade" in 1707. The legislation created a board of commissioners responsible for establishing trade policy and supervising the trade. They also supervised the activities of the Indian agent, a new office created by the same act. The agency represented the colony's most visible diplomatic connection with southeastern

Native America, entrusted with the responsibility of adjudicating differences between Indians and traders, policing the trade, and delivering diplomatic messages to and from Indian country.[2]

The regulatory legislation of 1707 was part and parcel of the market phenomenon already rippling along the frontier, and while its full economic consequences for southeastern Indians have not been recognized to date, historians have long considered 1707 a watershed year. For Converse D. Clowse, it marked the "dividing line between an Indian trade conducted informally and a regularized commerce," while Verner Crane saw it as a transformation of the Indian trade from a "profitable sideline" into a "mercantile interest second only to the exportation of rice." Scholars have traditionally agreed as well that the new regulatory legislation contributed, though indirectly, to the outbreak of the Yamasee War by failing to curtail trader misconduct and abuse. It is argued here, however, that South Carolina's regulatory apparatus played a central, even decisive, role in provoking conflict. Indeed, for a region prepared by the parching effects of market-driven change, South Carolina's efforts to regulate the Indian trade produced the perfect spark to ignite conflict.[3]

REGULATING DISCOURSE

South Carolina's new approach to trade regulation inevitably affected the ways in which the English and Indians spoke to one another. Although members of the Commons House of Assembly frequently expressed their desire to curtail "abusses" and "irregularities" committed by traders, the nature of the new legislation and its practical implications suggest that the real issue was not necessarily justice or fair play for Native Americans so much as control over the terms and content of Anglo-Indian diplomacy. By

empowering the Commissioners of the Indian Trade to license traders and supervise their behavior, the Assembly expressly intended
"to Constitute a power to hinder persons ffrom goieng to trade
amongst the Indians" except by their permission and according to
their rules. Controlling access to Indian villages meant more than
control of traders and a share of their profits. It meant control over
communication with the inhabitants of those villages and made
the Assembly, in theory at least, the official diplomatic voice of
South Carolina.[4]

The contentiousness that attended passage of the regulatory
act indicates just how ambitious it really was and how deeply the
colony's governing elites understood and struggled for the control
it promised. The Commons House of Assembly repeatedly found
its efforts rejected by the vetoes of Governor Nathaniel Johnson
and his council. The governor feared that his influence over the
Indian trade, and the gifts he received from Indian leaders, would be
reduced or usurped if the bill were passed. "Can I with any reason
in the world expect presents from the Indians," he complained,
"when they shall perceive I have no power either to aide or Serve
them?" In fact, he suspected that the legislation was "meant rather
to restrain your Govern'r than the Traders." The act did, of course,
transfer control over diplomacy and trade with American Indian
nations from the governor and his council to the Assembly. It thus
represented a major milestone in the general trend toward greater
power for representative assemblies in the southern colonies, and
it ushered in a new era in Anglo-Indian discourse.[5]

No case illustrates the extent to which trade regulation involved
the regulation of discourse better than that of Alexander Longe, a
trader working among the Cherokee Indians. In addition to blowing up a Euchee Indian in his store, he ran afoul of the Commissioners of the Indian Trade in 1714 when he assisted several of the

Cherokee headmen from the Overhill Towns (settlements on the western side of the Appalachian Mountains) in a slave raid against the Euchee town of Chestowe. Because the Euchees were allies of South Carolina, the raid and especially Longe's complicity in it threatened to destabilize the colony's alliance network.

The raid itself stood out as especially brutal, even in a ruthless and cruel era. A number of the besieged Euchees, trapped in their own "war house," chose to "kill their own people" to spare them a life of slavery or worse. Outraged over the incident, the commissioners spared no expense in prosecuting Longe and his compatriot, Eleazor Wiggin. For four days between May 4 and May 7, 1714, from dawn to dusk, the Commissioners of the Indian Trade heard the testimony of fourteen witnesses on the matter. Prosecuting Longe without angering the Cherokees was a delicate procedure, complicated by the commissioners' awareness that Cherokee initiative and involvement were never far below the surface of the proceedings. But they wanted Longe badly, and they wanted him for reasons that are not immediately evident in the trial records.[6]

In considering the issue, the commissioners focused heavily on Longe's personal grudge against the Euchees, dating back several years to a scuffle in which "some Euchees" had "torn off" his hair. Longe reportedly vowed that "he would never rest till the Euchees were cut off," and his handling of the Euchee warrior who came to his store for gunpowder certainly lent credence to the force of that vendetta. He was credited with suggesting that if the work was to be done, it needed to happen "before green Corn Time." Some witnesses claimed, moreover, that Longe had pretended to have a written order from the governor of South Carolina supporting the attack. When it became clear that Longe and his business associate, Theophilus Hastings, had also supplied the Cherokee war party with powder and shot and had received a portion of the Euchee captives taken in the attack, the commissioners concluded that Longe had been "instrumentall" in "incouraging" the Cherokees.[7]

The prominence accorded to Longe in the Chestowe affair by South Carolina officials is understandable, for they had long-standing concerns about his behavior in Cherokee country. If the Commissioners of the Indian Trade condemned him in 1714 for "incouraging" the attack on the Euchees, it was in part because they had not yet forgiven him for "stopping the Indians from marching against the Tusqueroras" in 1711. Ironically, Alexander Longe found himself at odds with the Charles Town government for both beginning and stopping wars. The key to resolving this paradox has nothing to do with traditional historiographical accusations of trade abuse or misconduct on the part of English traders but rather hinges upon two separate, interwoven dialogues proceeding simultaneously between the Cherokee Indians and the English: one involving the South Carolina government, the other with Alexander Longe.[8]

DECISIONS ABOUT WAR AND PEACE

Decisions about war and peace in the heyday of the Indian slave trade more often than not involved the prospect of war captives, and British traders hoping to purchase those prisoners naturally had a compelling interest in such decisions. Not surprisingly, they often attempted to influence matters by entering, as far as they were able and allowed, the local talks among regional leaders and warriors. Those discussions took place at any number of locations, including informal venues such as town plazas, where men and women often gathered for conversation, or at the trader's own warehouse or store. During the final stages of debate they also took place in more formal settings such as war or council houses, and English traders did their best to participate.

At the informal level, Alexander Longe's infamous demolition of a Euchee Indian undoubtedly functioned, intentionally or otherwise, as part of the local Overhill Cherokee conversation about how to deal with intertribal tensions with the neighboring Euchees. Shocking as it may seem from a modern perspective to "sett fier" to a pile of gunpowder and kill an innocent Euchee customer, it is important to recall that Longe did so in Cherokee—not Euchee—territory, and that the act was performed exclusively for a Cherokee audience. Indeed, the grisly demonstration survived in the records only because Cherokee observers gave testimony about it.

In the context of local debates about whether to send Cherokee warriors against the Euchees, Longe's "misconduct" must have announced a very loud English endorsement of plans to "cut of[f] Chestowe." In fact, in the context of a preexisting "difference" between the Cherokees and the Euchees and the latter's alleged killing of a Cherokee Indian, the incident may have been received among some Overhill Cherokee warriors as an act of sympathy, solidarity, and vengeance. It should be noted that the Cherokees far outnumbered the Euchees and would have constituted Longe's most lucrative consumer base. Making Cherokee quarrels his own might have been a good business strategy. Being a good businessman, he made certain that Cherokee leaders understood the probability that "there would be a brave Parsell of slaves if Chestowe were cut off."[9]

That Alexander Longe's participation in local Cherokee discussions ultimately came into conflict with South Carolina officials, however, points out a fundamental schism in the structure of Anglo-Indian discourse. Although it may not have been entirely apparent to the Cherokees as they considered Longe's "incouragement," the cacophony of British voices vying for Native American attention emanated from two distinct groups of men in two different places: the local trade talk of men like Pight, Probert, Lucas, and Longe, and the long-distance treaty talk of Charles Town.

Official diplomatic communication from the South Carolina government, as distinct from the local profit-centered chatter of individual traders, tended to focus more on matters of alliance and regional geopolitics. From 1707 onward, the colony's Indian agent generally served as the conduit for that discourse, conveying messages to the Cherokees and other southeastern Indian nations from the governor and council or Commons House of Assembly and vice versa. For different reasons, the starting and stopping of wars was a high priority at that official level as well, and the Tuscarora and Euchee crises represented the most pressing topics in the Cherokee–Charles Town dialogue from 1711 to 1714. South Carolina had made its wishes clear when the Tuscarora Indians attacked North Carolina in 1711. Native trading partners and allies were exhorted to rally to the defense of the northern colony, and many—including the Catawbas, various Carolina piedmont tribes, Yamasees, Lower Creeks, and a few Cherokees—responded with military assistance. Many Cherokee towns, though, declined to participate. The extent of Alexander Longe's influence over that decision is uncertain. English traders rarely if ever had the power to coerce war and peace in Indian country. Yet the trade itself provided Longe and others with some measure of influence, and the Charles Town government expected traders to use that leverage to further the colony's interests. Longe apparently did not.

Official communication between South Carolina and the Cherokees with respect to the Euchee Indians was more ambiguous. Although Governor Charles Craven, the council, and the Commons

House of Assembly recognized that a problem might be brewing with respect to the Euchees settled at Chestowe, they do not seem to have anticipated the possibility of a Cherokee attack. Instead, they expressed concern that the Euchees might be on the verge of "deserting" their settlements, particularly those on the Savannah River to the south of Chestowe, and perhaps moving closer to the French sphere of influence. The highly charged imperial rivalry between Great Britain and France during Queen Anne's War, 1702–13, potentially made this a political act with serious consequences for South Carolina. Carolina officials finally appear to have gotten wind of a proposed Cherokee offensive against the Euchees in early 1714, and the governor may well have sent a message advising against it. If so, later testimony suggested that the message did not receive prompt or widespread distribution, allowing a variety of rumors about its contents to circulate in advance of it. According to the "2d warrior" from the Cherokee town of "Echote" (Chota), the letter supported plans to "cut of[f] Chestowe." Another Cherokee warrior named Flint, meanwhile, claimed to have actual possession of "an Order for cutting off Chestowe." On the other hand, the Cherokee leader Partridge claimed there was "no Order from the Governor" and therefore refused to take part in the raid. If South Carolina officials opposed a Cherokee strike against Chestowe, that sentiment was not communicated clearly or effectively prior to the attack.[10]

The dual streams of British discourse entering Indian country, trade talk and treaty talk, originated in different places and often pursued different agendas. In many cases, as with Alexander Longe, the discourse of British traders was flatly incompatible with that of the Charles Town government. Sometimes the two voices became so garbled and intertwined that local Indian leaders had difficulty untangling the words of the governor from those of the traders. Yet the two classes of Carolinians themselves understood the dichotomy and engaged in a running battle to subordinate rival discourses to their own interests. For example, when South Carolina Indian Agent Thomas Nairne sent a deputy named John Dixon in 1713 with a warrant to free three Indian slaves unjustly detained by a trader named Thomas Welch, the trader responded by warning Dixon that "if he said any more to the Indians about itt, he had a gun ready charged for him." Welch's concern was not merely that the government opposed his actions but that the government's voice would reach the Indians and challenge his own explanation of events. Similarly, when the same John Dixon who served that warrant faced official opposition to his own trading venture, he responded by "tearing and burning the order." As punishment, the Commissioners of the Indian Trade ordered him to "make such publick Acknowledgement among the Indians as this Board shall direct."[11]

The conflicting agendas of Carolina's official diplomatic voice and the local dialogues of traders like Alexander Longe became most conspicuous with respect to decisions about the status of war captives. As discussed in chapter 2, the process by which slave status was ultimately formalized in an English legal context involved a complex, cooperative partnership between local Indian leaders and Charles Town officials. The latter nearly always deferred to decisions made in Native American council houses, even in the face of angry opposition from British traders. In fact, the *Journals of the Commissioners of the Indian Trade* contain only two cases out of many dozens between 1710 and 1715 in which the commissioners challenged a native decision about slave status. It was a dangerous thing to do, as Carolina officials undoubtedly knew, since it risked offending and alienating powerful allies. Significantly, Alexander

Longe's trial is one of those two rare instances in which the Charles Town government attempted such a thing.[12]

Although the commissioners' primary motivation seems to have been the subordination of trader influence to the government discourse in matters of war and peace, accusations against Longe implicitly threatened his Cherokee partners. By calling into question the propriety of his alleged "incouragement" of the Cherokee decision-making process, the commissioners challenged the validity of the decision itself and opened the door for questions about the status of the Euchee captives taken during the attack. The case, however, was hardly a study in logical progression. While the commissioners followed established patterns in securing native testimony, or hearsay evidence about native testimony, they harped insistently on Longe's behavior and assiduously skirted the issue of native initiative. In the end, the commissioners awarded punitive damages before handing down a decision, an indication that the conclusion was foregone. They declared all Euchee captives held by "white men" free and ordered them returned "to their own people." Those held by Cherokee warriors somehow escaped the commissioners' attention. By freeing only the captives held by white men, the commissioners wisely chose not to direct any criticism or condemnation directly at the Cherokees.[13]

Nevertheless, that criticism was implicit in the proceedings against Longe, and the commissioners' approach laid the groundwork for future misunderstanding and conflict with the Cherokees. Wishing to avoid a confrontation with the leaders of the Overhill and Middle Towns who had carried out the attack, South Carolina officials inadvertently created plausible grounds to suspect that they might eventually carry their prosecution of the case into Indian country. It was a legitimate, perhaps inevitable fear that could easily have been allayed by timely communication between

Charles Town and the Cherokees. The Commissioners of the Indian Trade had won their battle with Alexander Longe for control of the Anglo-Cherokee dialogue, but now, strangely, they stopped participating in it.

BREAKDOWN OF DIPLOMACY

Longe's trial in the spring of 1714 represented the commissioners' last meaningful effort to extend their influence into Indian country. That fall, the dual nature of Anglo-Indian discourse erupted into open conflict. The battle lines followed the same basic pattern as in previous disputes, pitting angry traders against the colony's regulatory regime. At the center of the controversy stood two men, Thomas Nairne and John Wright, whose relationship helped precipitate the complete disintegration of South Carolina's diplomacy with all American Indian Nations in late 1714. Although neither man by himself intended to compromise Carolina's diplomatic standing among southeastern Indians, together they produced a rare chemistry that managed to dissolve the colony's reputation utterly. Beginning as a simple competition for sole ownership of the Indian agency, which changed hands between them twice, their rivalry soon expanded into a vindictive conflict that ultimately transcended their personal enmity and drove a fatal wedge between South Carolina traders and regulatory officials.

The specific circumstances of the rivalry's inception, though compelling as human drama, are perhaps irrelevant to the current discussion. Wright felt himself wronged, first by his ouster as agent in 1712 and subsequently by Nairne's enthusiastic application of the regulatory laws to Wright's own trading ventures. Wright first sought legal redress through the Court of Common Pleas, where between 1713 and 1715 he became a master of nuisance suits, designed to harass and annoy his enemies. They followed a common formula, citing clauses of the new 1712 Act for Regulating the Indian Trade with such an emphasis on details and technicalities as to seem almost comical. He appears to have changed only a few key phrases and names from case to case in order to save time. Soon, other traders sympathetic to his cause also began filing suits, utilizing his exact format and targeting the same defendants. By the summer of 1714, Wright and his supporters were ready to move beyond nuisance suits and the Court of Common Pleas, to mount a more serious challenge to the colony's regulatory administration.[14]

Wright fired the opening salvos of that broader battle on June 8, 1714, when he submitted a list of "remonstrances" to the Commons House of Assembly, accusing Nairne of "irregularities & ill practices." Only four days later, another trader named John Pight revealed the full extent of the offensive when he too submitted a petition to the Assembly, this time accusing the Commissioners of the Indian Trade of exercising poor judgment in a case they had decided the previous year. Although the petitions were filed separately, it became clear as time went on that the two traders were coordinating their efforts, often drafting and submitting letters for their respective cases to the same people on the same or consecutive days and calling on a common pool of witnesses. Pight later testified that he had in fact spent much time at Wright's Goose Creek plantation during this period, a revelation that struck contemporaries as "very strange," since he was "notoriously known" to spend most of his time "in the Indian country."[15]

At the same time, Wright began to flout Nairne's authority openly on the frontier. When the agent locked up a cask of Wright's rum (an illegal commodity) in the mico's own "hous" at the Yamasee town of Pocotaligo, Wright sent two of his henchmen to take it back. They "broke open" the headman's house and carried away the rum. Nairne issued a warrant for their arrest, but the residents of Pocotaligo saw no immediate local action. And the real problem of bringing Wright and his supporters to heel was another matter entirely. For the Yamasee Indians, having seen both Nairne and Wright in an official capacity, the incident could not possibly have made sense. It signaled the disintegration of a coherent policy and voice from Charles Town. The two agents were at war with each other. Several questions must have passed repeatedly around Yamasee council fires in late 1714 and early 1715: which man is the official agent, which man is more powerful, which man's policy is best, and which man is to be believed?[16]

No answers to these questions ever came from Charles Town. Beginning in November 1714, when the Commons House began considering in earnest the complaints brought to it by Wright and Pight, Thomas Nairne was forced to neglect his duties as agent and remain in town to defend himself. Likewise, the Commissioners of the Indian Trade foreswore their normal business and devoted themselves exclusively to their own defense. Virtually no routine business was conducted by either the agent or the commissioners in the five months preceding the outbreak of the war. In essence, therefore, South Carolina ended all official contact and correspondence with all corners of Native America from November 1714 onward, creating an abrupt and utter diplomatic vacuum everywhere. The colony simply disappeared on a diplomatic level, and the trade that continued pulsing outward from it carried a confusing array of messages, depending on the factional loyalties of individual traders.[17]

In some cases those messages meshed eerily, or were made to mesh, with preexisting regulatory conflicts to caste suspicion on the aims of South Carolina officials. Alexander Longe, for instance, having been arrested for his participation in the slave raid against the Euchees, capitalized on the confusion in Charles Town by running away to seek refuge among his old friends in Overhill Cherokee territory. Longe knew perfectly well that the Commissioners of the Indian Trade had ruled to free only the Euchee captives held by "white men." But now he apparently sought Cherokee protection by conflating the actual charges against him for "incouraging" the attack on Chestowe Town with the implicit charges against his Cherokee partners that the commissioners had pointedly chosen to disregard. He warned that "ye Einglish was goeing to macke warrs with them and that they did design to kill all their head warriers."[18]

This was a message not only for Flint, an allied warrior named Cesar, and the "second warrior" of Chota—that is, for those who had carried out the attack—but also for Partridge, who had refused to participate and had even testified against them all. As Longe undoubtedly knew, British ignorance of local Cherokee politics and factionalism made believable the blanket threat of war against friend and foe alike. His version of events harmonized remarkably well with recent developments, played upon predictable Cherokee concerns, and went entirely unchallenged by the colony. Indeed, the ominous silence of Carolina's diplomatic voice undoubtedly spoke volumes.

Information filtering into Cherokee territory from other Indian nations lent support to Longe's allegations as well. When the Yamasees observed English preparations to build a fort at Port Royal on the edge of their settlements, their initial concern over the cessation of diplomatic communications turned to alarm. Again, Charles Town offered no official explanation, leaving the Yamasees to search for their own answers. Some apparently became convinced that Carolina was preparing for war, and a Yamasee delegation conscientiously made a circuit of their neighboring allies to warn them of the threatening English behavior.[19]

With the breakdown of diplomacy in late 1714, the trade was stripped of its political dimension just when this was needed most. The growing inflexibility of English trade behavior during the first decade of the century had placed an unusually high premium on competent diplomacy from Charles Town, first to smooth over the difficulties of intercultural exchange, exacerbated by recent market developments, and second, to reassure concerned clients and confirm valuable alliances. Its absence now proved fatal. As the diplomatic blackout continued into the spring of 1715, and English traders began arriving in native villages across the South to collect their debts, the tensions reached critical mass for some nations. After having made "severall complaints without redress," the "Creeks" (probably the "Ocheese" or Lower Creeks) finally issued an ultimatum that "upon the first affront from any of the traders they would down with them and soe go on with it." The Creeks, to be clear, did not simply kill the traders. They issued a warning clearly intended to be heard and passed up the trading path to Charles Town. It was an effort, born of desperation, to break through the diplomatic pall that had fallen over the colony and to elicit some sort of official response. Similar warnings emanated from the Yamasee settlements around Port Royal at the same time, and they had their desired effect. Carolina officials snapped to attention, stopped their bickering, and organized their first diplomatic overture in over five months. Given the importance and delicacy of the venture, it was entrusted to the colony's most experienced frontier diplomats: Thomas Nairne and John Wright.[20]

The fate of this famous effort at negotiation has become a favorite staple of Carolina lore, and the Pocotaligo encounter appears prominently in the introduction of the present study in large part because it has indeed become an iconic moment in southern history. The standard account of this incident, however, has not changed significantly since the publication of Verner Crane's *The Southern Frontier* more than seventy years ago. In account after account, Nairne's official message of peace and friendship and the amicable goodnight exchanges are followed by the harrowing massacre of the English delegates at dawn on Good Friday. In the traditional version, the attack is generally taken as proof that the Yamasees had already committed themselves to war and that Nairne had little chance of changing their minds. The friendly goodnight thus became a sinister façade, masking the Yamasees' deadly intentions.

Yet there is a face missing from this time-honored portrait: namely, that of John Wright. Only six months earlier, the Yamasees had seen the conflict between the two agents played out in that very town, with the break-in and recovery of the rum. Wright's presence now alongside Thomas Nairne at what may be termed "ground zero" of the Yamasee War inevitably raises a number of questions. Foremost among them: did he bring to Pocotaligo Town the same political agenda that had governed his actions for the last two years in the Court of Common Pleas and the Assembly?[21]

Carolina lore also holds that after the first pitched battle with the Yamasees, a note addressed to Governor Charles Craven was found on one of the fallen warriors. Rumored to have included an explanation of Yamasee motives, it was thought to have disappeared as quickly and completely as the musket smoke of that battle. The note, however, did and does exist. It has spent the last three centuries, astonishingly, tucked inside another letter in the British Public Record Office, where it was never catalogued on its own merit. Signed by the "Huspaw King," it was written in "gunpowder ink" and dictated by the leader of Huspah Town to a young English boy taken captive for precisely that purpose. True to legend, it is an explanation in the Yamasee Indians' own voice as to why they acted as they did. Amidst voluminous English, French, and Spanish sources, this represents the only extant primary document ever produced by the Yamasees themselves during this crucial period (see appendix).[22]

The first few lines of the note confirm the central role played by John Wright during those final hours of delicate negotiation. According to the Huspaw (Huspah) king:

> Mr. Wright said that the white men would come and fetch [illegible] the Yamasees in one night and that they would hang four of the head men and take all the rest of them for slaves, and that he would send them all off the country, for he said that the men of the Yamasees were like women, and shew'd his hands one to the other, and what he said vex'd the great warrier's, and this made them begin the war.[23]

Wright's message seems intended to stir up trouble and could hardly have been compatible with the official reassurance of peace and friendship proffered by Thomas Nairne. If he did in fact say these things, as the Yamasees asserted, Wright must have arranged a private meeting at some point that did not include the acting Indian agent. It would have been difficult while the main negotiations were still under way but less so once Nairne had said his friendly good-night and gone to sleep.

Regardless of the circumstances, it now seems clear that two separate, conflicting messages were delivered to the Yamasee Indians gathered at Pocotaligo Town: Nairne's message of peace and Wright's message of war. According to Spanish accounts of Yamasee testimony shortly after the outbreak of hostilities, the assembled warriors and headmen debated the problem throughout the night, unable to arrive at a consensus. Having seen both Wright and Nairne in an official capacity, they knew only that one of the two messages reflected the colony's true intentions. After much soul searching, and some rousing predawn oratory by a Yamasee warrior, they ultimately found it easier to believe the worst about the Carolinians. Even so, if English sources are to be believed, a number of Yamasees may have clung to Nairne's message of peace to the bitter end and lost their lives along with him. This was not an angry, reflexive outburst provoked by trade abuse or dependency, nor was it necessarily the first premeditated act in a grand Native American conspiracy to destroy South Carolina. Rather, it was an agonized, deliberate response to English diplomatic behaviors that can only be described as schizophrenic.[24]

Instead of assuming that the Yamasees orchestrated a massive conspiracy among southeastern Indian nations, therefore, it might be wise to consider a new set of questions. How and with whom, for instance, did they form an alliance network prior to the outbreak of hostilities, and why did those allies respond as they did upon hearing the news that the Yamasees had broken off relations with South Carolina? The question is complicated by the likelihood, as Steven Oatis has pointed out, that the unified native front perceived by Carolinians masked a series of interlocking alliance networks, each acting on its own set of diplomatic considerations.[25]

PART 3 **Fire**

5. The Heart of the Alliance

✳ ✳ ✳ ✳ ✳ ✳ ✳ ✳ ✳ ✳ ✳ ✳ ✳ ✳ ✳

The fire kindled at Pocotaligo eventually spread from the Carolina coast to the Mississippi River. Its rate of progress was not uniform, however, and the damage it inflicted was not indiscriminate. The closest allies of the Yamasees took up the war in relatively short order, but the Catawbas, Cherokees, Upper Creeks, and Choctaws delayed their entry into the war for weeks or even months after the first shots were fired. In addition, various groups appear to have pursued distinctive military and diplomatic objectives that set them apart from other participants. This chapter and the next seek to understand those differences and reconstruct the ligaments of the Native American coalition that took shape in 1715 and 1716.

Despite hysterical rhetoric about a "general revolt" or "concerted defection," South Carolinians came to recognize certain structural elements of the coalition besieging them. The colony's defensive efforts evolved to focus, of necessity, on attacks from "Southern Indians" and "Northern Indians," and Carolinians took pains to identify the specific tribes operating together in those two groups. References to "Southern Indians" typically included the Yamasees, Euchees, Savannahs, Apalachees, and Lower (Ocheese) Creeks. "Northern Indians" included the Catawbas and their Carolina piedmont allies. Significantly, Carolinians generally referred to the Cherokees in their own right, although recognizing that they sometimes cooperated with the northern Indians. White colonists

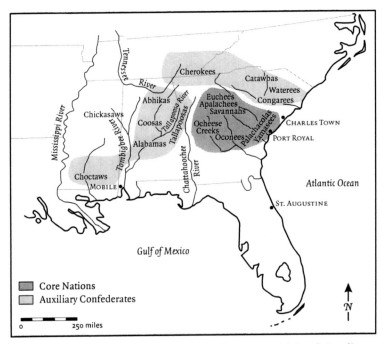

Map 2. Components of the 1715 Indian Coalition at war with South Carolina

were less aware of developments in what are now Alabama and Mississippi, where a third group of what may be termed "western Indians," the Upper Creeks and Choctaws, also fought to reposition themselves in the new anti-English South.

The behavior of those groups suggests a core of activist nations surrounded by auxiliary allies. The southern Indians struck the first and fiercest blows against South Carolina, often in concert with each other, and ultimately refused to make peace until long after the rest of the indigenous South had resumed trade with Charles Town. These nations, it is argued, had long-standing cultural and ethnic affinities that made them natural allies in wartime. As a result, they comprised a central core of highly motivated nations that subsequently drew less motivated neighbors into alignment with them. Those neighbors are referred to here as auxiliary confederates and are discussed in more detail in the following chapter: the northern Indians (Catawbas and their piedmont allies) and the Cherokees, Choctaws, and Upper Creeks (see map 2). They did not sever ties with South Carolina and realign themselves with the core nations at the heart of the alliance for some time. Indeed, even the mobilization of the core nations, as they are termed here, may well have been a chain reaction rather than a prearranged agreement.

CORE COMBATANTS

In early communications with South Carolina and Spanish Florida, the Yamasees made remarkable claims about the extent of their alliance. The Huspah king's letter to Governor Charles Craven, for instance, indicated that "all the Indians upon the main are comeing." Similarly, a joint Creek and Yamasee delegation to Governor Francisco Corcoles y Martinez at St. Augustine in May 1715, boasted pledges of alliance from 161 towns, represented by several knotted strands of deerskin. Frightened Englishmen and hopeful Spaniards generally gave credence to such pronouncements, but the Yamasees and their immediate allies were speaking in a highly charged diplomatic and military context. They undoubtedly sought to accomplish tactical objectives with such rhetoric rather than to portray their dilemma accurately. In making these extraordinary claims about the extent of their alliance, they probably intended to frighten Carolinians and fan the ambitions of Spanish officials.[1]

It is unlikely that the Yamasees tied those 161 knots as a mere diplomatic ploy to impress the Spanish, but it is even less likely that every Indian village in the South had committed itself to war against South Carolina prior to the outbreak of hostilities. The deerskin strands may have been produced during various English attempts to compile a census of southeastern Indians, which culminated in the 1715 census effort. If Carolinians employed Yamasee emissaries to assist in those efforts, knotted deerskins might have been a useful mnemonic device as they traveled from village to village. In addition, the census strands would likely have been kept at the Port Royal plantations of Thomas Nairne or John Barnwell, making them a conspicuous and perhaps choice object of plunder during the early days of the war. Significantly, the 1715 English census listed 160 towns as being engaged in trade with Carolina, ranging from the Choctaws and Chickasaws of modern-day Mississippi to the Overhill Cherokees in eastern Tennessee. The Yamasee figure of 161 allied towns was almost certainly derived, therefore, from the English census. As such, it may simply have been another way of saying "all the Indians upon the main."[2]

All the Indians did not come, of course, but the threat itself reveals a great deal about the Indians who issued it. The glaring solitude of Yamasee (and, by association, Lower Creek) voices in those early claims to a grandiose Native American alliance suggests not only the level of desperation they felt in the spring of 1715 but, more important, the probable inspiration and ethnic foundation for the alliance that eventually did take shape. By gathering together to discuss trade problems a few days prior to the war and appearing together in the first diplomatic efforts after hostilities had commenced, the Yamasees and Lower (Ocheese) Creeks demonstrated a deep and meaningful bond that existed in peace as well as war. In fact, it extended far back into the pre-Columbian history of the South and continued to bind towns as distant as Coweta and Chechesee together culturally even in the market-driven days of the deerskin and slave trades.

Today Pocotaligo continues to appear on road maps of South Carolina, but travelers passing through the region are hard pressed to find it. Locals, who pronounce the name with stresses on the first and third syllables, are apt to identify it only with a sweeping gesture of the hand in the direction of state highway 21. The exact location of the Yamasee town that surrendered its name to the area has never been determined. Yet the Pocotaligo River, a small, marshy tributary to the Broad, looks much as it must have on the morning of April 15, 1715, when an Englishman named Burage (identified elsewhere as Burroughs) escaped the fury of his Yamasee hosts by splashing across it. Wounded by a musket ball that "pierced his neck and came out his mouth" and another that entered his back and "lodged in his chest," he left his fellow Carolinians to their various fates and made his way as best he could through the marshes and woods of the tidewater down to the coast. The pattern of his wounds, resulting from shots fired from behind, suggests that Burage was not a man to tarry in an emergency. Before nightfall he managed to traverse the entire length of the Broad River, roughly thirty miles, from Pocotaligo Town to Port Royal Island.[3]

In doing so, Burage had passed through the most densely settled portions of the Yamasee homelands. Had he cared to observe it in his condition, he might have seen three centuries or more of southern history pass before him as he stumbled for safety. The Yamasee settlements fell into two basic divisions known to the English as the Upper Yamasee towns, consisting of six villages, and the Lower Yamasee towns, numbering four. These divisions roughly reflected the two ethnic components that lay at the heart of Yamasee identity. Most of the upper towns had formerly resided in the Spanish province of Guale, along the coast of present-day Georgia, and may have spoken a Timucuan or Muskhogean dialect, while most of the lower towns came originally from interior Georgia and may have been Hitchiti and Muskhogee speakers.[4]

Though newcomers to the Port Royal region, the Yamasees brought ancient connections with them. Among the lower towns, Altamaha (often written as Aratamahon by English observers), Okete (also Eketee), and Chechesee were fragments of the once powerful central Georgia chiefdoms that greeted Hernando De Soto during his 1540 march through the Southeast, recorded by Spanish chroniclers as Altamaha, Ocute, and Ichisi. Many Yamasees in the lower towns, moreover, had lived briefly with the proto-Creek villages of the Chattahoochee River Valley before migrating to the South Carolina coast in the 1680s, and some of them retained conspicuous links to those inland communities. Upon first arrival in the Carolina low country, for example, residents of "Cheachesee" lived only two miles from the town of Tuscagy, probably a "daughter town" of the famous Creek village of the same name, located at that time on the Ocmulgee River in central Georgia. The application of the name Yamasee to such a diverse collection of villages may well reveal as much about English perceptions of Native Americans as about the peoples to whom it was applied.[5]

If the English did not fully understand the historical connections that linked the towns and peoples with whom they did business, the language they used to describe these communities sometimes absorbed that knowledge inadvertently. Carolinians, for instance, preferred to use shorthand terms to refer collectively to the towns clustered along "Ocheese Creek," as the Ocmulgee River in central Georgia was then known. Using the geography of the region to simplify a confusing diversity of peoples, British traders variously referred to the Indians "settled att the creek" or to the "Ocheese Creek Indians." Thomas Nairne called them simply the "Ochessees." In time, of course, it became more common to refer to them as the Creeks. Yet a broad range of tribal groups, none of whom as yet called themselves Creek, established themselves on the river between 1690 and 1715. In addition to Muskhogee- and Hitchiti-speaking peoples from the Chattahoochee River, Chiaha Indians from Tennessee and remnants of the defeated Westos moved there as well. "Several family's" of Apalachee Indians even appear to have been present.[6]

The use of the name Ocheese in reference to the Ocmulgee River and the Indians settled on it between 1690 and 1715 may suggest some measure of continuity between the historic period and the prehistoric or contact period cultures previously in the area. In 1540, De Soto had marched northward along the Ocmulgee River through several towns of a chiefdom named "Ichisi." The site of the chiefdom's main town appears to have been the Ocmulgee mound site in Macon, Georgia. Even after the "Ocheese Creek Indians" moved back to the Chattahoochee River to become "Lower Creeks" in 1716, they continued to refer to the Ocmulgee River as "Ocheese-hatche" for the rest of the eighteenth century.[7]

Between 1690 and 1715, when the Ocmulgee became a thriving center of activity, native villages probably lined the river for several miles north and south of the mound site in Macon, where the trading path crossed. Scholars initially disagreed as to which town occupied the mound site itself, but the changing of the river's name from the Ocheese to the Ocmulgee (at least among South Carolinians), and consistent references to the site as the "Ocmulgee Old Fields," suggest that it may have been occupied by Ocmulgee Town. The Indians who lived there established themselves in the very midst of several imposing temple mounds, constructed between 950 and 1100 AD. The town appears to have functioned as an entrepôt for English trade with the surrounding "Ocheese Creek" settlements and also as a way station for trade intended for nations settled farther west. The trade path, a hard-packed dirt trail only a little more than three feet wide, entered the town from the northeast and led past ancient temple mounds and native houses directly to the doors of the trading post in the middle of town.

To facilitate business, English traders constructed a fortified warehouse where deerskins, merchandise, and perhaps slaves could be safely stored. The pentagonal structure measured 140 feet on its longest side and enclosed several smaller buildings. Artifacts associated with the trading house, such as a brass weight scale bearing the date 1712, probably used for weighing deerskins or gunpowder, and English pipe-stem fragments dating to about 1710, indicate that the facility functioned for several years before the outbreak of the war. The novelties of English trade thus entered the Muscogee economy through ancient and venerable arteries.[8]

In light of the Mississippian era legacies of the Yamasee towns of Chechesee, Eketee, and Altamaha, the Ocheese Creek continuities and their immersion in English trade relations take on additional relevance. In essence, the prewar Pocotaligo trade conference between the Lower (Ocheese) Creeks and the Yamasees brought together the descendents of central Georgia's legendary chiefdoms and the peoples then living in the shadow of their ancestral accomplishments. They spoke the same languages, made the same pottery, and many of them, in fact, had lived together prior to 1685. Indeed, even in the Carolina low country, residents of Chechesee could still visit residents of Tuskegee in a half hour's walk. The linear distance between central Georgia and Port Royal, South Carolina, so distinct on colonial era maps that depict the Lower Creeks and Yamasees as separate nations, may thus have circled back on itself in the hearts and memories of those who lived there.

The towns that lay along the trade path between the Yamasee and Ocheese Creek settlements reflected those connections. The "Palachacola" Indians, for instance, had once lived on the Chattahoochee River alongside other Lower Creek towns. In fact, "Apalachicola" was the standard Spanish name for the Chattahoochee settlements throughout the eighteenth century. In addition to documentary sources, ceramic evidence from archaeological work at the site of Palachacola Town identifies its inhabitants as former residents of the Chattahoochee River. When those towns migrated to the Ocmulgee River in 1690, however, the "Palachacolas" continued farther east along the path. They finally settled on the banks of the Savannah River about twenty miles from the coast, not necessarily because they intended to declare independence from the inland Lower (Ocheese) Creeks or coastal Yamasees but probably to secure a strategic location. The 1690–1715 location of Palachacola Town controlled "the usual place for . . . Indians to ferry or cross over the said River." It also proved to be "very serviceable in furnishing wth provisions the English men who go up that river in perryagues [pirogues] wth supplies of goods for the Indians & bring skins in returne for them." After the Yamasee War, it should be noted, South Carolinians occupied the site for similar reasons.[9]

Like Palachacola, Oconee Town migrated from the Chattahoochee River in 1690 but did not settle at Ocheese Creek with the majority of Lower Creek towns. Oconee Indians established themselves instead on the banks of the Oconee River near present-day Milledgeville, Georgia, about thirty miles east of the Ocheese Creek settlements. Archaeologist A. R. Kelly conducted excavations at the site of Oconee Old Town in the 1930s. Although he did not publish a report, the ceramic types recovered from the site have been identified by Mark Williams of the University of Georgia as consistent with styles indigenous to the Chattahoochee River Valley. In 1995 Williams used aerial photographs to identify the site of Kelly's excavations and conducted limited excavations of his own. He recovered a number of eighteenth-century trade-related artifacts such as small trade beads. Deeply involved in trade with South Carolina, the Oconees were at the same time enmeshed in the historical, linguistic, and ethnic connections that bound the Lower Yamasee towns, Palachacolas, and Lower Creeks together.[10]

At the center of this far-flung collage of interrelated villages lay the anomalous enclave of Savano Town. Located on the Savannah River near present-day Augusta, Georgia, the settlement was home to a diverse collection of refugees and conquered peoples. More than 1,000 Indians from three different nations were clustered here on the eve of the Yamasee War. The Savannahs, numbering between 67 and 150 warriors, 116 women, and 50 children, were dispersed among three villages. Nearby, more than 600 Apalachee Indians lived in about four villages, while about 130 Euchee (or Yuchi) warriors inhabited two villages slightly to the northward. The region functioned as one of the most important trade entrepôts in the Southeast, and the Indians settled there played a critical role in moving supplies along the paths that radiated outward from it. Because English traders rarely used packhorses prior to 1715, heavy packs of European merchandise or deerskins were carried "upwards of 700 miles . . . upon Indians' backs." Carolina Indian Agent Thomas Nairne, for instance, accompanied a convoy of twenty-five "Apalatchys that were burtheners for [his] fellow traveller" in 1708 on a journey into Chickasaw territory, a round-trip total from the Savannah River of over eight hundred miles.[11]

Perhaps the most distinctive attribute of the peoples settled around Savano Town is that none of them appear to have been very happy about living there. Even more unusual, they were not allowed to leave. The Apalachee Indians had been forced to relocate in 1704 from their northern Florida homeland after a Lower Creek military invasion led by Carolina Governor James Moore. According to Thomas Nairne, "nothing but downright force brought them over to our side." As many as four thousand of their countrymen had been sold into slavery abroad or on low-country South Carolina plantations, and the six hundred survivors settled around Savano Town were, not surprisingly, observed to "behave themselves very submissive to the government." In practical terms, of course, the primary reason for their submission was not the military power of the Carolina "government" but that of the Lower Creek and Yamasee warriors whose settlements flanked them on either side. The historian Alan Gallay has described them as being "in effect, hostages." In this context, it is impossible to resist the speculation that the Lower Creek towns of Oconee and Palachacola, posted on either side of Savano Town, may have functioned as sentry towns to monitor and control a captive population.[12]

Gallay's assessment may hold true for the other nations settled at Savano Town as well, although the reasons for their declining status are unclear. Indeed, the Savannahs had established their right of occupancy in the area by defeating the Westo Indians in 1681 and should thus have enjoyed greater autonomy than the Apalachees. Nevertheless, they expressed their unhappiness on several occasions during the first decade of the eighteenth century. In fact, they appear to have begun leaving the area shortly after the arrival of the Apalachees. The census figure of 150 Savannah warriors recorded in 1708 as compared with sixty-seven warriors recorded in the 1715 census, for instance, may reflect interim population losses due to out-migration. Their exodus, however, did not go unnoticed or unopposed. When a group of "revolted" Savannahs attempted to flee the region in 1707, the South Carolina Assembly dispatched an armed posse, once again under the leadership of James Moore, "to bring back the Savannahs." Likewise, when the South Carolina Commons House of Assembly heard rumors in 1712 that the Euchees were thinking about "deserting their settlements and goeing over to the French," it dispatched an observer to interview the headmen. Perhaps suspecting that their reassurances might not be genuine, he based his final report on the more reliable evidence "that they are planting as usual great quantities of corn." Even so, he "ordered the head men amongst them to give the governm't an account of themselves" by traveling to Charles Town to speak with the Assembly.[13]

The cordon that appears to have been drawn around the settlements at Savano Town could not have been accomplished by the unilateral desire of South Carolina, although the colony clearly participated in its enforcement. Rather, I argue that it grew out of the military alliance between the Lower Creeks and Yamasees and the devastating firepower they could bring to bear on their opponents. The historical record contains no written treaty of mutual defense or diplomatic accord between the two nations. It may be too much to say that the Yamasee settlements around Port Royal and the Lower Creek towns on the Ocmulgee River acted as coordinated nodes of power to exert control over a central tributary population prior to the outbreak of the Yamasee War. Yet the historical and ethnic connections between them suggest that Lower Creek and Yamasee identity and self-interest were overlapping categories. Those connections predated exchange relations with South Carolina and continued to influence the decisions made by individual towns about migration, settlement, trade, diplomacy, and military alliance as they became more deeply involved in the English trade.

It is not surprising then that the first native voices to break through Carolina's diplomatic paralysis in early 1715 came simultaneously from the Lower Creeks and Yamasees. Nor is it unusual that they corresponded with the same geographical range and set of towns that had been most vocal in protesting various trade practices over the previous decade. Having become, on average, routine participants in the Carolina trade network during the mid-1680s, by 1715 the Lower Creeks (including the splinter towns of Oconee and Palachacola) and Yamasees were more deeply engaged in trade and consequently more attuned to the tenor of the exchange relationship than any other groups in the South. The frictions of intercultural exchange, exacerbated by disturbing market trends, demanded a continuous dialogue between these nations and Charles Town and made the diplomatic breakdown of late 1714 all the more conspicuous. Their relationship shaped the terms of their participation in the deerskin and slave trades and, once the war had begun, it determined early patterns of violence in the Carolina low country.[14]

PATTERNS OF VIOLENCE

At one level, acts of warfare communicate the very obvious desire to harm or annihilate one's enemy. At another, however, the forms of that violence can also communicate the unspoken assumptions and objectives that gave rise to it. The first descent of the Yamasees upon the Port Royal area provided one such episode in symbolic violence, offered up in grand form for a live English audience. The first wave of warriors arrived "as night drew on," but they could find "nobody in the houses." Captain Burage's warning had given the settlers time to evacuate most of the island and board a ship that, fortunately for them, lay at anchor in the Port Royal River (probably Beaufort River). The perplexed Yamasees at length "came down to the water's edge," where they discovered several hundred refugees crowded on the boat. They kept up a continual volley of musket fire on the frightened Carolinians all night long and "continually repeated their diabolical war-whoop as they fired." Failing to inflict serious damage, however, they turned their attention the following day to the abandoned town. They gunned down horses and cattle and "sacked and plundered everything they met with," then they burned the houses, "dancing in a grotesque fashion, and uttering loud cries of joy."[15]

In performing this mayhem beneath the constant gaze of the island's inhabitants, the Yamasees did more than vent their rage on proxy victims. By destroying the trappings of domestic life, they put a public end to the life of the place. They claimed ownership for themselves and expressed their determination to make English reoccupation as difficult as possible. The killing of horses and cattle, in particular, capped a long-standing Yamasee dialogue with Carolinians about the disruptive influence of English cattle ranching on native agriculture and hunting. Yamasee violence against cattle, in fact, continued throughout the 1720s. Just as often, though, warriors preferred to lead domestic livestock away as plunder, understanding that such things could be traded for ammunition, weapons, or merchandise at St. Augustine, Pensacola, and Mobile. This was especially true of the Lower Creeks, who possessed more than five hundred horses by war's end. Some established their own cattle ranches and even kept tabs on the going market value of livestock in various French and Spanish ports. One Carolinian logically concluded that "ye war enricheth themselves and impoverisheth us." The first strike against Port Royal may thus have represented a symbolic performance in which the Yamasee desire to make a statement about ownership and land use took precedence over the tactical considerations of the war.[16]

The territorial aspect of that violence may seem too obvious to bear sustained scrutiny, but it raises questions about the basic considerations that motivated Yamasee warriors and their allies. A statement of ownership as overt as the one communicated at Port Royal required a firm sense of "title" and prerogative. It may well be asked whether warriors from the upper or lower towns would have felt empowered to act out such a declaration of ownership and control. Scholars have known for years that the Yamasees launched a two-pronged attack against South Carolina settlements in the first week of the war, one supposedly directed at Port Royal and another aimed at the plantations east of the Combahee River in St. Bartholomew's Parish. Yet there has been no effort to understand the tactical logic of Yamasee actions from a Yamasee perspective. For William Osborne, a minister for the Society for the Propagation of the Gospel in Foreign Parts, their thinking hardly needed to be explained. The Yamasees "divided themselves into two parties," he recalled in May 1715, for the obvious reason that they wanted "to kill & destroy all they could."[17]

Perhaps they had aspirations to "kill & destroy," but the Huspah king had claimed in his letter to the governor to have more specific objectives in mind as well. Warriors from Huspah Town joined a force of three hundred Yamasees who were "goeing to watch to take the fort at Capt. Woodward's and that at Well Town." Here again, there appear to have been two initial targets, just as English observers recognized. But they do not match up neatly with the scattered plantations of St. Bartholomew's Parish or the frightened residents of Port Royal watching the destruction of Beaufort from their crowded ship. Rather, Woodward's fort occupied the headwaters of the Ashepoo River and controlled the main path from Charles Town to the plantations clustered along the upper reaches of the Combahee River and thence into the Upper Yamasee towns. Wiltown, by contrast, occupied a valuable fording point on the Edisto River where Pon Pon Bridge was located (at that time, the Edisto was also called the Pon Pon River) and thus connected paths from Ashley River to Port Royal. It is possible, therefore, that two groups of warriors moved first to control the two main trade paths leading into the upper and lower towns and subsequently doubled back to St. Bartholomew's Parish and Port Royal respectively. Such a scenario might help explain how an Englishman with a musket ball lodged in his chest and a bullet hole in his neck managed to travel from Pocotaligo to Port Royal Island faster than the warriors who had shot him.[18]

The Huspah king's account may certainly be questioned on several levels. It is strange, first of all, that a Yamasee leader engaged in war with South Carolina should divulge the movement of Yamasee warriors in a letter to the colony's governor. Equally peculiar, he claimed that the Yamasees continued to "love" the governor, even as they killed his subjects. Charles Craven and the Indians, the Huspah king affirmed, "are like Brothers." The leader may have been playing a political game with future treaty negotiations in mind, or perhaps he merely sought to mislead English forces by seeding false information. The English, for their part, dismissed the note out of hand as "a ridiculous letter." Even the Spanish officials who later embraced the Huspah king as an ally complained that "when he talks of going to one place, he commonly goes to another." Given these concerns, the military information contained in his legendary note may be more suited to psychological speculation than elaborate tactical analysis.[19]

Nevertheless, the Huspah king's two targets make sense in light of the dual patterns of violence that emerged in the first week of the war, and those patterns continued into the summer and fall of 1715. Following the first major confrontation between Yamasee warriors and Carolina militiamen at the head of the Combahee River, variously known as the Battle of the Combahee or the Sadkeche Fight, several of the Upper Yamasee towns were overrun by

English forces and compelled to retreat. The lower towns soon joined them in a general evacuation. Yet as they departed, Yamasee Indians appear to have withdrawn in at least two directions. One group traveled down the coast of present-day Georgia to seek the protection of the Spanish at St. Augustine, while another, it is argued here, apparently moved inland to Savano Town. Although ethnic differences between upper and lower towns may have begun to blur by 1715, it is striking that the Yamasees retreated along the same two migration routes that had originally brought them into the Carolina low country decades earlier.[20]

The identity of the Yamasees who fled toward St. Augustine is well documented. A census compiled by the Spanish in 1717 indicates that they were predominantly residents of the upper towns. Pocotaligo was reestablished about sixteen miles from the Castillo de San Marcos as "Pocotalaca," inhabited by 98 Indians, while the Upper Town of Pocosabo reappeared in the Spanish records as "Pocasapa," inhabited by 173 Indians. Although it did not appear in a recognizable form in the 1717 census (though it may have been the "Oapa Nation" that merged with Pocotalaca), Huspah Town also relocated to the neighborhood of St. Augustine, whence the Huspah king kept up a teasing dialogue with Carolina officials for many years. Some elements of the Lower Yamasee towns may have sought shelter in Florida briefly as well, for a settlement named "Our Lady of Candaleria de la Tamaja," possibly a variant of Altamaha, appeared for the first time in 1717. The Spaniards identified the 163 residents as Yamasee language speakers.[21]

In addition to the predominance of the upper towns, the census of 1717 presents an interesting demographic problem with respect to the Yamasee retreat from South Carolina. It recorded only three villages containing a total of 427 Yamasee Indians as being present in Spanish Florida. The English census of 1715, on the other hand, had recorded a total of 1,220 Yamasees living in ten villages in the vicinity of Port Royal. If these figures are even remotely accurate, as they appear to be, nearly eight hundred Yamasee Indians did not make the journey to Florida. Put another way, 65 percent of the Yamasee Nation disappeared in transit between South Carolina and St. Augustine. This represents a colossal statistical discrepancy that no scholarly discussion has recognized to date, much less attempted to resolve. Even allowing for massive native casualties in the early days of the war, which the documents do not suggest, an enormous number of Yamasee Indians chose to retreat beyond the pale of European census takers. [22]

The identity of that second group of Yamasees and where they went is less clear, but South Carolinians suspected that many had retrenched at Savano Town among the Apalachees, Savannahs, and Euchees. Early discussions in the Commons House of Assembly about military retaliations against the Yamasees, for instance, focused on Savano Town rather than St. Augustine. Yet no census was produced to verify their presence there, and when they ultimately moved farther inland to merge with the Lower Creeks, as did the Apalachees and Euchees, they intentionally courted anonymity. By 1717, they were becoming increasingly invisible. Rather than establishing recognizable Yamasee towns as the residents of Pocotaligo and Pocosaba had done in Florida, Yamasees and Apalachees lived "dispersed" among the Creek settlements. They did this, it was said, because they did "not wish to exercise vengeance." Nor, it may be assumed, did they wish to have vengeance exercised upon them. [23]

In the summer of 1715, however, those inland Yamasees and their countrymen who had retreated along the coast were still intent on vengeance, and the targets they each chose to attack bore a striking resemblance to the territorial priorities initially suggested by the

Huspah king's letter. When warriors set out from St. Augustine or encampments along the coast to make war on Carolina, they did not strike indiscriminately as opportunities arose. They paddled upriver into the vicinity of the abandoned upper towns of Pocataligo, Pocasabo, and Huspah in order to burn plantations and carry away plunder along the Combahee River. In fact, the predictability of their movements led to disaster for the Yamasees on at least one occasion. Upon learning that "the Indians were at Combhee burning and destroying the plantations," the Carolina militia organized one of its few offensive expeditions of the war. They formed up at "the Pond Bridge" (at the headwaters of the Ashley River) and marched westward into the ravaged plantation districts, where they surprised a small raiding party "at one Jackson's house near the Ferry." This may have been the location of "Jackson's Bridge," as historian Verner Crane termed it, located where the trade path into the Upper Yamasee towns crossed the Edisto River. This was apparently as far away from Charles Town as the Carolinians felt they could operate on land. They next ordered a scout boat "to lay in wait at the mouth of the River" for other warriors, who appeared the following day. Most of those men "leapt overboard and swam ashore," but the Carolinians wisely fell back to Daufuskie Island "by which the Indians must of necessity pass." After two days of waiting, "they spy'd 8 perraugers coming." In the ensuing ambush, the Yamasees lost thirty-five warriors, and prisoners captured in the battle were compelled to reveal the location of coastal settlements on the Sapelo River.[24]

South Carolinians demonstrated more than an aptitude for fighting "like Indians" in those encounters. They acted on a set of fundamental assumptions about Yamasee military behavior that were subsequently verified on the field of battle. In order to confront warriors "on the Combhee," they knew that they would need to march along the path that led into the upper towns. They also felt certain that warriors operating along the upper town path would evacuate the area by water and attempt to withdraw southward along the coast. The aggressiveness of English forces and their willingness to commit men as far south as Daufuskie Island, moreover, suggest that they had a relatively low opinion of the number of warriors likely to be deployed in a water-borne assault against the Combahee River plantations or, for that matter, of the number of allies that might be operating with them.[25]

Successful as they were against raiders from St. Augustine, however, none of those insights proved helpful in defending against land-based Yamasee incursions from the interior. When six or seven hundred "Southern Indians" entered the Carolina low country in July, they traveled by the lower path connecting Port Royal to Charles Town and crossed the Edisto River at the Pon Pon Bridge. Once across the Edisto, they focused their attack on Wiltown (New London) just as the Huspah king claimed one of the two Yamasee parties would do at the start of the war. Failing to take the fort there, "they spread themselves down Stono River, and burnt all before them." When Governor Charles Craven moved to oppose them with an equal force of about seven hundred men, the Indians crossed back over Edisto River, burning Pon Pon Bridge behind them. The Carolinians made no effort to pursue them further on this occasion or to predict their movements in order to stage an ambush. In fact, they had no firm idea where the Indians had gone following the invasion, "not being able to discover them." Some suspected, however, that they had "gone to the Savana Town, and from thence to make incursions upon us now and then as they see fit."[26]

In contrast to the predictable Yamasee attacks on the Combahee River plantations, the descent of the southern Indians presented

Charles Town with more serious problems. The southern Indians did not disperse to burn and plunder deserted plantations in territory already conceded by the Carolinians; they crossed over the Edisto into inhabited land as an organized, disciplined body in order to challenge and threaten the colony. Although they attacked one of the two original Yamasee targets, moreover, the number of warriors who ventured their lives in pursuit of that objective in July 1715 far exceeded even the prewar strength of the united Yamasee Nation. This was, therefore, a true coalition of nations working together, and the use of the umbrella term *southern* to describe them suggests that English defenders recognized the multinational character of the assault.

Most important, however, the incursion appears to have been orchestrated in defense of another alliance network to the north. The warriors made their attack just as Governor Craven was leading his troops "away to the Sarraws and our other Northern Indians to strive to cut them off." As soon as he crossed the Santee River, the southern Indians marched over Pon Pon Bridge unopposed. Craven was forced to abandon his offensive to the northward and rush back to defend Charles Town. The diplomatic importance of this episode in the council discussions of Catawbas, Waterees, and other piedmont nations, who were thus spared an English military thrust, must have been immense.[27]

Whereas the Florida Yamasees made war alone, then, the so-called southern Indians represented a coalition of several nations working together toward specific Yamasee goals but also, by all appearances, to defend and influence other such coalitions in the greater Southeast. As such, I argue that they formed the heart of the alliance network that ultimately transformed the entire region as far west as the Mississippi River, and the July invasion of South Carolina suggests at least one of the ways in which they persuaded potential allies to join them or alternatively maintained allegiance from those already aligned with their interests. According to the minister Francis LeJau of the Society for the Propagation of the Gospel in Foreign Parts, those southern forces included warriors from the Yamasees, Euchees, Apalachees, Savannahs, and Lower Creeks. If so, their military alliance in 1715 was hardly surprising. It drew on long-standing connections that had shaped their behavior in peacetime for many years.[28]

The rhetoric of violence inflicted by the southern coalition east of the Edisto River was as significant as the identities of its component nations. Just as they had done at Port Royal in the first days of the war, they "killd all the horses & cattle & sheep." In all, they burned between twenty and thirty plantations, but in the midst of that destruction they spared the parish church of William Bull. Confronted with a structure that was devoted mainly to spiritual matters, they apparently limited themselves to "breaking a few of ye windowes & tearing off ye lining from one of ye best pews." The reasons for their restraint can only be inferred, but it may be significant that Creek warriors serving in the Vietnam War also sought to preserve Cambodian temples in a similar way, sometimes in opposition to white compatriots who were ready to throw grenades. In the latter case, at any rate, the temples were spared not from any fear of Cambodian reprisal or deep veneration of Buddhist doctrine but because they were judged holy places and thus worthy of respect and caution. If nothing else, the southern Indians' decision to spare Bull's church suggests that they were actively appraising targets both in tactical and spiritual terms and meting out destruction accordingly. Their decision to take possession of the red pew cloth, however, given the association of the color red with war for most Muskhogean-speaking peoples, would seem to have been an act of spiritual disrespect rather than mere plunder.[29]

Although the southern Indians were tied together by ancient cultural and historical connections, the mobilization of trade partners into wartime allies did not necessarily take place easily or overnight. The prewar meeting between Yamasees and Lower Creeks at Pocotaligo Town, it should be stressed, concerned Lower Creek proposals for modifying the trade, not for destroying it. When considering the prospect of war against Carolina, Lower Creek leaders faced a difficult decision that may not have been unanimous. In fact, they may not have had the luxury of making a considered decision. A story related many years later to the naturalist William Bartram suggests that popular outcry and mob activism may have brought the Lower Creeks into alignment with the Yamasees in spite of ongoing council house discussions. Traders from several towns had retreated to take shelter in one place "under the avowed protection of the chiefs of the town." While local leaders discussed the matter, however, "Indians in multitudes surrounded the house and set fire to it." Barring an overt display of contrition from Creek headmen, the massacre of "18 or 20" British traders would likely have committed the Lower Creek towns to war with South Carolina in and of itself. No apology was offered, but several leaders expressed misgivings about the war, including the powerful mico of Coweta, Emperor Brims. Even the prominent Lower Creek warrior Cherokeeleechee, who readily admitted to doing "the English all the harm he could" during the war, recalled that he was originally "averse unto it." There appears, moreover, to have been a constant pro-English faction of "malcontents" among the Lower Creeks throughout the war.[30]

Although some historians, notably David Corkran, have cited Lower Creek activism as the predominant factor in both the origins of the war and its subsequent prosecution, evidence suggests a more ambiguous Creek response at each level. A number of Lower Creek warriors acted in concert with the southern Indians in their June

1715 invasion across the Edisto River, but their participation in that and other actions did not overshadow the exploits of Apalachee, Euchee, Savannah, and Yamasee warriors. In proportion to their total military strength, in fact, Lower Creek efforts may have been fairly anemic. The documentary record reveals no Lower Creek groundswell of military support during the spring and summer of 1715. Instead, Emperor Brims of Coweta seems to have focused his energies primarily on diplomatic maneuvers to further Lower Creek interests in the region.[31]

Just as Creeks and Yamasees differed in their approach and enthusiasm for war, not all members of the coalition were happy with the outcome of the war or the terms of peace, even as they merged by outward appearances into the Lower Creek polity. In some cases, it may be possible to trace the outline of lingering Yamasee frustration in the behavior of ostensibly "Creek" warriors well into the 1720s. When delegates from the Lower Creek town of Coweta traveled to Charles Town to discuss the terms of peace in 1722, Governor Francis Nicholson politely requested that Creek leaders exert some control over "tew people of your nation" who had chosen to encamp on Port Royal Island rather than join the rest of the Creek entourage in town. Nicholson complained that their behavior toward the white residents of Port Royal was "very saucy." Worse still, the two warriors, despite being warned, continued to go about the island and "kill the people's Cattle." Seven years after the harrowing Yamasee performance at the start of the war, some "Creek" warriors still appear to have remembered that original message and clearly resented the repopulation of the island by English people and their livestock. British efforts to strike at the Florida Yamasees, moreover, invariably prompted Lower Creek complaints. As late as 1726, a frustrated emissary from South Carolina complained to Emperor Brims of Coweta that it had become increasingly difficult "to have Yamasees Killed, for as Shure as we Kill A Yamassee, he has a Relation or friend amonge The Creek's."[32]

THEMES, PATTERNS, PROBLEMS

Englishmen thus recognized the continuing ties between the Florida Yamasees and those who had merged with the Lower Creeks, yet the disintegration of the Yamasee Confederacy during its withdrawal from South Carolina indicates that there were also significant differences among Yamasees. The upper towns chose by and large to reestablish old ties to the Spanish in Florida, while the lower towns appear to have renewed their ancient connections to the Lower (Ocheese) Creek towns of the interior. Those decisions guided the trajectories of Yamasee retreat, on the one hand, and the targets selected for attack, on the other, when Yamasee and allied warriors returned to prosecute the war in the Carolina low country. Ultimately, those who moved inland to forge wartime alliances with Apalachees, Euchees, Savannahs, and Lower Creeks proved far more influential in transforming the geopolitics of the greater Southeast. As southern Indians, Yamasee warriors continued to focus their military efforts on objectives that had been important to them from the beginning, but they also began the work of making their cause the cause of other Indians in the region.

Scholars who viewed the Yamasee War as a conspiracy have felt no logical need to explain the cohesiveness of the nations who came together as the southern Indians in the spring and summer of 1715. Indians everywhere, in Verner Crane's account, joined forces as a result of their shared "resentment" of trader abuse and misconduct. Even scholars such as Crane, however, who posited unanimity of purpose among southeastern Indians, should have recognized the obvious problem presented by the disorganized mobilization of the alleged conspirators. Why, if they had arranged the uprising in advance, did the Catawbas and Cherokees fail to act promptly in support of the Yamasees? By Crane's own reckoning, there was no firm evidence that Catawbas and other "northern" Indians had killed the traders in their towns until early May. Northern warriors, moreover, did not move to attack the colony until June, fully two months after the eruption of hostilities at Pocotaligo. It is difficult to maintain the existence of a conspiracy in the light of such lengthy delays. More likely, Catawbas, Cherokees, Upper Creeks, and Choctaws faced a complex decision that they had probably not foreseen, and it took them some time to discuss it.

6. Auxiliary Confederates

✳ ✳ ✳ ✳ ✳ ✳ ✳ ✳ ✳ ✳ ✳ ✳ ✳ ✳ ✳

The core combatants were flanked on two sides by less enthusiastic "confederates," as Carolinians sometimes referred to them. To the west were the Upper Creeks (including Alabamas, Abhikas, Coosas, and Tallapoosas) and Choctaws, and the Cherokees and Carolina piedmont tribes lived to the north (see map 2, chapter 5). They were all peoples whose complaints appeared much less regularly, if at all, in the English records. Although they all eventually killed the majority of English traders working in their towns, only the Cherokees and Carolina piedmont tribes mounted additional attacks against the colony, and even they grew quiet by the end of the first summer. While the destabilizing effects of market influence and diplomatic breakdown must have shaken them, it is doubtful that these auxiliary participants would have struck at the English of their own accord. Their decision to do so ultimately depended on the interplay and compatibility of local concerns with the emergence of a powerful war movement among the core nations.[1]

In contrast to the Lower Creeks, Savannahs, and Yamasees, their confederates were generally influenced by two meliorating factors that set them apart in significant ways. First, they were relative newcomers to trade with Carolina. The English did not move west into Upper Creek territory until the mid-1690s, and Carolinians continued to regard the Cherokees as "but little known to us" as late as 1713. The Choctaws, meanwhile, remained outside the Carolina trading sphere until 1714. Although subject to the same market-driven changes as the core nations, the auxiliary confederates felt them less intensely due to their more limited involvement in the English trade. The only exception to this rule may be the Catawbas and other piedmont nations, who had been engaged in trade with Virginia before the establishment of South Carolina.[2]

Yet here a second factor of profound significance came into play. All of the auxiliary confederates enjoyed access to alternative sources of European goods. The Upper Creeks and Choctaws reaped the benefits of direct relations with French Louisiana, while the Catawbas and their Carolina piedmont neighbors routinely welcomed Virginia traders into their villages. Although geographically remote, Cherokee consumers also managed to acquire French goods via the Tennessee and Tallapoosa river systems and Virginia goods through Catawba middlemen. Competition with Virginians on the one hand and Frenchmen on the other forced Carolina traders to provide these groups with better terms; and because French and Virginia traders were still willing to purchase beaver pelts and other traditional staples of the old fur trade, these nations were spared the hardships of converting abruptly to an exclusive reliance on deerskins. Equally important, access to alternative sources of trade also brought rival French or Spanish diplomatic overtures into Upper Creek, Choctaw, and Cherokee villages. Understanding the participation of these nations in the Yamasee War thus demands a painstaking reconstruction of the contexts that guided local decisions about alliance and trade in 1715 and 1716.[3]

NORTHERN INDIANS

Where European trade was concerned, Waxhaws, Waterees, Sugarees, Shutterees, Catawbas, Congarees, Santees, and other residents of the Carolina piedmont occupied an enviable position. Equidistant from South Carolina and Virginia, they benefited from competition between traders from each colony and consequently received better than average prices and treatment. In addition, as noted, Virginia traders were still willing to exchange merchandise for a broader range of peltries than Carolinians, allowing piedmont Indians to continue trading fox, raccoon, wolf, cat, mink, and other furs when other southeastern Indians had converted exclusively to the deerskin trade. As a result, the Catawbas and other piedmont peoples rarely complained about the English trade, and their reasons for participating in the Yamasee War are not obvious.[4]

James Merrell has suggested that the very competition between Virginia and South Carolina traders that minimized trade-related tensions may also have led piedmont Indians to expect the English to work against each other, even in times of war. The failure of South Carolina and Virginia to send significant aid to North Carolina during the Tuscarora War of 1711–13 undoubtedly confirmed native perceptions of English divisiveness. Virginia traders continued selling arms and ammunition to the Tuscaroras throughout the war. Yet the decision to make war on Carolina in 1715 was a momentous decision, requiring the presence of specific objectives and motives. Expectations of English disorganization and divisiveness, important though they may have been, hardly explain the real motives of the Catawbas and their neighbors.[5]

The fact that several piedmont nations were already at war in late 1714 was probably more significant than vague perceptions of English disunity. The Iroquois indicated at a conference with Governor Robert Hunter of New York in September 1714 that their "young men that are the warriors" had taken up the "hatthett . . . against the flattheads subjects of Carolina." A number of these young Iroquois warriors were probably Tuscaroras harboring a grudge against the Carolina Indians who had defeated them in 1712 and 1713. Although the Tuscaroras did not officially move north to join the Iroquois until 1721, thus transforming the Five Nations into the Six Nations, they had been collaborating for some time. Indeed, as discussed in chapter 2, at least one Seneca emissary was discovered among the Tuscarora captives in 1713. Whether the warriors traveling southward to attack the Catawbas were Iroquois or Tuscarora or a combination of both, there was no mistaking the destruction they visited on piedmont villages. When prompted by New York officials to stop the attacks, the Iroquois merely responded that "peace oughtt to be made between the Christians of Carolina and the Indians." Although modern historians universally view the Tuscarora War as having ended decisively in 1713, the issue was evidently less clear to the Tuscaroras and their new countrymen the Iroquois. It must therefore have been unclear to the Waxhaws, Catawbas, and other piedmont Indians of Carolina, who found themselves still fighting the war well after the English thought matters had been put to rest.[6]

Nothing demonstrates the war footing of the Catawbas and their piedmont neighbors more tellingly than the account book of John Evans, a Virginia trader. His entries in mid-March of 1715, only a little more than a month before the outbreak of the Yamasee War, recorded a heavy volume of sales of military equipment. Although he also sold a few incidental items, such as knives, the overwhelming majority of his sales involved "powder" and "shott." On March 10, for example, ten of his eleven transactions involved either gunpowder or bullets, and an undated fragment even recorded the sale of "vermillian," a pigment often used as war paint. These sales may well be an indicator, as Merrell suggests, that the Catawbas were preparing themselves for a preplanned strike against South Carolina in concert with the Yamasees. At the same time, however, they were not at all unusual for a nation already engaged in war with the Tuscaroras and Iroquois. In fact, it would be more surprising if the Catawbas were *not* preparing to defend themselves in the spring of 1715, knowing that more attacks were likely on their northern front.[7]

Reliable allies were thus a matter of supreme diplomatic importance for the upcountry tribes of Carolina in early 1715, and Charles Town had proven itself a fair-weather friend. Whereas the Catawbas, Waxhaws, and others had honored their alliance with the English by attacking the Tuscaroras in 1712, the English were nowhere to be seen in 1715. Not only did they fail to send the military assistance expected of native allies; they could not even manage to send an official diplomatic greeting. The Yamasees and Lower Creeks, meanwhile, were busy in early 1715 bolstering a powerful alliance network capable of mobilizing several thousand warriors. Once that alliance network was called into action against the English in April, the decision facing the piedmont tribes was all but made for them. They knew that aside from the trade, which they anticipated continuing with Virginia, Carolina really had nothing to offer in terms of alliance. They also knew that they could not defend themselves against continuing Tuscarora and Iroquois attacks from the north unless they were on good terms with the Yamasee/Lower Creek alliance network to their south. In choosing to kill English traders and mount limited attacks on Carolina's northern frontiers, the Catawbas, Waterees, Congarees, Waxhaws, and others responded to a complex, localized set of diplomatic and military considerations that had virtually nothing to do with trader misconduct or trade abuse.

Even so, many piedmont nations may have remained uncommitted to the war for some time after it had begun. According to two Virginia traders operating in Catawba territory: "Neither that nation [Catawbas] nor ye others in their neighborhood had any

intention to quarrell with ye English . . . 'till they receiv'd advice
(whether true or false is yet uncertain) that some of their people
going to Charlestown with skins were cutt off by the English, and
upon that report, they, according to their natural principles of
revenge, murdered all ye Carolina traders in their towns."[8]

Whether the story was "true or false," or was perhaps itself
only a rumor, remains unsettled even today. If true, it could explain
why the Catawbas, who had no clear reason to make war on South
Carolina, at last committed themselves to the native alliance in
early 1715. That decision may in turn have swayed other piedmont
nations still considering neutrality. For some, opposition to the
growing momentum of the war movement may ultimately have
appeared more dangerous than opposition to South Carolina.

CHEROKEES

Cherokee villages were less deeply involved in trade relations with
South Carolina than were other tribes. Occupying the myriad remote
clefts and valleys of the Appalachian Mountains, many villages had
only just begun to receive the attentions of English traders and
may consequently have had relatively few causes for discontent.
The motives that drew Cherokee towns into military alliance with
the Creeks and Yamasees are not therefore immediately apparent.
Carolinians at first assumed that the Cherokees were not involved
in the war. Early meetings of the Commons House of Assembly in
May 1715 focused on plans to negotiate a Cherokee alliance. That
was placed on hold, however, when it was discovered that English
traders had been killed there too.[9]

Traders working in Cherokee country appear to have been as
surprised as anyone by the decision to make war on South Carolina. Many of the traders answered a friendly invitation to attend a

feast, where they were subsequently shot. Others, however, "with difficulty escaped . . . from the Indians" and made their way to Charles Town. They reported deep divisions among Cherokee towns over the issue of war with Carolina. Indeed, even with many of his friends dead, one of those escaped traders, John Chester, felt confident that he might "still prevail with some of that Nation, being assured that they are not against us."[10]

Cherokee military behavior during the summer of 1715 also suggested internal divisions and perhaps a lack of enthusiasm for the war. A contingent of Cherokee warriors fought alongside Catawba and piedmont forces in several early victories, most notably at Shenkingh's Cowpen in June. Yet the populous Cherokee towns could muster only seventy warriors to supplement more than four hundred Catawba and piedmont troops, and that small contingent soon retired for the remainder of the conflict when they learned that Carolinians had dispatched emissaries to Cherokee country to discuss peace.[11]

Given their lack of military commitment and apparent disunity, many Cherokee towns probably agonized over the initial decision to make war on South Carolina. With few recorded grievances about the prewar terms of trade, Cherokee leaders must have found the colony's lack of diplomatic communication from November 1714 onward a disturbing development. Had Charles Town managed to send even the most cursory affirmation of friendship, some of those debates might have taken a very different turn. In the ensuing silence, however, Alexander Longe's escape to Cherokee country and the misinformation he brought with him appears to have had some effect. As discussed previously, the Commissioners of the Indian Trade had sought to discipline Longe for his role in the Cherokee raid on the Euchee town of Chestowe, but they had stopped short of criticizing the Cherokee warriors who carried out the raid. With no reassurances coming from South Carolina, however, Longe may have managed to persuade many warriors that the judgment against him was also a judgment against them: that South Carolina intended "to macke warrs with them and . . . kill all their head warriers." Longe's message must have gained additional credibility once hostilities between the Yamasees and South Carolina began in April.[12]

EURO-INDIAN RELATIONS IN THE WEST

Upper Creek settlements along the Coosa and Tallapoosa river valleys in central Alabama and the Choctaws in central Mississippi were, like the Cherokees, relative newcomers to the Carolina trade network and may also have harbored fewer grudges than nations with a long history of interaction with the English. As among the core nations, ambiguities concerning credit and conflicts between European and native concepts of personal and communal property led to problems in Upper Creek territory as well. In 1713 the Alabamas were angered by the Indian agent John Wright's decision to give "several slaves to Mr. Gower [a trader] for debts which were not due from their owner but from other private persons." This incident resulted in the first serious dialogues between the Alabamas and the French, as the commissioners for the Carolina Indian trade well knew. Yet Wright's actions were not viewed as "abusive" or "unregulated." He was functioning as an official agent of the colony, legitimately empowered to supervise and police the Indian trade.[13]

Unlike the core nations, however, the Upper Creeks enjoyed regular access to French trade goods from Mobile, by virtue of the water carriage along the Alabama River. The resulting competition between French and English traders may have worked in their favor, just as competition between Virginia and South Carolina traders benefited the Indians of the Carolina piedmont. Yet in the case of the Upper Creeks and Choctaws, the struggle between France and Great Britain for control of the Southeast made the competition for trade much more than a mere scramble for profit. It became a matter of paramount political and diplomatic importance.

Whereas Spain had pursued an imperial policy based on spiritual conquest, French and English colonial officials recognized that, by the end of the seventeenth century, the Indian trade represented the key to imperial expansion in the Southeast. English strategists felt particularly confident in their ability to win allies by "furnishing them at honest and reasonable prices with the several European commodities they may have occasion for." They believed that the "enlargement of [his] majesty's dominions in those parts doth almost entirely depend . . . on the successfull progress of that trade" and rightly predicted that "the french could not possibly rival us if we made a right use of our advantage."[14]

The overwhelming success of the English on the frontier owed perhaps as much to the weaknesses and internal divisions of French Louisiana as it did to the skill and ruthlessness of English Indian agents and traders. France had suffered greatly during the War of the Spanish Succession, and Louisiana, easily the least important of the French colonial possessions, languished without imperial support for the first decade of its existence.[15] Without reliable assistance, the welfare of the colony depended to a large extent on the initiative and skill of local leaders such as Jean-Baptiste Lemoyne, Sieur de Bienville. The failure of the English to mobilize their native allies against the French was due partly to English mismanagement but also, according to historian Marcel Giraud, to "the great ability of Bienville."[16] Giraud argues that Bienville, unable to compete with the English in terms of presents and trade, nevertheless used his "personal qualities" to "reestablish in the most critical moments an equilibrium of forces, undoubtedly precarious, but sufficient to prevent the formation of the coalition sought by the British."[17]

After the War of the Spanish Succession, however, new leadership entered the colony. The French crown issued a monopoly over Louisiana to Antoine Crozat, and Antoine La Mothe de Cadillac received a commission as the new governor. He arrived in Mobile in June 1713, along with Jean-Baptiste du Bois Duclos, Sieur de Montigny, the new *commissaire ordonnateur*. Bienville remained in the colony as the king's lieutenant in charge of the garrison at Fort St. Louis in Mobile but retained little executive authority.[18]

The Crozat monopoly further hampered French effectiveness on the frontier. In addition to removing Bienville from a position of authority, it established a mercantile system that placed a higher value on short-term profits than on the long-term interests of the colony. Crozat fixed an arbitrarily low price on deerskins and raised the price of French trade merchandise, thus conceding the competitive edge to the English from the outset.[19] Under these conditions, Louisiana's commerce with southeastern Indians suffered. During the Crozat monopoly's first year of business, the colony exported only about 1,000 deer-skins to France in contrast to the 54,000 skins shipped annually from Charles Town to Great Britain.[20]

In many respects French Louisiana exemplified the classic colonial conflict between the applied policies of the metropole and the internal realities of colonial life. This conflict became highly personalized under the Crozat monopoly as Cadillac's quest for immediate company profits encountered resistance from Bienville and his supporters. The Bienvillist faction, of course, sought immediate profits also, but they pursued material gain for their own benefit, often at the expense of the monopoly. The dispute appears to have gone much deeper than a mere conflict of personalities. According to historian Carl Brasseaux, it represented a fundamental rift between the interests of mercantilism, as represented by Cadillac and the Crozat regime, and the indigenous interests of private enterprise.[21]

The Bienvillist faction included a majority of the Superior Council members. Duclos, the commissaire ordonnateur, also sided with Bienville against Cadillac on most occasions. His support provided valuable leverage since his position as director of the colony's accounts gave him control over the disbursement of funds and merchandise. According to Brasseaux, the pursuit of personal aims by Duclos undermined the policies of Cadillac and contributed directly to the eventual failure of the Crozat monopoly.[22]

In February 1714 Bienville and Duclos jointly petitioned the Superior Council for less oppressive regulations concerning the Indian trade, but Cadillac managed to defeat their efforts.[23] Bienville had apparently hoped by the proposed measures to make the Louisiana traders more competitive with their English counterparts. He probably expected to benefit personally through his participation in the trade as well. Regardless of his motivation, however, Bienville's knowledge of Indian affairs and his experience as a frontier diplomat gave him valuable insights into the economic realities of the Indian trade. Cadillac, on the other hand, brought to the Louisiana governorship a history of troubled Indian relations dating from his disastrous command at the Detroit post. He made no effort to acquaint himself with the subtleties of Louisiana's unique Indian relations and rapidly alienated many former French allies.[24]

In addition to the dampening effect of the Crozat monopoly's mercantile interests and the substandard diplomacy of Cadillac,

Louisiana's influence over southeastern tribes declined because the power struggle between Cadillac and the Bienvillist faction obstructed the distribution of gifts. In 1714 the French crown allocated a total of four thousand *livres* annually for presents to the Indians. Bienville received instructions to distribute two thousand livres' worth of the gifts to Indians living along the lower reaches of the Mississippi River, while Cadillac and Duclos were to cooperate in distributing the other half of the gifts to the Choctaw and Creek Indians.[25] This cooperation failed to materialize, however, as Duclos began using his position as commissaire ordonnateur to restrict Cadillac's access to supplies. Carl Brasseaux suggests that opposition to Cadillac by Duclos extended even to "embezzlement of royal funds and mismanagement of the provincial warehouse."[26]

In 1714 the English capitalized on these handicaps by compromising the very bulwark of Louisiana's frontier defenses, the French-Choctaw alliance. A contingent of between twelve hundred and two thousand Alabama, Abhika, Tallapoosa, and Chickasaw warriors, led by "a party of twelve Englishmen," marched into the midst of the Choctaw settlements and intimidated many towns into accepting English trade relations. Later French reports indicated that the English and their allies may well have been invited into the region by Conchak Emiko, an influential Choctaw headman who probably sought to bolster his position by tapping into the lucrative English trade. The show of force, combined with Conchak Emiko's support, brought twenty-eight Choctaw villages into the Carolina trade system. "Only those of Loucha and Echicahae," according to the journal of Jean-Baptiste Bernard de la Harpe, "remained hostile to the English." Shortly afterward, a French emissary dispatched to assess the situation apparently encountered in the "grand village des Chactaws" a group of English traders who triumphantly "mocked the governor of Louisiana and the 40 or 50 rascals who were there with him."[27]

French authorities, primarily Jean-Baptiste Lemoyne de Bienville, observed the growing influence of the English with alarm. One Englishman in particular caught the attention of the French. In 1714 Pryce Hughes, probably a participant in the Choctaw visitation, circulated "through all the Indian villages in which there were Englishmen," then visited the Natchez and began traveling south along the Mississippi River "to make an alliance with the Houmas, Bayagoulas, Chaouachas, and Colapissas."[28]

Concerned over his intentions, Governor Antoine La Mothe de Cadillac issued orders for Hughes's arrest. The French caught up with him at his campsite on the banks of the Mississippi River, where they "found him sketching" and conducted him to Mobile.[29] There Bienville discovered that Hughes carried an official commission from the governor of South Carolina that purported to lay claim to lands as far west as the Mississippi River, presumably by right of Carolina's proprietary charter. According to Bienville, he "made no secret about saying that the Queen of England was going to send them five hundred families this autumn to settle on the St. Louis [Mississippi] River and provisions for three years."[30] Hughes had indeed petitioned Queen Anne in 1713 for support of a Welsh colony to be established "near the mouth of the Mesisipi," but he undoubtedly exaggerated the extent of the queen's support.[31] Nevertheless, an entry in the *Journals of the Commissioners of the Indian Trade of South Carolina*, dated November 21, 1713, made reference to Hughes's "designated Journy among the Indians."[32] The commissioners ordered "that a letter be writt" to ensure "that Mr. Hughs have al possible incouragement given him."[33] This may well have been the document recovered by Bienville a year later.[34]

The issuance of Hughes's commission in November 1713 makes it extremely likely that he indeed took part in, and possibly organized, the Choctaw visitation of 1714. Bienville probably questioned him on this and related matters and became convinced that the South Carolinians had embarked on a comprehensive and threatening new frontier strategy. "By all the measures the English of Carolina are taking," he warned, "we cannot doubt at all that they have the intention to seize this country completely."[35]

The first step in the solution to these problems for the French came unexpectedly in early 1715. Investigating reports that a silver mine had been discovered in the Illinois region, Cadillac left Mobile in February 1715 on an eight-month journey. He departed, according to Bienville, "without saying where he was going and without leaving me any orders."[36] Two months later, Bienville received a sealed packet of instructions from Cadillac advising him "to oppose the plans that the English of Carolina have of taking possession of this country."[37]

Bienville probably delighted in such instructions, but he hardly needed them. He and Duclos had consistently defied the governor while he was present, and his absence now gave them a prime opportunity to pursue their own interests unopposed. With or without authorization, Bienville began trying to "reconcile to ourselves all our Indian allies who have taken the side of the English since the arrival of Mr. de Lamothe whose conduct has greatly alienated the minds of all the Indians . . . , and I flatter myself that I shall bring them back to our side if Mr. Lamothe delays three or four months longer on his journey."[38]

He claimed that Cadillac had instructed him "to use . . . all the presents that come from France."[39] This assertion ranks as one of the most significant remarks of the episode. It may indicate that Bienville distributed his two thousand-livre portion of the year's four-thousand-livre allowance all at once. Moreover, with the full cooperation of Duclos, Bienville may also have succeeded in distributing the other half of the annual gifts that had been a point of contention between Duclos and Cadillac, thus flooding Creek and Choctaw villages with a sudden windfall of merchandise.

Bienville then took a step that could not possibly have been condoned by Cadillac. He persuaded a group of village headmen who had come to negotiate with him—probably Choctaws, Alabamas, Abhikas, or Tallapoosas—that he "was still commandant," and "that Mr. de Lamothe would not come back here any more." Far from being a private bargaining ploy, the hoax apparently involved the entire garrison and settlement of Mobile. In order to authenticate Bienville's claim, the Indians went around the settlement themselves and "inquired of the officers and inhabitants to whom [Bienville] had given word whether it was really true that Mr. de Lamothe would not come back again." Everyone seems to have cooperated, "knowing that all the nations had received English among them only because of the bad reception that Mr. de Lamothe had given them." Bienville requested that the Indians "bring [him] those English traders who were among them," offering as an additional incentive his permission "that they could pillage all their merchandise."[40]

The pronoun *ils* ("they") unfortunately remains a point of some uncertainty in these documents, making it difficult to identify the nations involved, and the chronology surrounding the Mobile conference may never be completely understood. Bienville reported success in weaning the Alabamas, one of the four main branches of the Upper Creeks, away from the English trade in the summer of 1715. "The Alabamas," he claimed, "are beginning to come here to trade and I am sending some Frenchmen to them." When he wrote this, however, the Yamasee War had been under way for several months. Significantly, he reported the acquisition of the Alabama trade as a routine matter of commerce and diplomacy unrelated to other Indian nations or South Carolina. Had the war been a preconceived, region-wide conspiracy against the English, as generally represented, it would surely have been apparent as such to Louisiana officials by late April. Nevertheless, Bienville seemed entirely unaware of it as late as June. He did not report the Mobile conference, moreover, until September, so it is impossible even to determine whether the Alabama breakthrough resulted from Bienville's hoax or predated it. The earliest known reference to the Yamasee War by a Louisiana official dates to September 1715.[41]

Frustrating as the French correspondence may be, it nevertheless suggests that Upper Creek and Choctaw participation in the Yamasee War did not commence promptly in April when the Yamasees launched their deadly attacks against South Carolina. The historical record does not reveal a specific date on which Choctaw and Upper Creek towns committed themselves to war with South Carolina, nor does it offer detailed information about the motives that prompted those decisions. For these reasons, an in-depth analysis of Upper Creek country during the Yamasee War will need to wait for a more capable researcher. But events in Choctaw country may offer some insight into the Upper Creek problem.

CHOCTAW-EUROPEAN DISCOURSE

If Choctaw emissaries witnessed Bienville's semi-comic hoax at Fort Mobile, as seems probable, it was neither their first nor last exposure to French stratagems. The Choctaws were the most populous nation in the colonial South, poised strategically north of the fragile settlements of French Louisiana; their loyalty could not be left to chance. Both Bienville and Cadillac resorted to des-

perate measures to dislodge the English traders from the "grand
village" of the Choctaws in 1715. Initially they tried to intimidate
the Choctaws by sending armed parties of Chickasaw warriors to
speak with them, but deadly skirmishes erupted. The gravity of the
situation ultimately forced Cadillac to abandon his expedition to
the Illinois country and return to Mobile. Once back, he attempted
to manipulate internal Choctaw familial politics by inviting the
brother of the "great chief to kill his own brother as the author of
all these troubles." Cadillac even promised to install the man in
his brother's place.[42]

Suggestive as these references seem, they do not do justice
to the complexity of Choctaw diplomacy or the finesse required
of French officials. Bienville knew perfectly well, if Cadillac did
not, that there was no single "grand village" or "great chief" of
the Choctaws. The Choctaw confederacy functioned diplomati-
cally as three distinct entities, sometimes four: the western district or Okla Fallaya, the eastern district or Okla Tannap, and the
Sixtowns district or Okla Hannali. Some sources, especially in
later periods, also referred to the Chickasaway Towns, which lay
to the southeast of the other districts and were generally the first
towns encountered by French parties traveling from Mobile into
Choctaw territory. All these districts regarded the Mississippian
era mound site of Nanih Waya (in northern Mississippi) as their
spiritual center, but it was no longer inhabited in the early eighteenth century and served no practical role in negotiations with
Europeans. Instead of a single grand village, each district had its
own constellation of "village clusters," influenced but not controlled
by more dominant central towns. In the eastern district of Okla
Fallaya, for instance, the town of West Yazoo traditionally played
a leading role in matters of diplomacy, while the eastern district
often followed the leadership of the town of Concha. Cadillac's

reference to a grand village undoubtedly referred to one of these regionally dominant towns.[43]

Despite the ambiguities of the French documents, some of the nuance of Choctaw-European relations can still be recovered. La Harpe's report that twenty-eight towns allied themselves with the English, for instance, suggests that the confederacy must have been divided in its loyalties, for it included between forty and fifty towns all told. Later French sources claimed that most of the remaining anti-English towns belonged to the more southerly Chickasaway and Sixtowns districts, which actively took up the French cause by threatening military action against their northern neighbors. Cadillac's effort to inspire the "brother" of Conchak Emiko to kill him, moreover, apparently bore fruit. The headman was indeed assassinated by Chicacha Outlacta, who subsequently carried his brother's head to the French at Mobile as a demonstration of his friendship.[44]

This morbid transfer of political authority had as much to do with Choctaw traditions of chiefly power and inheritance as with French diplomatic cleverness. Ethnohistorian Greg O'Brien has argued that the conceptual foundations for political authority among the Choctaws changed profoundly as a result of contact and trade with Europeans during the eighteenth century. Chiefly power initially drew its legitimacy from spiritual sources and had deep roots in the redistributive societies of the Mississippian period (ca. 900–1550 AD). Accordingly, the material benefits that proceeded from a leader's successful management of spiritual forces merely served as confirmation of his power. Trade goods were thus viewed as the result rather than the source of his power. However, O'Brien argues that by the end of the eighteenth century, Choctaw political authority had come to rest more on the ability to procure and manage European trade as an end in itself, as the primary source of chiefly power. If so, then Conchak Emiko's ordeal offers a suggestive glimpse into early eighteenth-century Choctaw uses of chiefly power in practical matters of diplomacy with Europeans.[45]

His initial decision to allow English traders into Choctaw villages probably involved a complex assessment of power relations in the greater Southeast. Because Choctaws already enjoyed access to muskets, ammunition, and other merchandise via French Louisiana, it is unlikely that they suddenly felt a pressing desire for English trade goods. The influence of English trade posed a graver, more mysterious problem for them. Conchak Emiko and the inhabitants of the eastern district of Okla Tannap had been under attack by English-allied slave raiders for years (principally Upper Creeks and Chickasaws), and those attacks undoubtedly increased following the 1704 destruction of the Apalachee mission system in northern Florida. It is easy for modern historians to trace those attacks to their root cause: the Atlantic economy's demand for unfree labor. It could not have been so clear to Choctaw leaders or the men and women who looked to them for answers. In response to these pressures, Conchak Emiko drew on his own spiritual power in an effort to bring external threats into harmony with the Choctaw world.[46]

It hardly matters whether the 1714 visitation of English traders and their Upper Creek and Chickasaw allies entered Choctaw territory at Conchak Emiko's invitation, as French sources seem to suggest, or whether he acted under duress upon their arrival. Either way, he staked his reputation on the English alliance. After the withdrawal of Upper Creek and Chickasaw warriors, moreover, English traders in Conchak Emiko's village depended as much on his continued spiritual and political power as he did on the ascendancy of English economic power. Consequently, the English mockery of Cadillac's representative, belittling the governor and the "40 or 50 rascals" in French Louisiana, was not merely a private communication between Europeans. It functioned as a political performance to reassure Conchak Emiko and persuade Choctaw observers still uncertain about the new alliance that English power was greater than French power.

In this context the outbreak of the Yamasee War may well have created an island of residual English trade influence in Choctaw territory, inhabited for some time by both the doomed English traders and the hapless Conchak Emiko. The cessation of official diplomatic communication from Charles Town in late 1714 gave way to the total disruption of trade the following spring. As news of developments in the East filtered into Choctaw country, English traders must have tried desperately to counter the information with local displays of bravado and gift giving, while Conchak Emiko called on every source of spiritual power at his disposal. In the end, the truth of the matter may have become too overwhelming to resist. According to the Penicault narrative, the key moment came when the French took action against Pryce Hughes, who had probably been one of the English leaders of the armed expedition that had opened the Choctaw trade in the first place. Shortly afterward, the Choctaws "killed the English that were in their village and pillaged the warehouse they had there." Whether Conchak Emiko died with them or not, he died for the same reason.[47]

By attacking the English traders in their midst, Upper Creek and Choctaw villages committed a political (and perhaps spiritual) act, intended to convey a message to the "core" nations, Bienville, and their own people. It signaled a realignment of alliances, communicated in the simple, time-honored formula of trade with allies and warfare with enemies. That message sent, however, they did little else. In nearly every case, "warfare" for the western nations who took action against South Carolina in 1715 meant primarily the cessation of trade and symbolic violence against the representatives of that trade.[48]

The Chickasaws undoubtedly experienced similar problems and considered the same solutions, but they followed a different path. A handful of English traders survived the Yamasee War in Chickasaw country, and that remarkable fact has traditionally set the Chickasaws apart in the secondary literature as the only nation in the Southeast to remain nominally allied with or at least neutral toward the English. Recently, however, the historian Alan Gallay has warned that Chickasaw loyalties may not have been so clear. Their commitment to the English prior to the Yamasee War, he points out, remained uncertain. In 1708, for instance, the South Carolina Indian agent Thomas Nairne recorded his frustration over the Chickasaws' unwillingness to commit themselves to an exclusive and binding alliance with the English. While some English traders survived the war, moreover, some died, and postwar Chickasaw disclaimers that Lower Creek warriors from the town of Coweta had crept into their villages and killed the traders can be read in several ways. Gallay clearly considers it a case of Chickasaw equivocation, and he is probably right.[49]

Even so, as the only nation in the South in which Carolinians survived the Yamasee War in situ, the Chickasaws were an anomaly. Traders in Chickasaw country inhabited an island of residual English trade prestige much like the one that may have preserved the Choctaw headman Conchak Emiko and his English guests for some time. The difference, of course, was that the tide of public disbelief in the power of English trade, even after months of diplomatic silence and news of war, never entirely overran the Chickasaw homeland. Their precarious diplomatic position in the region made the English alliance more important to them by far than it was for the Choctaws. Indeed, in spite of numerous efforts to pursue alliance and trade with French Louisiana, the Chickasaws had seen too clearly by 1715 that the French, for all their good intentions, had committed themselves first and foremost to the Choctaws. Failing to hear from the English during the diplomatic blackout created by the Nairne-Wright controversy in Charles Town, the Chickasaws had dispatched a delegation to the English capital. After being ignored by Carolina officials for several days, the delegation eventually received a formal declaration of friendship and alliance. It was the only such assurance given to a southeastern Indian nation in the five months prior to the Yamasee War. It mattered enough for them to walk five hundred miles, and they remembered it once they returned home.[50]

The Chickasaws reached different conclusions than other nations in the South, but their reasoning was very similar. They responded to external diplomatic problems according to internal needs and realities. Despite their long trek to Charles Town, they were not necessarily more committed to an English alliance for its own sake than was Conchak Emiko of the Choctaws; nor, in all likelihood, were they any less willing than his brother, Chicacha Outlacta, to cut their losses had circumstances demanded it. Even as a dissenting voice, the Chickasaw example conformed to the general pattern among the auxiliary confederates; it was a local decision that sought to preserve local stability and serve local interests in the midst of bewildering external instability.

CONFEDERATES AT WAR

The ligaments of those multifold local interests became painfully apparent as the war with South Carolina burned into the late summer and fall of 1715. The appearance of solidarity that so astounded and terrified the British in April, May, and June slowly revealed its fragile underpinnings from late summer onward, as the strain of the conflict began to wear on various members of the coalition. By autumn Carolinians were pleased to learn from the testimony of captured native prisoners that "the different nations of Indians ... grow jealous of each other, & begin to quarrell among themselves." Robert Maule, and perhaps many other colonists, considered this a consequence of God's intervention and gave thanks to "divine providence" for having "in a surprising manner infatuated their councils." Carolinians celebrated such "quarrells" because they held out the possibility of salvation for the colony, but they also revealed a great deal about the behavioral mechanics of the coalition as it existed in 1715 and 1716.[51]

Signs of serious distress appeared first among northern auxiliary members of the coalition. Cheraws, Catawbas, and other tribes of the Carolina piedmont and coast suffered the most severe losses of the war during the summer of 1715, losing sixty men in a pitched battle with Colonel George Chicken in June and another eighty to forces under Maurice Mathews in July. By native standards, these were catastrophic numbers that simply could not be sustained. More ominous still, Governor Robert Hunter of New York persuaded the Iroquois to step up their war on South Carolina's enemies (the same war he had tried to persuade them against the previous year, when the "flatheads" were still considered allies of Carolina). By September, Mohawk and Seneca raiding parties were regularly terrorizing the Carolina piedmont. Hard-pressed by European and Indian foes alike—and, perhaps to their surprise, unable to trade freely with Virginians—Cheraws and Catawbas began making overtures for peace and trade to Governor Spotswood of Virginia before the summer was over and effectively ended military engagements with South Carolina that fall, though a formal peace was still months away.[52]

At the same time, the core combatants to the south of Charles

Town found it increasingly difficult to acquire ammunition once English trade relations had been severed. The Spanish at St. Augustine attempted to keep the Yamasees in arms, and an English prisoner held for a brief period during 1715 among the Lower Creeks, probably on the Ocmulgee River, recalled that "divers parties of Indians came in with ammunition from Moville and Pansecola." Yet such efforts ultimately fell short, and many warriors reluctantly laid aside their muskets in favor of their old native weapons. English defenders noticed the transition during the summer of 1715 and rejoiced that many of their enemies now "had only bows and arrows."[53]

With ammunition growing scarce, the core nations and their northern auxiliaries appear to have revised their original strategy during the fall of 1715. Instead of large forces being sent to besiege English garrisons or waylay relief columns, small raiding parties began to strike by surprise along the tattered fringes of British settlement. According to one Carolinian, "they pursue their old method of bush-fighting and one or other of our scouts are daily shot down without ever seeing an enemy and without prospect of being reveng'd by ye rest."[54]

South Carolinians began the war in dreadful ignorance about the extent of the native coalition, but they soon perceived its basic structure and moved to exploit its weaknesses. Increasingly, they saw the Cherokees as the key to their salvation. These powerful residents of the Appalachian Mountains and foothills had participated in several of the early attacks on Carolina, generally in joint operations with piedmont tribes such as the Catawbas. Yet by October they too had become weary of the war, and rumors began filtering into Charles Town "concerning the Cherikees a most potent nation as if they were willing to be reconciled to us."[55]

Carolinians tested the waters by sending two former traders

up the Savannah River to parley with the Cherokees, promising them each five hundred pounds upon their return "if they succeed." Nothing was heard of them for some time. Then a few weeks later, the men reappeared alive and well, accompanied "in a submissive manner" by 128 Cherokee Indians. They proceeded to Charles Town and concluded a truce and alliance with the English, solemnized by native ceremonies. The Indians even promised to join forces with the Carolinians in an expedition to attack the Creeks and their allies, but they represented only one of several factions within Cherokee society. Others, principally the Lower Cherokee towns clustered around Tugalo at the headwaters of the Savannah River, still refused to make war on other members of the coalition. When the promised military assistance failed to materialize, Carolinians feared that the war's conclusion might be as far away as ever.[56]

In late December 1715, Colonel Maurice Moore gambled the colony's future on a desperate bid to secure a meaningful, broad-based Cherokee alliance. Moore led three hundred soldiers, black and white, directly into Tugalo Town. His show of force coincided significantly with Creek efforts to persuade the Cherokees to remain faithful to the native coalition. As Moore was presenting his arguments to the principal headman of the Lower Cherokee towns, known as the Conjuror, a Lower Creek delegation from Coweta was presenting counter-arguments. The Creek negotiators sought to convince the Conjuror that a joint Creek-Cherokee ambush of Moore's forces could drive the English out of the region entirely, and they were surely right. Here was a moment when the future of the South literally hung in the balance like the fog of the delegates' voices in the cold mountain air.[57]

In the end the presence of three hundred English troops proved sufficient to drive a wedge between the Creeks and Cherokees, never the closest of friends even in times of peace. In January 1716 a contingent of Cherokee warriors made their decision in stark fashion, possibly under the influence of alcohol, by massacring the very Creek delegation that had come to negotiate under a flag of truce. The native alliance rapidly shattered along traditional lines, as blood feuds flared up again among old enemies. Creek war parties began preying on Cherokee victims as well as on the English, while the Catawbas and other Indians of the Carolina piedmont, unwilling to make war on the Cherokees, made peace at last with South Carolina.[58]

For the weary colonists of South Carolina, news of the Cherokee decision was regarded as a "wonderfull deliverance," signaling the war's inevitable end. For Indians still at war with the British, however, it was a devastating blow. Particularly among the Creeks, who lost thirteen headmen at Tugalo, the incident would not soon be forgotten. Years after the Creeks had made peace with South Carolina, they continued to nurse their resentment against the Cherokees. English efforts in 1726 to make peace between the Creeks and Cherokees, for instance, found Emperor Brims of the Lower Creek town of Coweta unreceptive, "for them men that was killed by the Cherokeys of mine when the white people were there is not over with me as yet, nor never shall be while there is a Cowwataid living."[59]

Seeking to end hostilities with the English, the Cherokees did little more than substitute one enemy for another. After January 1716, Creek war parties increasingly targeted Cherokee towns rather than the already ravaged plantation districts of South Carolina. Besides the direct attacks, Cherokee efforts to move trade along established paths often fell prey to Creek raiding parties as well. Nor did Creek resentment diminish once they had concluded a peace with the English. For the next three decades, Creek depredations exceeded in severity and frequency anything the Carolinians could possibly have managed.[60]

In addition, the 1716 Cherokee-English rapprochement triggered a series of diplomatic aftershocks that extended as far away as the Illinois country. Cherokee emissaries immediately set out to bolster their alliance network in early 1716 and to prepare for the opening of a new front against the Lower Creeks. Logically enough, they sought to use the promise of a resumed trade with the English as a bargaining ploy. The records do not allow a complete view of this diplomatic effort, but it is clear that the Cherokees traveled up the Tennessee River to approach the Illinois "on behalf of the Governor of Carolina" and persuade them to "receive the English in their village." On this occasion, the Cherokees suffered the same treatment they had just visited on Lower Creek delegates at Tugalo Town. The Illinois Indians killed three of the Cherokee emissaries and "burned two of them alive." Recognizing perhaps that English trade had not yet regained its former luster, the Cherokees responded to the Illinois setback by sending negotiators to Mobile to reconfirm their friendship with the French. They also launched a vicious retaliatory raid against the village of Kaskaskia, where they took a dozen French "habitants" prisoner in addition to an unspecified number of Illinois captives.[61]

These Cherokee initiatives came shortly after the Louisiana governor, Antoine La Mothe de Cadillac, had visited the Illinois country, and some of the French could not help wondering if his inept diplomacy had provoked the attacks in some way. What is more, Cadillac had been so anxious to return quickly to Mobile "that he had refused to accept the calumet of peace that they wanted to sing to him" at various Indian Nations along the way. This constituted a "tres gros insulte," according to Bienville, especially when it came from the governor of French Louisiana himself. As a result,

Europeans who descended the Mississippi River immediately after him met with an unusual degree of hostility. "Two Spaniards and an Irishman," for instance, "were wounded at night by several arrow-shots by the Arkansas or Yazoo Nation." The Natchez Indians, who occupied the eastern banks of the Mississippi River in portions of modern-day Mississippi, went further and "assassinated the first four voyageurs [French traders] that went to them after Mr. de Lamothe." Unaware of the renewed Cherokee-English alliance and the ambitious Cherokee efforts to rebuild a pro-English trade network, Bienville concluded simply that "Mr. de Lamothe has inspired war in all the nations established on the St. Louis [Mississippi] River."[62]

By the summer of 1716, however, even Cadillac's bitterest enemies could see that something more than the governor's usual incompetence was at work. "The English of Carolina are beginning to win back all their Indians," Commissaire Ordonnateur Duclos lamented in early June. "Entire villages that had massacred Englishmen," he claimed, had been utterly destroyed "without sparing either women or children." South Carolinians themselves certainly had no power to exact such vengeance, and there are few recorded instances of Carolinian offensives aside from strikes against the Catawbas or Yamasees. The Cherokee violence at Tugalo and Kaskaskia may have fueled rumors of deadly English retributions that could threaten Indian nations far inland. Duclos and others in French Louisiana feared that southeastern Indians were "intimidated by these examples" and were thus "seeking to become reconciled to the English."[63]

Cadillac's refusal to smoke the calumet as he descended the Mississippi River in late 1715 thus coincided with growing indigenous concerns about a possible resurgence of English trade influence, made credible by Cherokee initiatives in early 1716. His journey took on a political significance that no one in Louisiana completely understood and, as a consequence, inadvertently created a cascading diplomatic crisis that followed him all the way back from the Illinois country to Mobile. The crisis became so acute that the French ultimately prepared themselves for anticipated attacks from the Alabama Indians, who "in order to make their peace with the English" were rumored to be sending as many as a thousand warriors "to destroy entirely Fort Louis." On two occasions in the summer of 1716, an overwhelmed Cadillac allowed his "fright and fears" to get the better of him when news of Alabama and Upper Creek movements reached Mobile. In each instance, he pathetically "assembled all the soldiers and settlers who were then at Fort Louis around his house to defend him alone in case of attack."[64]

THEMES, PATTERNS, PROBLEMS

The Yamasee War as it unfolded from the Carolina piedmont to the Illinois country thus consisted of a series of diplomatic aftershocks and realignments in which the indigenous peoples of the region continued to seek ways of adjusting themselves to the new order and vice versa. English, French, and Spanish observers saw portions of this phenomenon, but none of them saw the whole drama or comprehended its enormity. Few of the French, least of all the frightened Governor Cadillac, understood the resurgence of anti-French sentiments in 1716. Those hostile postures conformed entirely, however, with the anti-English postures adopted by auxiliary confederates a year earlier. They were diplomatic adjustments to a complex network of alliances in which South Carolina and Louisiana figured as important but by no means decisive influences.

Each of the auxiliary participants faced a complex set of local considerations that defy generalization. Common elements shaped their decisions, to be sure, such as prospects of alternative trade, market influence, the ambiguous silence of Carolina's diplomatic voice, and finally the unambiguous clamor of warfare in April. But the nature and value of these elements differed from region to region, involving a thousand threads that wove differing local realities. The enduring marvel of the Yamasee War may be that in so many cases they all led to the same solution: political alignment with the core nations and token "war" with South Carolina.

PART 4 Ash

7. Monsters and Men

✳ ✳ ✳ ✳ ✳ ✳ ✳ ✳ ✳ ✳ ✳ ✳ ✳ ✳ ✳

In August 1715 Governor Charles Craven appeared before the South Carolina Commons House of Assembly to discuss the Indian war that had set the colony's plantation districts ablaze in mid-April. He gave voice to the anguish of many Assembly members who had lost friends and loved ones in those attacks and attempted to make sense of the calamity that had descended on them so suddenly. Whereas many Carolinians had initially assumed that only the Yamasee Indians and their immediate neighbors were involved, it had become apparent, he explained, that "these monsters of man kind" had formed "a general confederacy and alliance."[1]

If Craven and other Carolinians had finally come to realize the full extent of the danger confronting them, the governor's language nevertheless revealed a deeper problem with which Carolinians had difficulty coming to grips. The "monsters" at war with the colony were also "of man kind," and many of them lived within the colony itself as free "settlement Indians" or slaves on low-country rice plantations. In desperate need of military allies, scouts, and labor, white Carolinians could not yet afford to extend their racial epithets and anger to all Indians indiscriminately. As a consequence, they spent much of their time attempting to distinguish the supposed "monsters" from the men. Coupled with the Charles Town government's extensive efforts to enlist and arm African slaves in the war effort, the Yamasee War became much more than a simple military contest. In many ways it became an early exercise in "racial profiling" and ultimately a testing ground for new racial definitions, boundaries, and policies that set the tone for the colony's emerging plantation regime. While portions of the present chapter discuss the fires of the Yamasee War, therefore, the primary objective is to trace the patterns of ash they left behind.

CAROLINIANS AT WAR

Perhaps as much as the struggle for survival itself, the psychological terror of being surrounded by supposed "monsters" drove Carolinians to reconsider the human landscapes they inhabited. Various shades of fear, some verging on panic, pervaded the correspondence of South Carolinians throughout the summer of 1715. By July the mere prospect of being "massacred by savages" had ceased to do justice to the threats they saw before them, and colonists began to speculate instead about "perhaps . . . being rosted in slow fires, scalp'd and strick with lightwood, and other inexpressible tortures." Most correspondents chose to leave the details of "such acts of barbarity" to the imagination of their readers, noting that "even to relate ye manner is shocking." Yet others could not help filling in the gaps. After promising not to "alarm you with a relation of the barbarous cruelties of the heathen upon the English in Carolina," for instance, John Squyre went on to describe reports of Indians "spliting open the women's young children before their eyes, whom they tormented and rosting them and making the mother eat a part of it." "Nor yet shall I trouble you," he assured his audience again, "with the occasion of the Heathens doing so, only I may say . . ." The unrecorded conversations and rumors that circulated among the refugees crowded into Charles Town that summer must certainly have mirrored in many respects the contents of the few letters that escaped the colony. It is impossible to say how much of this rhetoric was the predictable result of wartime propaganda or panic and how much of it was truth, but it is clear at least that white Carolinians were in the process of painting themselves as innocent victims, as virtuous martyrs confronting an inhumane and ultimately inhuman enemy.[2]

In creating such an emotionally charged contrast between their own humanity and the inhumanity of their Native American enemies, Carolinians were not unusual. Virginians reached a similar level of hyperbole in the 1620s during conflicts with the Powahatan Indians, and New England colonists set the standard during the Pequot War of 1637. Indeed, the historian Jill Lepore has argued persuasively that the wartime rhetoric produced during King Philip's War in 1675 and the popular histories that subsequently codified that rhetoric played a decisive role in the process of self-definition for New Englanders. Not only did the winners write the history in that case, but the ordeal of surviving and making sense of the war produced some of the defining myths of American exceptionalism. All of these conflicts hardened English attitudes toward non-English peoples and created an increasingly inflexible and divisive frontier.[3]

Yet in the case of South Carolina, the sweeping oversimplification so natural to wartime mobilization stumbled on a home front that displayed a level of racial and ethnic complexity unmatched in other British colonies. Embedded among Carolina's far-flung plantations were numerous free "settlement" Indians such as the Edistos, Winyahs, Stonos, Cussas, and Itewans, who "lived interspersed amongst ye English." The original inhabitants of the region, these small nations had learned to adapt themselves to the uninvited influx of Indian, African, and European populations beginning in the 1670s. They initially welcomed the English establishment of Charles Town as a counterbalance to the military power of the inland Westo Indians, and in many ways the outbreak of the Yamasee War presented them with a new version of that same challenge: how to manage their relations with more powerful neighbors in order to preserve a measure of local autonomy. In the spring of 1715 they chose again to ally themselves with South Carolina, just as they had in 1670. Warriors from several of these "settlement" nations fought alongside white Carolinians and armed African slaves in critical battles early on that halted the first Yamasee offensives into the Port Royal settlements.[4]

By summer, however, even the settlement Indians began to reconsider the wisdom of their support for South Carolina. Perhaps the withering pressure applied by other Indian nations or the desperate conditions within the colony gave them pause. More likely, they were alienated by the growing anti-Indian rhetoric of white Carolinians. Though willing to accept their military assistance, colonists expressed growing doubts about the reliability of their last remaining allies. They suspected, for instance, that the settlement Indians were "only spyes upon or proceedings & gave intelligence of all yt past among us to ye enemy." July brought horrifying confirmation of such fears for many Carolinians, when Captain Thomas Barker and thirty of his men died in an ambush on their way to "compel . . . or force" another small nation called the Congarees to join the Carolinians. English survivors of the ambush recognized the leader of the native forces as one of their former comrades in arms, a "war captain" who had fought alongside them against the Yamasees "at ye battle of Combahee." He had reportedly separated from the main Carolina force only the day before "wth a promise to meet ym ye next day." And so he did. It may well have signaled the settlement Indians' formal declaration of war against the colony. By the middle of July, at any rate, the only nations still allied with South Carolina, the "Cassaw's, Itewans, & Winyau's," had officially "revolted to the enemy."[5]

The challenge of self-preservation forced Carolinians to confront the practical dilemmas of their slave society at almost every turn. Operating under severe martial law, for instance, they augmented their forces in 1715 by moving "to press several of the inhabitants and several slaves" into involuntary military service. They even appointed a "press-master" to speed things along. Most of Carolina's military initiatives, as a result, involved multiracial forces such as the one commanded by Governor Charles Craven in the summer of 1715, which consisted of "100 white men and 100 Negroes and Indians." Indeed, according to historian Peter H. Wood, "Negroes may never have played such a major role in any earlier or later American conflict." At the same time, however, depositions given by Yamasee warriors to the Spanish in St. Augustine indicate that African-American slaves were also negotiating and cooperating with Indian raiding parties. In some instances, they even entered into alliances with Native Americans and commenced their own private wars against the colony. Thus, just as white settlers questioned the loyalties of their few remaining Indian allies, they also harbored fears about the enlistment of African slaves, even those deemed "trusty." "There must be great caution us'd," several planters warned in 1715, "lest our slaves when arm'd might become our masters." Carolinians became so concerned about that danger that they even refused to send female slaves to Virginia in exchange for white recruits, as originally agreed, because they feared that "the Discontent such usage would have given their husbands to have their Wives taken from them . . . might have occasioned a Revolt also of the Slaves." The internal consequences of using African slaves to defend against external threats were thus never far away from Carolina's military planning.[6]

Simultaneously, the colony's internal labor system contributed in several frightening ways to the external threat. The Cherokee alliance that ultimately saved the colony in 1716, for instance, was initially delayed by a "parcell of lies" circulated in Cherokee country by two escaped African slaves. Those rival versions of truth undoubtedly struck deep and painful nerves among colonial officials, nerves still smarting from the conflict with Alexander Longe, and they were not soon forgotten. A full two years after the alliance with the Cherokees had finally been concluded, Carolinians were still concerned about the influence of African slaves beyond the colony's borders. A ship returning from Charles Town in early 1718 brought news to Lieutenant Governor Bennett of Bermuda that "the inhabitants there were very apprehensive that the Cherikees Indians in conjunction with the negroes (many haveing already run away from their masters into the woods) would invade them." The view was the same from Virginia, where Governor Alexander Spotswood saw the anti-English activism of escaped slaves of all races as one of the principal dangers confronting South Carolina. As a precondition to opening negotiations with the Catawbas and other piedmont nations in 1715, he demanded "that they deliver up to me Pompey an Appalatchee Indian slave and Pope a negro slave, belonging to So. Carolina, who I understand have been very active in doing mischief to the English."[7]

The colony's labor system came into play as Carolina negotiated with potential Native American allies as well. Shortly after losing their last internal native allies in the summer of 1715, Carolinians acquired their first ally outside the colony: the Tuscaroras. Although, in truth, the Tuscaroras had been fighting the Catawbas for some time, colonists could not help reassuring themselves in August 1715 that they had "now come to our assistance." The irony of the situation could not have been clearer. The same colony that had sought to destroy the Tuscaroras by massing its native allies in

1713 now begged for help from Tuscarora refugees against those former allies. Whether they appreciated the irony or not, there is little question that the Tuscaroras understood the situation and remembered that hundreds of their people had been enslaved by the Carolinians. To make amends for that unpleasant reality, the South Carolina Commons House of Assembly quickly enacted a remarkable piece of legislation, unthinkable in peacetime. It issued a blanket resolution granting the Tuscaroras "the liberty of redeeming what Indians of their nation are now slaves in this province." The Assembly ensured their right "of carrying . . . home againe" not only all the Tuscarora slaves within the colony itself but also those "to be taken in the war," apparently referring to individuals still held captive by neighboring Indian nations.[8] It is unclear whether the Assembly acted spontaneously or in response to a specific demand from the Tuscaroras. Either way, it transformed the Yamasee War in one small corner of the Carolinas into a war of liberation.

Although Tuscaroras probably represented a decided minority within the Indian slave population at the time, they were by no means a rarity. Even the former Indian agent John Wright, killed during the early days of the war, had owned a slave named "Tusquerora Betty." Clearly antagonistic to the English reverence for property rights, the wholesale emancipation of Tuscarora slaves must also have rattled the sensibilities of planters who owned Indian slaves of other nationalities. According to some studies, this included as many as 26 percent of all South Carolina households in 1715. Had the Assembly attempted such a thing in peacetime, it would certainly have met with angry opposition. In the fall of 1715, however, with most of the colony's plantation districts in ruins, the legislated exodus of the Tuscaroras generated no recorded criticism.[9]

DEMOGRAPHIC DEFENSE

Even so, state-coerced emancipation posed serious legal and racial problems for the colony's plantation regime, and it is clear that white Carolinians were thinking about them. In 1715 the Commons House of Assembly drafted an act that sought to legislate out of existence the racial category of mustee, traditionally used by low-country planters to designate slaves of mixed African and Indian ancestry. They now evidently found it problematic. In order to avoid "all doubts and scruples that may arise" about the definition and valuation of these slaves, the act ordered that "all and every such slave who is not entirely Indian, shall be accounted and deemed as negro." The importance of this first official effort to eradicate the connecting link, or middle ground, between Indian and African slaves cannot be overemphasized. While the language of the law cited practical, monetary concerns over the appraisal of different types of slaves, the very nature of the act revealed a much more ambitious agenda. It sought for the first time to create a clear and legal demarcation, however arbitrary, between Africans and Indians. Moreover, by declaring that all mixed-race slaves be "deemed as negro," it effectively maneuvered the gravitational pull of slavery to that side of the line, with far-reaching implications for the subsequent development of white racial ideology.[10]

At the same time, a similar effort to clarify racial boundaries by legislative action was under way in North Carolina. Having endured years of violence during the Tuscarora War, inhabitants of the Albemarle region witnessed a resurgence of violence in the fall of 1715 as several coastal tribes took up arms against the colony again. As late as the summer of 1716, in fact, North Carolinians were still complaining about "the Indians being broke out." In the midst of this distress, the North Carolina Assembly in 1715 sought to gain control over the colony's racial composition by passing a restrictive marriage statute. "White" colonists who married "any Negro, Mulatto, or Indyan Man or Woman" were to be fined fifty pounds. While similar in substance to Virginia's infamous 1691 legislation, the North Carolina statute was not merely a control measure for the emerging slave regime. It was a clear response to endemic Anglo-Indian conflict. According to the historian Kirsten Fischer, the 1715 statute "codified a growing intolerance for cross-cultural unions and strengthened definitions of racial difference." Fischer is correct in regarding the statute as a consequence of the Tuscarora War, but it was also a response to the ongoing Yamasee War and continuing violence within North Carolina. The simultaneous discussions of racial boundaries in both the North and South Carolina assemblies, moreover, suggests a region-wide reexamination of such issues that transcended colonial borders and was driven by a shared experience. In this respect, the Tuscarora and Yamasee wars should really be viewed as linked events.[11]

White Carolinians thought about such things because they believed their survival depended on it. The hyperbole of wartime rhetoric and associated wartime racial legislation all coincided with a chronic need to identify and control the colony's internal and external enemies. Even while they were still sorting monsters from men, South Carolinians began to formulate a defensive strategy based on those new racial definitions. The historian William S. Willis of Columbia University first articulated that strategy in a seminal article published in 1963. A frightened white minority, he argued, "segregated Indians and Negroes from each other" in order to preserve themselves against the combined threat of those "two exploited colored majorities." Willis viewed the Yamasee War as the launching point for the new strategy of "divide and rule," as did the historian Peter Wood in his classic monograph, *Black*

Majority, published nearly ten years later. In each case, however, the war figured mainly as a chronological benchmark, notable only for its blunt shock value in alerting Carolinians to the demographic dangers surrounding them. The Yamasee War indeed gave birth to the policy of divide and rule, but it did far more than merely frighten white settlers into a defensive posture. It frightened them in several specific ways that were rooted in the colony's multiracial countryside as it existed in early 1715. Those specific fears, in turn, generated specific responses. In addition to giving birth to the policy of divide and rule, I argue that the Yamasee War gave it final shape and form.[12]

It is impossible to establish a precise chronology for events that were so intertwined and mutually reinforcing, but the process of identifying enemies so evident in 1715 and 1716 appears to have led quickly to a comprehensive set of race-based responses beginning in 1715. Coincident with the realization of their minority status in 1715, Carolinians sought to preserve the colony's white population by requiring a passport for those wishing to evacuate. That emergency measure was immediately followed by legislation in 1716 to augment the white population by encouraging "the importation of white Servants." Every year thereafter, the Assembly passed new legislation toward the same end, offering special "Privileges, Exemptions, and Encouragements" to entice white (and preferably Protestant) settlers into the colony. They even sought to "appropriate the Yamasee Lands to the use of such persons" in the summer of 1716 but were stymied in that effort by the Lords Proprietors, who continued to guard their land rights jealously.[13]

In addition to wanting to bolster the colony's white population, Carolinians also felt a pressing need to govern white behavior in ways they had not previously considered. The Assembly's "Act for the Better Ordering of white Servants," ratified in December 1717, reflected both the concerns of a nascent slave society and the specific threats posed to it by the Yamasee War. Having suffered the wrath of runaway slaves like Pompey and Pope, white colonists placed special emphasis on stopping white servants from running away "in company" with slaves. White servants who committed such an offense were to "be deemed a felon, and the punishment of a felon be inflicted on him accordingly, without Benefit of Clergy." Just as they had sought to legislate racial boundaries by defining the offspring of Indian and African unions as "negro" in 1716, moreover, they moved to create a clearer boundary between white and black. The act prescribed harsh punishments for "any white Woman, whether free or a Servant, that shall suffer herself to be got with Child by a Negro or other Slave or Free Negro." Likewise, white men who produced offspring with nonwhite women were to "undergo the same penalties as white Women."[14]

The historian Peter Wood viewed this 1717 act governing white servants as the first legislative response of Carolinians to the "black majority" around them, but the act was clearly preceded by similar legislation and born of the same needs. All of these measures focused on a specific set of racially motivated concerns, not all limited to African Americans, and they all occurred within two years of each other as the colony fought for survival during the Yamasee War.[15]

Those war-related efforts, it should be stressed, continued well into the 1720s. In fact, the Yamasee War itself continued throughout the 1720s, if at a much reduced level, and white Carolinians lived with that reality. Unfortunately, the desire to draw clear chronological boundaries around historical events has led historians to underestimate the continuing havoc and emotional strain of the war. The Cherokees and Catawbas made their peace with South Carolina in 1716, but the colony did not achieve a formal peace with portions of the powerful Lower (Ocheese) Creek Nation until 1718, and that peace apparently counted for little in some parts of Creek country. As late as 1722, Carolinians were still trying to persuade the Creeks that they had negotiated a "lasting" and "thorough" peace. And while the Charles Town government made repeated overtures to the Yamasees, offering to "be friends with them, and forgetting all that is past," the Indians gave no quarter. As members of the Governor's Council observed in 1722, the Yamasees "have ever since continued our open and avowed enemies, and now very often murder and ruin her Majesty's subjects."[16]

Not surprisingly, most of the murder and ruination occurred in and around the old Yamasee homelands, and those exposed areas to the south of Charles Town became, as a consequence, the testing ground for many of South Carolina's new racial policies. Although early efforts to use the Yamasee lands to attract white settlers were opposed by the proprietors, the same concerns about the colony's racial composition found expression in several proposals for defending the frontiers. In 1722 the Commons House of Assembly took action against absentee landlords holding acreage "in and about Port Royal" who apparently wished to keep their property but were afraid of actually occupying such an exposed frontier. The act threatened fines and possible forfeiture of the property for owners "who shall not have a white Man who shall personally appear" whenever local alarms required the mobilization of the militia. Owners of property around Port Royal thus needed to have at least one white resident for every thousand acres of land within eighteen months of the ratification of the act.[17]

Recognizing that a number of white colonists had deserted Carolina to escape financial difficulties, the Assembly also passed legislation to create incentives both to keep them in the colony and, just as important, to move them to key locations where they could help stabilize the frontiers. Hence, "no Process, Writ, or Execution" was to be undertaken "for any Debt, Duty, Contract, or Sum of Money whatsoever" against anyone who settled within twenty miles (or "three runs") of Fort Moore on the eastern side of the Savannah River, the old location of Savano Town. The same immunities were granted to individuals who settled near the fort at Palachacola Old Town on the Savannah River and at Beaufort Town on Port Royal Island. These were more than narrow efforts to defend the marches. The act explicitly cited the complex of fears that had plagued Carolinians since 1715. Members of the Assembly worried that the continued desertion of white debtors would further "expose this Frontier Colony to the Incursions of the Indians, Insurrections of the Negroes," and possibly even attacks from French and Spanish forces.[18]

DECLINE OF INDIAN SLAVERY

Those attempts to exert control over the colony's social fabric took place in the midst of a significant demographic shift in South Carolina's slave labor force. Because the Yamasee War effectively ended the Indian slave trade, few new slaves came into the system thereafter. As a result, natural demographic factors came to the forefront. As might be expected of a population in which 75 percent of members lived on plantations where they had no access to potential partners from their own race, Indian slaves began declining in number immediately.[19] The rate of household ownership of Indian slaves, derived from a survey of South Carolina will transcripts, fell from a prewar level of 26 percent between 1710 and 1714 to about 21 percent for the five-year period following the war, 1715–19 (see table 1).[20] Between 1720 and 1724 the rate of ownership dropped drastically to about 11 percent. Thereafter the decline continued at a more moderate rate throughout the 1720s, falling to about 7 percent for the five-year period 1725–29. Ultimately the percentage of households owning Indian slaves leveled out during the 1730s at about 2 to 3 percent.[21]

This absolute decline in the population of enslaved Indians concealed a more complex pattern of demographic change. Planters who owned multiracial labor forces often resorted to unwieldy terminologies to express the composition of their holdings. Christopher Smyth, for instance, bequeathed to his grandson "all & singular the negroe & Indian slaves," while Robert Daniell left his wife Martha "all my slaves, whether negroes, Indians, mustees, or molattoes, both male & female." Where slaves were identified by name and bequeathed to particular relatives, however, it is likely that they held special value for the family and may have been intended for use within the household as personal servants. Such was the case when Henry Bower drafted his will in 1724. He stipulated that his wife be allowed to select from his slave holdings "a young negro or Indian woman which of them she will (such as understands house business)." Similarly, Robert Stevens in 1720 left his wife "a negroe girl . . . to be solly att her comand." Indian and African children were often given to children or grandchildren of similar ages and genders, perhaps in an effort to foster personal attachments. Mary Crosse thus bequeathed her "Indian girle slave, named reigner," to her daughter in 1699, while ten years later Thomas Dalton gave "an Indian boy called Thomasse" to his son.[22]

The percentage of Indian slaves identified in this manner, relative to Africans, offers a unique perspective on the occupational demographics of Indian slavery. It suggests that the clear intent of the Commons House of Assembly's racial legislation found practical expression in the occupational decisions made by low-country planters in the waning phases of the Yamasee War and

Table 1. Rate of household ownership of slaves, 1690–1739

Years	Number of wills	Households with Indian slaves (%)	Households with African slaves (%)	Households with mustee slaves (%)
1690–94	30	2 = 6	4 = 13	0
1695–99	23	1 = 4	6 = 26	0
1700–04	14	2 = 14	5 = 36	0
1705–09[a]	14	6 = 43	8 = 57	0
1710–14	46	12 = 26	15 = 32	0
1715–19	43	9 = 21	15 = 35	2 = 4
1720–24	133	15 = 11	61 = 46	5 = 4
1725–29	122	9 = 7	47 = 38	7 = 5.7
1730–34	167	3 = 1.8	63 = 38	4 = 2.4
1735–39	185	6 = 3	77 = 41	6 = 3

Source: Will Transcripts, vols. 1–4, SCDAH.

[a] There is good reason to believe that a larger sample of wills would produce a more moderate result.

its aftermath. Whereas white Carolinians had routinely utilized Indian slaves for domestic service prior to the war, they increasingly appear to have consigned them to field work afterward. From an estimated prewar high of 34 percent of slaves bequeathed by name to family members, and thus likely to be engaged in domestic labor, Indian slaves appeared as probable domestic laborers at a rate of only 22 percent in the five years following the war, 1715–19, and fell further to 10 percent between 1720 and 1724. By the second half of the decade, 1725–29, the number of Indian slaves likely to have been working within the household had fallen to only 3 percent. This rate of decline far exceeded the general rate of decline in the ownership of Indian slaves, suggesting that the system of domestic occupational roles of Indian slaves as seen prior to the Yamasee War broke down long before Indian slaves themselves disappeared from low-country plantations.[23]

New social dynamics between Indians and white Carolinians may well have forced Indian slaves out of the household and into the fields after 1715. Although inventories reveal a moribund population of enslaved Indians during the 1720s, they do not indicate a rate of decline as pronounced as the disappearance of domestic servants from the will transcripts. They suggest, instead, stagnation and moderate decline. It is clear, moreover, from the relative monetary values assigned to Indian and African slaves in postmortem inventories from the 1720s that Indians were considered much less desirable. The reasons for this price differential are unclear, but they may have been related to white anxieties about the use of Indian slaves. One of the glaring differences between the will transcripts and other records, even prior to the Yamasee War, is the lack of male Indians in the wills and their relative abundance in postmortem inventories and census records (see tables 2 and 3). Since the wills were heavily biased toward domestic servants,

Table 2. Population statistics for Indian slaves

Years	Total population of Indian slaves	Women (%)	Men (%)	Children (%)
1703	350	43	29	29
1708	1,400	43	36	21
1722–27	1,100–1,280	37	31	32

Source: Population figures for 1722–27 are derived from a survey of postmortem inventories. Based on 169 inventories, Indian slaves represented 7 or 8 percent (depending on how slaves not identified by race are apportioned) of the entire slave labor force, which stood somewhere between twelve thousand in 1720 and twenty thousand in 1730. I have taken sixteen thousand as a mean figure for 1722–27. See WIMR, 1722–1724, vol. 58; 1722–1726, vol. 59; 1724–1725, vol. 60; 1726–1727, vols. 61A and 61B, SCDAH. Figures for the years 1703 and 1708 are based on information in a report of the "Governor and Council to the Lords Proprietors," September 17, 1708, RBPRO, 5:203–10.

the relative absence of male Indian slaves in this record series may indicate that Indian men were never widely trusted to work closely with the planter's family. If so, the outbreak of the Yamasee War must surely have strengthened existing prejudices. The rapid disappearance of all Indians from the immediate domicile after 1715 may therefore be viewed in part as a defensive measure, perhaps intended to preserve not only the safety of the planter's family members but also their peace of mind.[24]

Did white Carolinians intentionally distance themselves from their Indian slaves by relegating them to the fields? Unfortunately, the evidence does not conclusively answer this question. According to Winthrop Jordan, English colonists used "the separate meanings of *Indian* and *negro*" to "triangulate their own position in America." Before they could do this, however, they first had to separate the "meanings of Indian and negro," and evidence suggests that many white South Carolinians were in the process of doing just this after the Yamasee War. As slave names suggest, low-country

Table 3. Survey of South Carolina postmortem inventories

Years	Estates	Estates with Indian slaves	Estates with African slaves	Estates with mustee slaves	Total no. of Indian slaves	Total no. of African slaves	Total no. of mustee slaves	Total no. of unknown descent
1722	12	5	8	2	8	51	2	0
1723	40	11	34	5	21	231	5	62
1724	32	5	22	2	14	369	5	88
1725	39	14	32	4	34	284	7	6
1726	35	11	25	3	28	241	10	102
1727	11	4	10	2	16	96	2	14

Source: WIMR, SCDAH.

Note: Slaves listed as "unknown" in this table were not identified by race in the inventories. Since Indian and African slaves carried very different values, however, appraisers were careful to distinguish between them. Large numbers of slaves, valued collectively without reference to race, were probably African.

planters tried mightily to draw Indians into the category of *slave* by divorcing the individual's identity from that of free relatives on the far side of the frontier. Nevertheless, the connection must have remained vividly apparent to all concerned. In 1700, for instance, white Carolinians were alarmed to discover that two Indian slaves had attempted to incite a neighboring Indian nation to attack the colony. They apparently told their free Indian acquaintances that "a great many nations of Indians had already agreed & confederated to make war & cutt off all the white men." Concerns over this sort of collusion between free and unfree Indians must from the outset have driven English efforts to deny Indian slaves those vestiges of their former lives deemed threatening. After the horrors of the Yamasee War, white conceptions of the Indian as enemy may have grown too persuasive to allow even guarded confidence any longer in the Indian as nanny.[25]

As was the case prior to the war, moreover, the pressure exerted by free Indian nations outside the colony continued to set Indian slaves apart from African slaves. Just as the Assembly had granted freedom to all Tuscarora slaves in 1715, it continued to sublimate the property rights of slave owners to the external demands of diplomacy well into the 1720s. In 1727 for example, the Cherokee Nation formally petitioned the government of South Carolina for the return of two Cherokee children, a boy and a girl, who had been sold into slavery. The Commons House of Assembly moved quickly to appease the Cherokees but encountered difficulties in dealing with the new owners of the children. Mrs. Bohannon, the owner of the boy, demanded that the Assembly pay her the inflated sum of 170 pounds for her loss, which the Assembly regarded as a "gross imposition on the publick." With respect to the other child, it met with stubborn intransigence from a Mr. McNobney, who "absolutely refus'd on any account to part with the girl."[26]

Confronted with what it regarded as the "hight of arrogance" in McNobney's defiance, the Assembly found itself caught between the anger of the Cherokees on the one hand and the legal proprieties surrounding the forceful confiscation of property on the other. Ultimately, McNobney's ire appeared less threatening than that of the Cherokees, and the Assembly simply issued a "warrant to take into custody the sd boy and girl." As in previous incidents of government intervention, the Assembly's action must have troubled owners of Indian slaves generally. Yet as we have seen, by 1727 Indian slavery had been steadily declining since 1715, with the rate of household ownership falling from a high of 26 percent in 1715 to a mere 7 percent in the late 1720s. Hence, whereas the Assembly's decision concerning the Tuscaroras had threatened a quarter of the colony's slaveholders during the Yamasee War, similar action discomfited only a small minority in 1727.[27]

Despite those developments, many Carolinians were by all indications just as eager to acquire Indian slaves after the war as they had been beforehand. Even while hostilities continued with many tribes, the Commissioners for the Indian Trade authorized traders doing business with the Cherokees to accept "all such manner of truck, as skins, furrs, *slaves* or other vendible commodities, as is customary to receive from Indians" (italics mine). They initially felt it might be prudent to restrict the trade in male Indians to boys under the age of fourteen years but, perhaps unsatisfied with the number of slaves brought in, quickly amended that instruction in late 1716 to allow traders the "liberty" to buy male slaves "at any age not exceeding thirty years."[28]

If the colony's demand for unfree labor ultimately gave white Carolinians the courage to begin purchasing male Indians older than fourteen once again, it could not revive the dwindling external market for the "product." As discussed previously, the Indian slave trade may have been in decline for several years prior to 1715, due both to the depopulation of Florida and the efforts of several northern colonies to reduce the importation of Indian slaves. The outbreak of the Yamasee War accelerated that trend by providing additional confirmation for many northern colonists that the risks attending the use of Indian slaves were unacceptably high. Only three months after the outbreak of hostilities in South Carolina, Connecticut officials expressed concern over the "considerable number of Carolina Indians" coming into the colony. Above all, they feared that rebellion might prove infectious among Connecticut's free Indian population, and that "our Indians may be tempted to draw off to those enemies." The Connecticut governor and council accordingly agreed to a complete prohibition against any further importation of "Carolina Indians" and made additional arrangements for any slaves who happened to arrive in port thereafter to be "put into the strictest custody . . . to prevent their communication with any Indians in this his Majesties colony."[29]

In addition to reducing South Carolina's export markets among other mainland colonies, the Yamasee War struck a more direct blow at the slave trade by destroying the primary means by which it was conducted: the traders. These individuals functioned as intermediaries between the Indian groups wishing to sell war captives and the merchants and planters of Carolina who sought to buy them. In many cases traders lived in Indian villages and possessed extensive ties to local communities. They encouraged slave raids and extended credit and supplies to outfit the raiding parties. One trader, Anthony Probert, even had his own raiding party and apparently sent "his slaves to war" to capture new slaves. In the first week of the Yamasee War, the vast majority of English traders died, perhaps as many as ninety men. Their loss deprived South Carolina of practical knowledge, experience, personal networks, and paraphernalia, without which the slave trade could not function.[30]

Few if any serious attempts were made to repair and resume the Indian slave trade after 1715. By contrast, the African slave trade, functioning independently of South Carolina, remained undamaged by the war and proved more than capable of servicing the labor needs of the colony's expanding economy. In the three years between 1717 and 1719 alone, over fifty ships transported 1,519 African slaves to Charles Town, a figure that may approach or even exceed the total population of Indian slaves prior to the Yamasee War.[31]

The Indian slave trade, with its machinery and personnel wiped out, its principal slaving regions either depopulated or dangerously well armed, and its export markets rapidly evaporating, thus offered little real competition to the trade in African slaves. It failed even to maintain the enslaved Indian population at the prewar level. With few new slaves coming in after 1715, natural demographic forces and attrition steadily reduced the number of Indian slaves already working on Carolina plantations until, by the 1730s, they had become a rarity, appearing in only 2 to 3 percent of all households. It is reasonable to assume that economic forces and demographic realities might ultimately have ended or curtailed the Indian slave trade and the use of Indian slaves in South Carolina had the Yamasee War never occurred. Yet the abruptness of the decline in the war's aftermath tends to suggest that it served to accelerate the process greatly and may even have initiated it. Had it been left intact, the machinery of the slave trade would likely have continued to function for many years beyond 1715, though perhaps with diminishing effectiveness. It is even possible that a naturally sustainable enslaved Indian or mustee population might have developed as a permanent adjunct to African slavery. That the

Indian slave trade ended as it did, and that Indian slavery ended with it, was the result both of natural demographic forces at work within the colony and the intervention of historical forces in the form of the Yamasee War.

THEMES, PATTERNS, PROBLEMS

The decline of Indian slavery after 1715 effectively ended South Carolina's experimentation with a multiracial labor force and committed white planters thereafter to an increasing reliance on African slaves. It seems clear that this transition had an enormous impact not only on the subsequent evolution and character of the plantation regime but also on the formation of white concepts of ethnicity, race, and "place," possibly facilitating a greater degree of precision in the differentiation between Indians and Africans. As is suggested by efforts to establish a legal distinction between African and Indian slaves and the possible expulsion of Indians from the immediate domicile following the Yamasee War, white Carolinians may have been struggling with conceptual and social developments that paralleled the changing demographics of the enslaved labor force.

The extrication of Native Americans from involvement in slavery, both physically and conceptually, represented an essential step in the process of triangulation Winthrop Jordan has proposed. From 1715 onward, Carolinians stopped trying to bring Africans and Indians together under the unified mantle of slavery and instead began a prolonged effort to keep the two groups apart and, equally important, opposed to each other. If the fear of a "black majority . . . gradually deepened," as Peter Wood has argued, it did so after receiving a sudden and compelling start during the

Yamasee War. In its early stages, moreover, white apprehensions of a black majority were intimately conjoined with fears of external Native American enemies, internal Native American enemies, and the complicated internal and external threats attendant on their multiracial slave labor system. The 1717 legislation that Wood identified as the first defensive response of white Carolinians to their minority status was in fact preceded by a flurry of related legislation that simultaneously sought to address perceived threats from the slave labor force and free external enemies. In the space of two years, therefore, South Carolina engineered a set of racial policies that guided its treatment of both African Americans and Native Americans for the next century.

8. New Patterns of Exchange and Diplomacy

* * * * * * * * * * * * * * *

The apprehension that white South Carolinians felt with respect to their minority status within the colony as well as in the greater Southeast was not immediately apparent to Native Americans as negotiations for peace commenced. The first Cherokee delegates to visit Charles Town in 1716 appear to have entered the colony with considerable trepidation. Observers of the emissaries described them as behaving in a "very submissive manner." Whatever their initial concerns may have been, however, the Cherokees found themselves "greatly caressed by the Governour" during their visit and went home with "considerable presents . . . of fine laced cloaths, hats," and other items.[1]

In a very short time, the Cherokees reassessed the terms of their alliance with the English and began to assert themselves with greater confidence. Subsequent Cherokee visits to Charles Town grew less and less "submissive" and more explicit about the material needs of Cherokee warriors. Throughout 1716, South Carolina had "no allies of any importance but the Cherikees," and that status gave them unprecedented bargaining power. By early 1717 Cherokee influence had reached a level that clearly disturbed some Carolinians. "We buy their friendship at too dear a rate," members of the Commons House of Assembly complained in January 1717, "if the wellfare of the colony did not depend on the same." They resented the financial hardships of maintaining the Cherokee alliance, but at a deeper level they also chafed at the imbalance of power. "The demands they make are so unreasonable," they observed, "that we may properly say, we are become their tributaries."[2]

The same dynamic emerged as South Carolina sought to reestablish peaceful relations with the Catawbas and their piedmont allies and especially with the powerful Creek Confederacy, to which many of the "Southern Indians" had fled. Members of the Commons House wrestled, for instance, with the need to maintain the colony's dignity even as they desperately sought to end hostilities with the Lower Creeks. They rejected a proposal for peace talks on the Savannah River mainly because they feared it might "neither be safe nor honorable" for the English to travel "so far out of the settlements amongst them." The Creeks rejected the talks for their own reasons. As a result, peace negotiations and postwar discussions about trade and diplomacy became the scene of intense struggles to influence the new terms of engagement, and Native American voices spoke more loudly and carried greater influence in those conversations than they had at any time prior to the war. Much trivial bickering emerged in the various dialogues that restored peace to the South in 1716 and 1717, such as the debate about the proper venue for negotiations; but deeper themes of paramount concern to Cherokees, Creeks, and Carolinians found expression as well. They reveal a period of vibrant interaction in which ideas were tested and old values adjusted to address new challenges. The dialogues are remarkable in themselves as examples of "frontier exchange," but their broader historical significance stems from the outcomes and understandings that emerged from them: new patterns of trade and diplomacy worked out mutually by Indians and Europeans.[3]

ENGLISH PRIORITIES IN RESTORING TRADE

South Carolina officials moved carefully in reestablishing the trade, retaining centralized control of virtually every aspect of it for three years after the resumption of trade with the Cherokees. In an unmistakable effort to "administer" the trade, they established a series of publicly owned factories to which native hunters brought their deerskins, thus eliminating the private trader entirely for a time. Their reasons for doing so centered more on the security of the colony than the maximization of profit and, as security became less precarious, on tactical countermeasures to offset French and Spanish influence among the Cherokees, Creeks, Chickasaws, and Choctaws. The factory system proved impractical on several levels and eventually gave way to a less regulated system of trading companies and independent traders. In their determination to make "public" ownership of the Indian trade a success, however, the commissioners of the trade engaged in a revealing dialogue with Native Americans that forced all sides to bring into the open their concerns about the new postwar terms of exchange. As they debated the locations of proposed factories, prices of goods, the range of goods to be sold, and methods of transporting those goods, South Carolinians revealed a continuing apprehension about rival discourses from within the colony as well as some new concerns that had not previously been present in their dealings with native trade partners, while American Indian leaders took issue with aspects of market participation that had troubled them even before the war.[4]

The Commons House intended for the factory system to exert control over the conversation with Native American allies and clients, just as it had sought to do in its 1707 regulatory act. Members of the house undoubtedly remembered the Alexander Longe affair and understood the damage that mixed messages and misinformation could wreak upon even the simplest diplomatic initiative. They therefore established stringent rules of discussion for factory employees, whether they served fulltime as "storekeepers" or temporarily as "messingers." All public servants engaged in the Indian trade took an oath to "keep secret and not divulge the Debates and Resolutions" of the officials in charge of the trade. Naturally, the clerk for the Commissioners of the Indian Trade swore to a more specific oath, promising not to "eraze, alter, or deface any of the Papers or the Journal belonging to this Board" unless they received "the Commissioner's order" to erase and alter the documents. Factors operating in the field were warned "not to promise or engage the Word of the Government." Such efforts to control the protocols and content of communication with Native Americans grew directly out of similar pre–Yamasee War efforts and continued to be a major source of concern after the factory system collapsed.[5]

Nowhere did South Carolina's centralized trade system more closely approach the model of "administered" or "treaty" trade, perhaps, than in its handling of the Winyah factory on the Santee River. Too few Winyah Indians resettled among the colony's plantation districts after the Yamasee War to guarantee the colony a profitable return on a trade store. Yet the Commissioners of the Indian Trade chose to locate a "small factory there, to ingage those Indians to continue among them." They did so solely because the presence of the Winyahs had "been found beneficial to that part of the province, for their Safety, by keeping the Negroes there in Awe." The tactical importance of providing a trade to the Winyahs, regardless of its economic benefits, manifested itself in the sacrifices that South Carolinians were willing to make. Because the store could not be expected to support itself financially,

one Santee River resident "offered to manage that Trade, gratis."
When Indians in the area experienced a bad harvest, moreover,
the commissioners purchased a shipment of corn for them at five
shillings per bushel.[6]

As an instrument of the public weal, therefore, the Indian trade
sometimes reflected war-related efforts to manage the colony's
internal social landscape. By using the trade to position native
people as a bulwark for the enslavement of both Indian and African
laborers, the commissioners embarked on a complex maneuver
that required an equally complex racial calculus. The manipula-
tion of the Winyah trade occurred, it should be remembered, in
the context of new racial legislation to create a clearer boundary
between Indians and Africans and at a time of changing demographic patterns within the low-country slave population. The racial
considerations that created the Winyah factory in the first place
revealed themselves in other matters of trade with neighboring
Indian nations to the north of the Winyahs. When the commissioners attempted to send supplies by boat up the Peedee River in July
1716, for instance, they requested that the proposed factor of the
Winyah store, Bartholomew Gallard, "assist us with some Wineau
Indians, for rowing of the Periago designed for the Northward
Indian trade." Their plans ran aground when he "sent us Negro
slaves." The commissioners thanked him but explained that "we
expected you would send some Wineau Indians instead of them."
Failing to secure the desired Winyahs for the trip, they ultimately
hired two Indian slaves from John Barnwell as "oarsmen."[7]

Such racial calculations had not yet been set in stone, however,
and circumstances occasionally forced the commissioners to allow African slaves to participate in the trade, especially when they
possessed special skills that could not be easily duplicated. As

Carolinians moved to reestablish trade relations with the Creek Indians in 1718, they found themselves in need of the services of Alexander Mackey's "Negro Man Timboe." His fluency in one or more of the Muskhogean languages made him indispensable as a "linguist" for the Creek trade, and he rendered "extraordinary service" in that capacity in Creek country for five months. But even the involvement of specialists like Timboe became increasingly problematic in the 1720s, and by 1731 the informal operating procedures that had emerged in 1716 were finally codified in law. From that point onward, anyone who employed "any negro or other slave, in the Indian country, or in rowing up or down any boat" was subject to a fine of one hundred pounds.[8]

The historian William S. Willis discussed the Winyah episode as a prime example of the new policy of divide and rule, but he did not place it in the context of trade management. That context, however, is crucial. The novelty of using free indigenous populations to control enslaved African populations emerged as a simultaneous corollary to an equally novel development: the use of an administered trade to influence native behavior. All these innovations, moreover, emerged under the tutelage of the planter-dominated Lower House of Assembly, where the merchant interests that had played a significant role prior to the war had largely been subdued. Within a remarkably short time, therefore—slightly more than a year after the massacre at Pocotaligo Town—planter interests managed to subordinate the Indian trade as an independent economic sector and place it in the service of the plantation economy. This was not a gradual development resulting from growing white anxieties about the black majority, on the one hand, or from the natural evolution of the plantation regime, on the other. It was a stunningly rapid development that grew specifically out of the historical contingencies of the Yamasee War.[9]

CHEROKEE-ENGLISH DISCOURSE

Just as South Carolinians reevaluated the importance and tactical value of the Indian trade between 1716 and 1719, American Indians also expressed specific needs and priorities about the terms of the new exchange relationship with Charles Town. In what may have been the first transaction of the new trade era, the Cherokees appear to have made a concerted effort to broaden the range of commodities that the English were willing to purchase. Knowing full well that the trade in beaver pelts had been defunct since the disastrous 1703–4 trading season, the Cherokees nevertheless loaded burdeners in the summer of 1716 with fifteen packs containing 473 "Bever Skins" and absolutely nothing else. It is doubtful that such a large shipment of beaver pelts had ever been sent to Carolina, even in the early days of the trade when the colony routinely exported more than a thousand beaver pelts per year. It was certainly the last major effort to revive the beaver trade, and as the first effort to initiate new trade with South Carolina following the Yamasee War, it stands out as being especially meaningful. Although Charles Town took the pelts and paid the burdeners who had carried them, subsequent shipments of beaver skins from the Cherokees fell back in line almost immediately with market reality, and that reality was grim. There really was no external market for beaver skins at the time, and South Carolina made little effort to export them. Again and again, the Commissioners of the Indian Trade opened the public storehouse in Charles Town to sell the beaver skins to local hatters, "or as many of them as will buy the same," at the token rate of ten shillings per pound. Even then they could rarely get rid of the skins and usually put the rest up for auction. Nothing but the surpassing diplomatic importance of the Cherokee alliance in 1716 could have compelled them to exchange European trade goods for such an unattractive product.[10]

That shipment of beaver skins also spotlighted the issue of transportation. Prior to the war, trade goods had always been carried on the backs of Indian burdeners, and the initial postwar shipments to and from the Cherokees and Catawbas followed the established pattern. It had worked moderately well prior to 1715, but the English and Indians alike found problems with it in 1716. The Cherokee shipment of beaver skins, for instance, had left the trade store in the Appalachian foothills in fifteen packs of pelts, but the packs arrived in Carolina on the backs of twenty-one Cherokee burdeners. Somewhere on the trade path, the pelts had clearly been repacked to allow six additional burdeners to receive compensation for their labors. The commissioners grudgingly paid the burdeners, "being unwilling at first to have any Difference with them." But they were resolved "not to make this a president." They advised the Cherokee factor, Theophilus Hastings, "for the Future to agree positively with the Indians, how many Burdeners are to be paid."[11]

In spite of such agreements, Indians and Englishmen continued to test each other. In September 1717 officials in charge of the Indian trade discovered more than 150 deerskins missing from a shipment carried down by Catawba burdeners. A closer inspection revealed that the factor's brand on many of the remaining deerskins had been "visibly raced out with a Knife or some such instrument." As a result, the Charles Town factor who processed the shipment had unwittingly purchased the doctored skins a second time "before he discovered that Secret." The commissioners advised the Catawba factor to brand the deerskins more firmly so that the mark could "not be easily cut or rubbed out," but they decided not to confront the Catawbas about it "at Present, for good Reasons."[12]

Some storekeepers feared that the commissioners' leniency made the problem worse. According to one factor working in Cherokee territory, "their not being call'd at no time to a Strict accot. at such times as they went down . . . they at last was so embolden in their Roguery that they thought it no Crime but would go away by the Cattawbas and game away their Packs of Goods and come home without any of it as unconcern'd as if they had an authority so to do." When he confronted them about the practice, the Cherokee burdeners reminded him that "they was not [his] Goods they belong'd to the Governmt." Since the officials in Charles Town who claimed ownership of the packs "said nothing to them," they asked, "why did [he] trouble himself so much about it"? South Carolina's reluctance to engage the Cherokees forcefully on these and other issues, the factor concluded, "gave them good reason to think we was afraid of them, and that we was oblig'd to take all wrongs that they should offer us."[13]

Episodes such as these were framed in part around a basic dialectic between the economic priorities of South Carolinians, who naturally sought to minimize transportation costs and maintain reliable account books, and the priorities of indigenous deerskin producers and burdeners, who sought, just as rationally, to reduce risks and maximize the benefits of their involvement in the exchange. That tension was present before the Yamasee War as well, but solutions to it emerged from private relationships between individual traders or trade partnerships and various town leaders. Traders seeking to enlist native burdeners prior to 1715 routinely balanced the need to minimize their expenses with the rival need to maintain good relationships with influential leaders and, in many cases, to satisfy the expectations of kinship and lineage obligations imposed by their native wives. Only in rare instances did the Charles Town government step in to regulate or adjudicate agreements for transporting trade goods. By taking the Indian trade into its own hands after the war, South Carolina inherited the challenge of working out those transportation agreements and, in the process, transformed them into affairs of state with daunting diplomatic implications.[14]

There is no question that Charles Town officials, still uncertain about the colony's survival in 1716 and 1717, recognized the perils of engaging native allies and trade partners in honest discussions about transportation problems. They chose in most cases to absorb the inefficiencies and avoid potentially destabilizing confrontations. Having failed to resolve the problems by a variety of stop-gap measures—including a tracking system in which each burdener received a ticket listing "the number of his Pack and Quantity of Skins &c. therein contained" prior to setting out—Carolinians ultimately retreated altogether from the challenge of creating a collaborative method for transporting trade goods. After the Catawba incident, the commissioners launched a comprehensive effort to avoid the use of native burdeners and "wholy make Use of Pack-horses." They did so to solve basic logistical problems but also because they did not want "to be subject to such delays and inconveniences from the Indians."[15]

Having removed private traders from the trade, it might be argued, Carolinians now sought to remove Indians as well. Yet they were not responding solely to the "villany" of burdeners who scratched out the factor's brand on deerskins in order to sell them a second time. The commissioners' decision to utilize packhorses also grew out of clear messages of discontent from Cherokee and Catawba burdeners. As the Creek-Cherokee war intensified in 1717, even the prospect of surreptitiously reselling a deerskin could not offset the hazardous nature of the burdener's work. Although Creek warriors agreed to a "truce" with South Carolina in late 1717, Cherokee and Catawba burdeners remained legitimate targets even as they carried "the publick's" deerskins on their backs.

On October 21, for instance, a party of twenty-one Cherokee burdeners came under attack from Lower Creek warriors from Coweta Town. The Creeks "killed some of them in the Flight" and "wounded and robbed" the rest, making off with more than seven hundred deerskins. On another occasion the influential Cherokee leader Charitee Hagey of Tugelo Town, also known as the Conjuror, was killed by Creek warriors while traveling home from Charles Town with a group of burdeners. Incidents such as these made it difficult for Cherokee and Catawba leaders to recruit burdeners, "the Indians being informed that the Paths were way-laid by the Creek Indians." In the spring of 1718, Catawba leaders explained to Charles Town officials that they disliked the Carolina trade because it required them "to carry Burdens; which is the cause of their losing many Men." The Catawbas went on to praise Virginia traders for bringing them trade goods "upon Pack-horses . . . and carrying Home their Effects upon their Horses, which gives the Indians no Trouble at all in Dealing with them."[16]

Scholarly discussions of the Indian trade in the era of the Yamasee War rarely consider the mode of transporting trade goods, yet it posed one of the principal problems for the Carolina Indian trade in the two years following the war. Verner Crane assumed that the trade had been conducted primarily by packhorse all along. The appearance of burdeners after the war, he speculated, occurred "because the unsettled state of Indian affairs made it too risky to send horses." Kathryn E. Holland Braund in her work *Deerskins & Duffels*, by contrast, recognized that trade goods had been carried by Indian burdeners prior to 1715, but she incorrectly assumed that market forces had naturally brought about the transition to horses in the decades following. Based on the evidence considered here, the Yamasee War marked a clear and rapid transition point between two distinct transportation regimes: a prewar system characterized by the collaboration of private traders and native leaders that utilized Indian burdeners, and a postwar system administered solely by South Carolina that relied on packhorses.[17]

Market considerations framed the dialogue at many key moments in the transformative process, but they were not the driving force behind it. It was not a shrewd economic choice, for instance, for Native Americans to accept higher-priced goods transported by packhorse and in the bargain to concede control over the movement of goods. (For historians interested in the progress of trade dependency, however, it may be significant that the Cherokees had the latitude to make such decisions in 1717 and 1718). Nor was it prudent for South Carolina to invest heavily in the purchase of packhorses at a time when the colony faced massive war-related debts and defense expenditures. Instead, the process originated in the human needs and frustrations of the parties involved and proceeded through a mutual series of rejected proposals to address those problems. In this context, Native Americans apparently sought to offset the hazards of transporting trade goods by increasing the number of burdeners on the path and increasing the remuneration they might expect upon arrival. South Carolinians sought to challenge those attempts by creative accounting and ticketing schemes. In the end, horses appeared on southern trade paths not because the market demanded them but, rather, because they offered one way of maintaining diplomatic relations among key groups of people who were willing to make economic sacrifices to maintain those relations. If a middle ground existed in the eighteenth-century South, packhorses were surely among its earliest inhabitants.[18]

Other outcomes of postwar Anglo-Indian dialogue reflected a more conspicuous resistance to the market. Price agreements between South Carolina and its native allies, a classic feature of treaty or administered trade, also grew out of indigenous concerns about the terms of exchange and constituted one of the most durable modifications of the trade for the remainder of the colonial era. Although many historians consider them a standard feature of the deerskin trade, the earliest set price schedules date only to 1716. The Cherokees were the first to extort such an agreement from Charles Town in April 1716, when they negotiated a list of permanent prices for all items "as they are allways to be sold." Prior to this, Anglo-Indian exchange rates had been determined by the market mechanism of supply and demand, requiring Indians to "bargain," "deale," and "agree for" purchase prices. The Cherokee breakthrough was followed in short order by a fixed price agreement with the Creek Indians in 1718. Thereafter, South Carolina's exchange rates were always established at a fixed level by treaty.[19]

It may also be significant that accusations of "cheating" on the part of English traders appear in the records only *after* fixed price schedules became a regular feature of the Indian trade. Although such accusations have commonly been assumed to have been part of trader "misconduct" prior to the Yamasee War, relatively few traders were in fact ever accused prior to 1715 of tampering with scales, watering down rum, or other familiar eighteenth-century forms of underhandedness. Such behaviors appeared primarily after the Yamasee War and may thus represent an effort on the part of English traders, themselves not immune to the market mechanism of supply and demand, to maintain a profit margin in an era of inflexible exchange rates. Native Americans, it should be noted, also used unorthodox trading practices to circumvent the price schedules when it served their interests.[20]

After two years of dialogue concerning the transportation of goods, prices of goods, and a host of attendant details, therefore, Cherokees, Catawbas, and Carolinians had worked out a number of new trade practices that became hallmarks of the Carolina deerskin trade for much of the eighteenth century. Surprisingly, however, the process of restoring normal trade relations seemed to take a step backward in 1718. Rumors of a planned Cherokee invasion swept through the South Carolina low country, and many Cherokee communities openly expressed their fear that Carolinians intended to make war on them again. Some Cherokee towns became overtly "inofficious to the white Men that dwell among them, refusing to supply them with Provision or Necessaries." Anti-English sentiment reached such a pitch in some parts of Cherokee country that factory storehouses were broken into and despoiled in the towns of Chota, Quannesie, and Tunnissee. What concerned Carolinians most about the affronts was that "those who did it was head Men, and was not asham'd to own it."[21]

South Carolina's truce with the Creek Nation in late 1717 and the resumption of trade with Creek towns in 1718 undoubtedly created much of that tension. In light of continuing hostilities between the Creeks and Cherokees, some Cherokee leaders viewed the colony's willingness to supply their enemies with muskets and ammunition as an ominous sign. Following the death of the Conjuror on the trade path, in particular, the Cherokees accused the English of encouraging the Creeks in their attacks. For their part, Creek leaders manifested a thorough distrust of the English even as they moved to reestablish peaceful relations with South Carolina, and they made a point of maintaining diplomatic relations with the French of Louisiana and the Spanish of Florida. Anglo-Creek discussions thus commenced at a time when the primary focus of dialogue had moved beyond the practical issues of trade and transportation that had occupied English-Cherokee relations since 1716. Creek negotiations with South Carolina focused to a greater extent on issues of regional geopolitics.

CREEK-ENGLISH DISCOURSE

Recent studies of South Carolina's relationship with the Creek
Nation in the aftermath of the Yamasee War have unearthed important new documents and cast new light on the restoration of
peace in the Southeast. Joshua Piker's *Okfuskee: A Creek Indian Town
in Colonial America*, for instance, reevaluates the famous "Articles
of Friendship and Commerce" between Governor Robert Johnson
of South Carolina and key leaders from Upper and Lower Creek
towns. Although the "Articles" have traditionally been cited as the
defining document that ended hostilities in 1717, Piker's excellent
detective work demonstrates that they were actually drafted and
signed in 1732, long after the Creeks and the English had resumed
peaceful relations. Published in the same year as Piker's book,
Steven Hahn's *The Invention of the Creek Nation* revisits the legendary Creek "neutrality policy" that managed to play off European
powers as counterweights against each other for much of the
eighteenth century. Utilizing documents from Spanish archives,
Hahn challenges ethnohistorians such as Michael D. Green and
Kathryn Holland Braund, who see Creek neutrality as primarily a
result of intertown factionalism rather than as a unified foreign
policy. For Hahn, Creek neutrality grew directly out of a specific
diplomatic decision in 1718, which he refers to as the "Coweta
Resolution."[22]

By adding these new dimensions to the discussion, however,
Piker and Hahn have posed new problems that have not yet received
serious consideration. In dating the "Articles of Friendship and
Commerce" to 1732, many years after the conclusion of peace, Piker
nevertheless maintains that the document represented a milestone
in Creek-English relations. In his view, the signature or mark of
"Fannemiche" as the headman of the Upper Creek town of Okfuskee

served to reaffirm a special political and kinship tie between the Okfuskees and the English that had supposedly been ritualized in a 1708 ceremony. According to Piker, that tie was achieved via the traditional office of "Fanni Mico," which served among the Chickasaws and perhaps also the Creeks as a means of maintaining peaceful relations and communication between allied nations. Accordingly, he suggests that the appearance of "Fannemiche" on the 1732 articles capped a fifteen-year effort on the part of the Okfuskees to restore their alliance with the British.

It is an intriguing possibility, but at a practical level Piker's argument seems to depend rather heavily on the continued absence of the actual text of the 1717 Creek-Carolina treaty. The "Articles of Friendship and Commerce" may not have been signed in 1717, as Piker demonstrates, but it is clear that a treaty of some sort in which Upper Creek leaders participated was indeed concluded in November of that year, the text of which has since been lost. Should that document resurface in the archives, Piker's thesis, at least in regard to the 1732 embassy, may need to be modified if Fannemiche's mark appeared in 1717 as well. At the same time, his argument seems to clash with Hahn's assertion that the Coweta Resolution of 1718 launched a new era of studied and intentional Creek neutrality. How is it possible that Creek Indians simultaneously pursued a "doctrine of neutrality" while doggedly maintaining the existence of a special relationship with the English?[23]

There is no question that Creek diplomacy entered a new phase after the Yamasee War. Beginning with the appearance of two Muscogee messengers at the Savannah River in early 1717, Creeks and Carolinians began an extended dialogue about the terms of peace, alliance, and trade that came to involve Spanish and French negotiators as well. Accordingly, Hahn has argued that "the year 1717 witnessed the birth of a multilateral diplomacy" for

the Creek Nation. Creek efforts to draw representatives from all
the European powers into a single conversation, centered more
often than not on the town of Coweta, certainly had few precedents
in southeastern colonial history. In that respect, Creek diplomacy
in the post–Yamasee War era reflected a changed power relationship in which Muscogee leaders possessed a greater ability to
control the terms, locales, and content of their encounters with
Europeans than they had enjoyed prior to the war. The substance
of those multilateral conversations, however, revolved primarily
around traditional Creek conceptions of alliance, friendship, and
exchange, on the one hand, and earnest attempts on the part of
Creek negotiators to understand European approaches to those
vital topics, on the other. In the end, it is argued here, Creek leaders modified their approach to alliance and trade to incorporate
certain European usages, but this did not constitute a "doctrine
of neutrality." The Coweta Resolution of 1718, moreover, though
remarkable in its own right, came as an afterthought to Creek
foreign policy adjustments that had already been made. Indeed,
had Carolina met its diplomatic obligations in a timely manner,
there would likely have been no need for it.

The central problem for Muscogee leaders contemplating peace
with South Carolina in 1717 and 1718 appears to have been the
colony's alliance with the Cherokees. Again and again, the glaring problem that Cherokee warriors were using English muskets,
powder, and shot to attack Upper and Lower Creek towns emerged
as a complicating factor in negotiations for peace. Most recorded
instances of Creek communication with South Carolina leading up
to the restoration of trade in November of 1717 included a complaint
about Carolina's assistance to the Cherokees and a request for the
return of Creek Indians captured and enslaved by Cherokee war
parties. When Creek leaders failed to show up for scheduled peace

talks on June 6, 1717, for instance, they sent a man named Bocatie to explain to the English that they could not "come to make a peace before their corn is ripe." Bocatie also reiterated that the Creeks, though eager to resume peaceful relations with South Carolina, were still at war with the Cherokees and Catawbas. The connection between the two statements should have been clear to most eighteenth-century Indians. War parties traditionally operated during the summer, and they often targeted women tending or harvesting the corn fields because these women worked too far away from the village to receive timely assistance. When such attacks were anticipated, warriors stayed home to defend their families. By linking Creek-Cherokee hostilities and the agricultural cycle with the need to cancel negotiations, Bocatie must certainly have intended to chastise Carolinians for their support of Cherokee raids.[24]

The Creek leaders who sent him did not want to leave any room for confusion, so Bocatie visited Deputy Governor Robert Daniell in Charles Town to deliver the message "that the great men of his nation gave him in charge." Having postponed the peace talks because of the need to defend against Cherokee raids, the great men requested "that the slaves taken in the expedition of Col. Mackey and brought down to the Cherokees may not be sold." The Creeks made no overt criticism of South Carolina. It was unnecessary to finish the obvious line of reasoning implicit in the request. Creek scouts had identified the specific Carolina agent who had assisted a specific Cherokee raid. They likely knew whose relatives had been captured in the assault, and they definitely knew where the captives were being held.

In that simple request, Muscogee headmen effectively implicated South Carolina in Cherokee raids and made the restoration of peace contingent on the colony's treatment of Creek captives. "When they come down," Bocatie informed the governor, "they will buy and free them." He did not say when they might be coming. But for those among the English willing to hear what the Creek understatement made all the more audible, peace depended on a good deal more than simply not selling the Creek captives. It depended on not taking them in the first place. As a sign of its good intentions, and of course a tacit acknowledgment of the colony's guilt, Governor Daniell gave Bocatie "two Indian women belonging to the Creeks" to take back with him.[25]

Even so, the corn did not ripen that year until November, when Ouletta, the "son" of Emperor Brims of Coweta, led a Creek delegation to make a formal peace in Charles Town. Once again, Cherokee raids and the fate of the Creek captives taken in those raids became a central point of discussion. The "agreement" that finally emerged required the Carolinians "to deliver to them the slaves taken by the Cherikees, who they desire to carry with them." Yet this time the Creeks did more than make a point. They made a commitment to resume peaceful trade relations despite South Carolina's trade relationship with the Cherokees. This indeed was a novel development, for the Creeks traditionally regarded trade as a hallmark of alliance. Exchange had previously been possible only with allies, and allied nations bore the responsibility of reciprocal military assistance or, at the very least, forbearance from collaboration with known enemies. South Carolina could be expected to meet none of those time-honored requirements in November 1717, but Ouletta and the headmen who came with him either found a way around those technicalities or forced the Carolinians to modify their relationship with the Cherokees enough to justify peace. Without the actual text of the agreement, it is impossible to say which occurred. Either way, the Creeks agreed to a peaceful relationship that did not entail a firm and binding military alliance. As is discussed later in this chapter, however, they insisted that Carolinians forbear from actively aiding Cherokee warriors even as they found ways to accept the colony's trade relationship with their enemies.[26]

In the interval between the cancellation of peace talks in June and the resumption of trade in November, several important developments had taken place in Creek country. First, an English delegation led by John Musgrove and Theophilus Hastings took the audacious step of traveling unannounced into the heart of Lower Creek territory in late July. They encountered a red flag of war at the town of Kasita, but members of a pro-English faction welcomed them at Coweta. The "Chieftaness Qua," in particular, "opened her arms, and with wailing and sighs celebrated their arrival." Although a formal peace was still months away, the advocacy of Qua and others led the mico of Coweta, Brims, to condone the renewal of kinship ties to the English. This was accomplished by the marriage of Coosaponakeesa, later famous as Mary Musgrove, to the son of John Musgrove. Though it represented an important step toward the normalization of relations between the Creeks and South Carolina, Musgrove's breakthrough was largely personal. The Commons House of Assembly conceded as much in its decision that the presents given to him were his property alone and not Creek presents to the colony.[27]

A second diplomatic milestone occurred just after Musgrove's visit, when a Spanish emissary from St. Augustine, Diego Pena, traveled to several Creek towns to confirm and strengthen the Creek-Spanish alliance. Where Pena had been received with rejoicing and affirmations of alliance the year before, however, his appearance in September 1717 found the mood very different. His reception by Brims of Coweta, in particular, gave him cause to doubt the reliability of the Creeks as allies. He was appalled to find that the English had been allowed back into the town. In fact, some of the English may have made a point of "passing the place" where Pena was meeting with Brims, where they "instigated a thousand indecencies." Brims assured Pena "that he had not invited them," and he countered the Spaniard's complaints by observing that Pena "was as white as were (the English)." He then suggested that the Spanish "should reach an agreement with the said English," indicating that he and probably other Creek leaders had begun to view European diplomatic customs in a new light.[28]

Such reconsideration of European diplomacy emerged as a clear and urgent point of concern for the Creeks over the next year. When Spanish delegates led by Don Juan Fernandez de Orta traveled to the Tallapoosa settlements in March 1718, one of Brims's nephews, Chipacasi (elsewhere "Seepeycoffee"), arranged a meeting with the Spaniards late at night in hopes that they could help him "to settle a dubious point which had plagued him for various days past." Chipacasi could not understand "why the Spaniards, who were such good Christians, remained at peace with the English, who were such bad men." He did not ask "the question idly," he explained, because he would soon come to power by the "consent of Emperor Brims and the acclamation of all nations." Decisions about alliance and trade would therefore fall to him, and he wanted the Spanish emissary to give him advice "on how to proceed, and on Spanish methods." Nor was that apparently his first effort to explore the Spanish approach to diplomacy. "He had inquired of other Indians who dealt with the Spanish" about those issues while in St. Augustine "on several occasions."

The Spaniard informed him that they "preserved the peace with the English because the King has so ordered it." To this Chipacasi then inquired whether the king planned to declare war soon on either the French or the English, but the emissary could not assure him that war would be declared. "Well then," Chipacasi replied, "in case he takes such a step . . . you may count on it that I, and all my subjects, will be on your side. I promise you that. And, if you so desire, I shall furnish whatever assurance you may require that I will do as I say, whenever the opportunity arises." In the interim, though, Creek leaders would have to find a way of maintaining peaceful relations with people they would ideally have preferred to keep as enemies.[29]

The Creek determination to come to grips with European "methods" also manifested itself in nonverbal approaches to diplomacy. In 1717 Muscogee delegates who met with Europeans in St. Augustine (April) and Charles Town (November) altered their appearance to conform with local fashions. Traditional Creek clothing and dancing were in evidence as well, but key negotiators took pains to dress as Englishmen or Spaniards, as the case required. This had not been a standard practice for Creek delegates previously. Indeed, when Ouletta arrived on the outskirts of Charles Town to begin peace talks in November, he had no wardrobe. In order to make a proper English impression, he was forced to send ahead "to have a present of clothes sent up to him, in order to come down and make his appearance." Cross-cultural dressing of this sort suggests that Creek headmen were actively engaged in using European images and cultural forms to help communicate or add legitimacy (in European eyes) to Creek ideas. In that respect, it is reminiscent of the cultural borrowing used in French-Algonquian diplomacy to create what historian Richard White has termed the middle ground. At the same time, however, this "diplomacy of mirrors," another of White's phrases, could also advertise the cultural framework within which the terms of peace would be discussed and understood. If so, insisting on European terms of peace could serve as a caveat and disclaimer for Creek emissaries, who knew too well that Carolina was not worthy of peace on Muscogee terms.[30]

To what extent did new understandings and tactics translate into new foreign policy objectives? Even as they donned sombreros and pursued multilateral discussions, Creek leaders also engaged in very traditional forms of diplomacy in pursuit of objectives that would have been familiar to former generations. When Seneca and Mohawk warriors arrived in the spring of 1717 to seek an alliance with the Creeks, there was little need to question them about their approach to diplomacy or to rationalize the agreement in novel terms. The Iroquois were at war with both the Cherokees and Catawbas, and so were the Creeks. Muscogee leaders could be certain that Seneca warriors would not lead Cherokee war parties to their towns, as Alexander Mackey had done. Nor were the Seneca firm allies of the English any longer, since the Iroquois had embarked on their own policy of neutrality toward European powers in 1701, signing treaties in both Montreal and Albany. The historian Steven Hahn has even suggested that Creek diplomacy may have been influenced by advice from the Iroquois.[31]

If the Iroquois did discuss the benefits of a neutral posture toward Europeans, the Alabama Indians were not persuaded. They went a step further than the rest of the Upper Creek towns by forging a special relationship with French Louisiana in 1717 that remained firm until the ouster of France from North America in 1763. Although they represented the least populous contingent of the Upper Creeks, the Alabama towns occupied a strategic location at the confluence of the Coosa and Tallapoosa Rivers, which gave them unique diplomatic leverage in negotiations with the French. Accordingly, the French-Alabama alliance probably came as close to meeting traditional Creek expectations as could be hoped. The French committed themselves to the Alabamas in body and spirit by constructing Fort Toulouse near the town of Pakana in the summer of 1717. A token garrison of French soldiers maintained the fort solely for the convenience of the Alabamas, providing them with generous presents, trade, and even free blacksmithing services when their muskets needed repair. In addition, the garrison dutifully mustered to assist the Alabamas when needed. The alliance clearly met the needs of the Alabamas, and a half century later, when English traders had long been established in virtually every Creek town, there were still none in any of the Alabama towns.[32]

A similar commitment to traditional diplomatic relations may have been at work among more northerly Upper Creek towns as well, where the residents of Okfuskee Town labored to maintain a unilateral partnership with the British. Although rebuffed by the Alabamas, Carolinians may have succeeded in establishing a trading factory at Okfuskee as early as 1718. Josh Piker has argued that the town functioned as a liaison to the British throughout the 1720s, and there is indeed much evidence that both the Charles Town government and other Upper Creek towns recognized Okfuskee as a reliable, even obligatory, British ally during that period. The relationship may have been based on fictive kinship ties initiated prior to the Yamasee War, as Piker suggests, but his own work offers another possibility as well.

The same diplomatic orientations that took shape in Upper Creek country in 1717 and 1718 continued to distinguish the foreign policy priorities of southern towns such as the Alabamas from those of more northerly towns like Okfuskee even after the removal of the French in 1763. After the Great War for Empire, the Okfuskees, Okchais, and many other Abhika and Tallapoosa towns continued to seek trade relations with South Carolina by way of the lengthy overland trade path, despite the availability of the same British goods at lower prices via the Alabama River and

Pensacola, because they did not want to be reduced to mere clients of the Alabamas. If the control of trade paths and the political power they conferred within the Confederacy influenced Upper Creek diplomacy in the second half of the eighteenth century, those factors might have been at work in 1717 as well. Whatever the internal reasons for their actions, Upper Creek diplomacy in the aftermath of the Yamasee War continued in many cases to seek traditional alliances with Europeans. It is difficult, at any rate, to see an overt policy of neutrality at work in the behavior of Okfuskee and the Alabama towns.[33]

Nevertheless, developments elsewhere in Creek country may have hampered Okfuskee's efforts to reassert traditional forms of alliance. Piker suggests that the town probably did not immediately fix the mark of "fanni mico" on a treaty with the English at the end of the Yamasee War. Rather, it took "fifteen years of concerted effort by the Okfuskees to reestablish relations with the British." The English themselves were not the obstacle to the restoration of the Okfuskee partnership. Carolinians, for instance, requested permission in 1727 to build a fort at Okfuskee to counter the influence of Fort Toulouse, but the project met opposition from several quarters within the Confederacy. If Piker's portrait is accurate, there must have been forces at work to postpone a unilateral alliance with the British. Such countervailing forces could have taken several forms. Okfuskee's foreign policy goals could have been thwarted inadvertently by inter- and intratown factionalism. They could also have been thwarted by a careful management or perhaps cultivation of factionalism by influential leaders, or squelched outright by a purposeful neutrality policy. Over the years scholars of Creek diplomacy have argued in favor of all of those options, with Steven Hahn most recently seeking to move the discussion back toward David Corkran's "Doctrine of Neutrality," though with a deeper appreciation of factionalism. Since the debate seems presently to pivot on Hahn's depiction of the Coweta Resolution, it may be wise to revisit that historical moment in some detail.[34]

DISCOURSE AT COWETA

In March 1718 the world came to the Creek town of Coweta. Spanish dignitaries who had been visiting the upper towns dropped what they were doing and hurried east to Coweta to forestall the restoration of peaceful relations with Carolina, spurred by the arrival of English dignitaries seeking entry to the town. As representatives of the two empires competed for the loyalties of the Creeks, moreover, a Frenchman from Fort Toulouse arrived with a letter from Jean-Baptiste LeMoyne, Sieur de Bienville, expressing praise and admiration for Coweta's mico, Brims, whose "fame had aroused an intense desire" in Bienville to meet him. Toward that end, the mico was invited to Mobile, where, as chance would have it, "three vessels from France had arrived, loaded with exquisite objects, very well suited to serve as presents." A boat was waiting at Fort Toulouse, in fact, to carry Brims downriver, and the French stressed that the presents were his to keep "even if he stayed only long enough to smoke the peace pipe." In response to this remarkable confluence of European suitors, Lower Creek leaders, and perhaps a few Upper Creek leaders, assembled in council to discuss what should be done. According to Steven Hahn, the Creeks reached a momentous decision after about a week of deliberations: the Coweta Resolution, committing themselves to neutrality with all three European powers.[35]

Consider, however, the first moment of this unfolding drama: the moment, that is, when Creeks and Spaniards in Upper Creek country jointly received the news that the English had arrived on the outskirts of Coweta. What could it mean and what should be done about it? The Spanish were informed that the "Emperor" of Coweta "had denied the English permission to visit him." Thus the English were represented as unwelcome guests, and the Indians expressed alarm that the Carolinians had sent such a large party of thirty men. The people of Coweta feared, they claimed, that "this party was being followed up by others." From his discussions with Creek leaders, the Spanish emissary, Don Juan Fernandez de Orta, reported their general sentiment that "the English were coming solely in order to take revenge surreptitiously." They therefore requested that Orta write a letter to the captain of an expedition of fifty Spanish soldiers just setting out from St. Augustine "to press him to hurry" to Coweta. In consultation with Creek leaders, Orta advised them against their plans to "take away all their baggage," fearful that his presence at this violent act might provoke an international incident. At length, he agreed to their request that he go with them to Coweta to "find out what the English were trying to do."

The Spanish emissary might have been less willing to oblige them had he known that the Creeks, far from denying "permission to visit," had specifically requested during the Charles Town peace talks a few months earlier that the English send a delegation to Coweta. Their purported concern about the size of the English expedition, thirty men, would likely have struck him as insincere had he known that they had actually requested "fifty white men." Not knowing that Charles Town's financial distress made it impossible to outfit more than thirty men, however, the Creeks felt certain that they would be "followed up by others." Orta would surely have been appalled to learn that the Lower Creek leaders with whom he was consulting had demanded this English visitation in order "to show the French and the Spaniards that they do not want friends to assist them notwithstanding all their lies and stories to the contrary." At the same time, he might have recognized the language, since the Creeks also wanted fifty Spanish soldiers to visit Coweta because they felt "it was important that the English should see their friends and defenders."[36]

Seeing perhaps a little more deeply into the encounter than Don Juan Fernandez de Orta, modern scholars should approach the discussions at Coweta with extreme caution. First and foremost, the debate over the meaning of what happened there in February and March 1718 must abandon the presumption that the Creeks were responding to European initiatives. From beginning to end, the Europeans assembled at Coweta were responding to Lower Creek issues that had been apparent for some time. In short, this appears to have been an encounter engineered by Muscogee leaders to serve Muscogee ends. They clearly manipulated the English and the Spanish into position on this occasion, and the arrival of the French officer in the midst of it all could hardly have been coincidental. Certainly, the decision to have Bienville's flattering letter to Brims "read in the presence of Don Juan" was a calculated presentation. From this perspective, the episode seems less about a new diplomatic policy formulated in response to European overtures than a new method of reiterating old concerns.[37]

The themes for the various strands of conversation at Coweta had been established prior to the arrival of European delegates. The Creek dialogue with the Spanish merely elaborated on Chipacasi's late-night consultation about "Spanish methods" of alliance. Why did the Spanish remain "at peace with the English," and would the king "order war waged against the English and the French?" As the encounter at Coweta evolved, Lower Creek leaders presented those problems to Orta again and again in different ways. They expressed an "almost unanimous" intent to attack the English and take their goods, but Orta feared that such an act "would be blamed on him." As a result, he counseled the warriors to deal peacefully with the English or else to "proceed by themselves." "If he were not present," the Spaniard explained, "they could do what they wished." He ultimately agreed to go with them to Coweta only on condition that they first seek to discover what the English wanted before attacking them. The Creeks, of course, already knew. Once in Coweta, Orta again counseled caution, to which the Creeks complained that "they were not accustomed to dragging out their negotiations in this manner, and they asked him at once to decide on a course of action." Frustrated that they "had already forgotten the course previously agreed upon," Orta again urged them to send a messenger to learn what the English wanted. When it was disclosed that the English had come "to conclude the formalities of peace," he advised Chipacasi to summon Brims and all the other leaders for a meeting at the "royal dwellings," at which they would "discuss and determine a plan of action."[38]

At last, Creek leaders had forced the Spanish to put their alliance into practical action. They "yelled loudly and beat on the drum" to summon everyone together, and Orta confirmed that the time had indeed come to make a "final decision as to the English." The Creeks came to the meeting with "their weapons in hand." It was no game. Creek warriors carried their muskets into the council house. They wanted the decision to have consequences, and Orta understood that he might "lose his life," given the unpopularity of what he had to say in certain quarters. Nevertheless, he advised them not to harm the English, since they had "come in peace." He suggested Brims should explain to the Carolinians "that since they were friends of the Spanish they would also be their friends." That advice, it should be noted, bore a marked resemblance to the language and intent of what Steven Hahn has called the Coweta

Resolution, which emerged from another council meeting later in the month. There seems little doubt, at any rate, that Creek warriors had come prepared to continue the war with South Carolina if their Spanish allies had risen to the challenge. Hearing Orta's counsel of peace and friendship, however, they initially "had nothing to reply." They had tried hard to prompt the Spanish into acting the part of traditional military allies. After a period of silence, Creek leaders finally suggested that "since they were not to take their goods away from the English, they wanted to barter for the merchandise."[39]

Only at that point did the Lower Creeks allow the Carolina delegation to enter Coweta, and they made the reasons for their hostility toward the English very clear even as they discussed peace. The Creek-English dialogue at Coweta hammered away at exactly the same theme that Muscogee leaders had emphasized in the previous year as they waited for their corn to ripen: Charles Town's assistance to the Cherokees. The discussion at Coweta was able to proceed, in large part, because the English negotiators had complied with Creek demands made during the Charles Town talks that captives taken by Cherokee raids be returned to them. The transfer of those captives may have eased tensions somewhat, but it also made English-Cherokee collusion all the more obvious for those assembled to witness it. When the English broke a knife to symbolize the return of peace, therefore, Chipacasi brought out two bows and two arrows. He broke one set of weapons to mark the peace with South Carolina but left the other whole and "laid a blood-stained knife upon it." He did this, he explained, because the Creeks "were still at war with the Chalaquies." Chipacasi made it clear, moreover, that "if the English aided their enemy in violation of the peace, without hesitation they would wage war against them as well." In fact, having performed the ceremonies of peace,

Chipacasi could not help haranguing the English a little more. At the "same instant that they appeared to negotiate a peace," he said, "the English were furnishing arms and ammunition to the Chalaquies and exhorting them to deal cruelly with the Cavetas."[40]

What happened next may have been a coincidence, but it may also have been one of the most cunning diplomatic ploys of the age. With the English peace only a day or two old, a messenger reported that "a large number of Chalaquies warriors had been seen twenty leagues away en route to attack these provinces." The news created an uproar in Coweta and led many to call for the execution of the Carolina delegates "in the notion that they furnished the leadership." Seeing that they needed help to defend themselves, Orta now "donated seventy-five pounds of powder, a thousand balls, some gun flints, and vermillian" to the Creeks. Not wishing to be outdone, the French at Fort Toulouse rushed "two barrels of powder, balls" and vermilion for war paint to Coweta. The Indians appeared to be "pleased and encouraged" by these developments, and Creek war leaders wisely "sent out scouts to report everything." After the English had endured this tension for some time, the scouts "returned with the information that the Chalaquies had withdrawn." If it was a coincidence, it was one of the few unplanned developments at Coweta that month. Intentionally or not, the message this turn of events communicated to the Carolinians, "whose doom would have been sealed had the Chalaquies continued to advance," was precisely the message that Chipacasi and other Lower Creek leaders had been sending to them for the last year.[41]

If Lower Creek leaders were considering a policy of neutrality during this episode, it does not appear to have been their first preference. They were deeply interested in communicating traditional Creek notions about friendship and alliance and aggressively sought to bring European diplomatic behavior into conformity with those ideals. Once European delegates had departed from Coweta, however, Creek leaders gathered in the town to discuss their options. No clear record of the debate survives in either European documents or Muscogee oral tradition, but one of the participants later informed the Spanish of the final decision on March 23. The Indians "had resolved to remain at peace with the English, Spanish, and French garrisons, and had thereupon gone back to their provinces." In this version, the outcome of the assembly seems little more than a ratification of the advice given previously by Don Juan Fernandez de Orta.

Steven Hahn contends that the decision went a good deal further than that, initiating a new Creek diplomatic policy. He bases his argument on a letter that added a few words to the decision, reporting that the Creeks would live in peace with all three European powers even "if by some accident one should commence war upon the other." If his translation is accurate, that certainly would have represented a novel and far-sighted development. In this anglicized form, however, the phrase seems jarringly at odds with the immediate problems confronting the Lower Creeks. As preceded by the conditional "if," the resolution suggests that they were concerned over a future course of action in the event that Europeans declared war on each other. That, however, was never an issue at Coweta in the weeks leading up to the meeting. Indeed, such a declaration of war would have simplified matters for the Creeks. Chipacasi's conversation with the Spanish emissary, Orta, conveyed no uncertainty about what to do in case the Spanish declared war, only impatience that it had not been declared yet. Their problem, then, was not how to proceed in the event of future inter-European hostilities but, rather, what to do in the present until that desirable state of affairs came to pass.[42]

Although it seems more in keeping with the context of preceding events, this understanding of the March 1718 Coweta Resolution presents some difficult problems as well. First, although the Creeks could not have known it at the time, a decision to remain neutral until one European power declared war on another would in effect have committed them to neutrality until at least 1738, when the War of Jenkins' Ear at last erupted. It would be difficult for modern observers to tell the difference during those two decades between a permanent Creek policy of neutrality and a temporary neutrality that was contingent on European diplomatic decisions about peace and war. Second, the Creeks did not remain neutral until 1738. After many years of troubled relations with South Carolina, Creek diplomacy appears to have reached a turning point in 1728, when most Creek towns embraced the English while simultaneously adopting a hostile stance toward the Spanish. Many Creek leaders, moreover, including the Fannimingo of Okfuskee Town, committed themselves to a formal English alliance prior to the founding of Georgia in 1733.[43]

Steven Hahn regards the 1728 Creek-English rapprochement as a sign of Emperor Brims's waning influence and the erosion of his "political ideal" of neutrality by factionalism, but there is a clear link between the resurgence of pro-English sentiments in Creek country and South Carolina's military behavior. Led by Colonel James Palmer, Carolinians marched southward to St. Augustine in early March and attacked the Yamasee town of Nombre de Dios, just under the walls of the Castillo de San Marcos. They killed thirty Yamasees outright and surrounded the survivors and their Spanish allies in the stone fort. The Spanish fired canons ineffectually but declined to sally from the Castillo in defense of Nombre de Dios. Before leaving, Palmer and the Carolina forces burned the little chapel in the Indian town and razed the houses to the ground. If warriors in Creek country had been waiting for one European power to strike another, Palmer's raid gave them what they wanted.[44]

The attack occurred, moreover, in the midst of a diplomatic initiative from South Carolina. Recognizing that the Lower Creek towns continued to maintain friendly relations with Spanish Florida and the Yamasees at St. Augustine, the English suspended all trade to the towns along the Chattahoochee River in February 1728. Significantly, the emissary charged with carrying Carolina's message into Creek country, Charlesworth Glover, chose to begin his mission by traveling directly to the Upper Creek town of Okfuskee, where he could rely on the pro-English sympathies of the town's leadership. In many ways, then, the modern historiographical tension between Joshua Piker's portrayal of Okfuskee's prolonged struggle to restore the British alliance following the Yamasee War and Steven Hahn's Coweta Resolution found expression in Glover's mission. The British cannily sought to use the loyalty of Okfuskee and other Abhika and Tallapoosa settlements to force the Lower Creeks to abandon their neutral stance.

In March 1728, therefore, the cessation of trade and news of Palmer's raid combined to present Lower Creek leaders with a powerful dilemma. No European monarchs had declared war. But the attack on St. Augustine was an act of war nevertheless, and it was coupled with trade relations in a way that must have spoken to traditional Creek ideals of alliance. Although many Lower Creek leaders may secretly have mourned the pathetic military performance of the Spanish at St. Augustine, they responded quickly and resolutely to the new state of affairs. Barely two weeks after the raid against St. Augustine, Spanish officials and soldiers traveling through the Lower Creek towns of Eufala and Apalachicola, where some of their staunchest supporters resided, found themselves unceremoniously taken into custody. By mid-April, English observers reported that the Creeks had "stopped the path to Augustine," and shortly thereafter all but one of the Lower Creek towns sent out war parties to strike at the Spanish and their few remaining Yamasee allies. In doing so, Creek leaders responded to recognizable diplomatic cues from South Carolina in the traditional manner expected of Indian allies; they ended trade and declared war.[45]

I would argue that the Coweta Resolution in 1718, rather than embracing neutrality as a matter of principle, can be interpreted as a dialogic response to a specific sequence of conversations. The Lower Creeks may well have been disillusioned by Europeans in general. They may even have been tutored in that disillusionment by Iroquois emissaries, but they had not yet abandoned the dream of bringing European neighbors into compliance with Muscogee diplomatic customs. Their decision "to remain at peace with the English, Spanish, and French garrisons" in 1718 grew out of the failures of those "garrisons" at that time to meet the basic requirements expected of Creek allies. The search for reliable allies, however, remained a vital matter of concern for all members of the Creek Confederacy, and Europeans were still an important part of that effort.

THEMES, PATTERNS, PROBLEMS

By abstaining from traditional alliances with Europeans in the decade after the Yamasee War, then, Lower Creek leaders may not have been breaking with tradition but, rather, insisting on it. They had studied European approaches to diplomacy, and they put those new understandings to work in multilateral discussions with South Carolina, Florida, and Louisiana, but they continued to bring traditional Muscogee ideals to bear on those talks. That the talks did not result in the sort of military alliances that would have been condoned by former generations of Creek leaders can be attributed more to the failure of Europeans to meet traditional Creek expectations than to the emergence of new diplomatic objectives. Clearly, Creek leaders in the aftermath of the Yamasee War felt empowered to demand European compliance with the traditional terms of alliance.

That sense of empowerment influenced Cherokee discussions with South Carolina about the postwar terms of trade as well. Although in the long run they were unsuccessful in their efforts to revive the beaver trade, Cherokees managed to negotiate the first set price schedules and spurred the transformation of the transportation system by which goods traveled. These were fundamental changes in the practical operation of the trade that became hallmarks of the frontier exchange economy through midcentury. In making these compromises, moreover, South Carolinians increasingly came to view the Indian trade as more than a profitable economic activity. It became a means of maintaining both the security of the frontier and the colony's internal social landscape. As such, the Yamasee War spurred distinct antimarket modifications on both sides of the frontier that had profound implications for the development of the region.

Conclusion
New Problems

On February 1, 1733, nearly half a century after the inland Yamasees had arrived at the same location to commence their troubled relationship with South Carolina, James Edward Oglethorpe and 106 British settlers debarked at Yamacraw Bluff, near the mouth of the Savannah River. As they began to busy themselves with the work of establishing the colony of Georgia, they were greeted amicably by a small band of Indians, hardly more numerous than the colonists themselves. At their forefront "came a man dancing in antic postures with a spread fan of . . . feathers in each hand as a token of friendship, which were fixed to small rods about four foot long, set from top to bottom with small bells . . . which made a jingling, whilst the king and others followed making a very uncouth hollowing." As Oglethorpe moved to greet the Indians, "the man with his feathers came forward dancing and talking, which . . . was repeating a speech, the acts of their chief warriors, and at times came close and waved his fans over him and stroked him on every side with them." This performance lasted about fifteen minutes, after which the "king and all the men came in a regular manner and shook him by the hand."[1]

When Tomochichi, the "king" of this small band, shook hands with Oglethorpe, a circuit of sorts was completed. The two men had come to Yamacraw Bluff for different reasons, but for both of them those reasons all found their way back ultimately to the Yamasees and the Yamasee War. Oglethorpe and the first Georgia colonists, inspired though they were by philanthropic motives, were guided to the Georgia country by imperial stratagems that grew out of the need for more secure frontier defenses after 1715. Tomochichi and the Yamacraws, by contrast, had been forced to retire to the area as exiles.[2]

Tomochichi made it clear that he had once been associated with the Lower Creeks, but he gave few details as to why or when he had parted ways with them. It was clear, however, that something had propelled him out of the Muscogee homeland. "I came here poor and helpless," he explained in an early meeting with Oglethorpe, "to look for good land near the tombs of my ancestors." When several Lower Creek headmen arrived to negotiate with the English in May, they made reference to his past in vague, poetic terms. According to Yahou-Lakee (probably Yahola Kee), the mico of Coweta, Tomochichi and his people were "little birds" who had been scattered asunder by the "eagle." It is impossible of course to know exactly what he meant. But the reference drew on powerful Creek traditions that revered the eagle as a symbol of peace. The following year, when Tomochichi met with King George in London, he explained that the eagle "flieth all round our Nations," and its "Feathers are a sign of peace in our Land." He thereupon handed the king a bundle of eagle feathers as confirmation of the peace between the English and the Indians of Georgia. That he and his Yamacraw followers had somehow been scattered by the same peace suggests the uniqueness of his position in southern colonial history.[3]

As Oglethorpe would soon learn, Tomochichi and the Yamacraws were essentially the only Indians still living in Georgia. There may have been a few families living along the banks of the Savannah River near present-day Augusta, where Charlesworth Glover observed "8 men, 12 women, and 10 children" as late as 1725, but for the most part the region was uninhabited. In the aftermath of the Yamasee War, native groups across the sub-Appalachian Southeast abandoned their homes to seek strength in numbers, combining forces for protection against external foes. They traveled to the Chattahoochee River, the Catawba River, the Tallapoosa, St. Augustine, even Pennsylvania and New York, where the Savannahs finally found a home among the Tuscaroras and Iroquois.[4]

Tomochichi, however, had a turbulent past, possibly rooted in the violence of the pre–Yamasee War Indian slave trade, which may have made it difficult for him to fit into the new "peace" circling the South in the 1720s and 1730s. In 1706, for instance, complaints had been made against English traders who purchased ten slaves from "an Indian named Tomichee . . . which were ffree and which he or they knew to be ffree and made slaves of them." On another occasion, an Indian identified as "Toomichau," despite "knowing them to be ffree," had sold "7 Waucoogau free people" into slavery. When he spoke to the Georgia Trustees years later, Tomochichi acknowledged that "when he was Young, he took delight in War and hunting, and did not mind the Instructions of the Old Men."[5]

Having been scattered like "little birds" by the "eagle," Tomochichi and the Yamacraws had little choice but to marry their fortunes to those of Oglethorpe and the new colony. Yet their case was an exception. The same "eagle" that had scattered the Yamacraws succeeded in gathering the majority of sub-Appalachian Indians together, and Oglethorpe, to his credit, quickly recognized the difference. He valued the friendship of Tomochichi, but he was wise enough to invite the various headmen of the Creek Nation to confer with him in Savannah shortly after his arrival. Oglethorpe understood that it was their collective permission for the Georgia settlers to use whatever "land they did not use themselves," and not the "antic" dancing of the Yamacraw shaman, that conferred real security upon the colony.[6]

The treaty concluded in May 1733 between Oglethorpe and the Creek Indians illustrated the extent to which the native South had changed. If the Georgians had arrived before 1715, they would have found themselves surrounded by numerous disunited Indian nations, none of whom could lay sole claim to the region or exercise the sole authority of granting or rescinding land use rights. By 1733, however, the situation was reversed. The Georgians came to a country that was virtually devoid of human habitation but that fell under the purview of a single Indian nation several hundred miles away: the Creek Confederacy.

The South that Oglethorpe encountered was scarcely older than his colony, born only eighteen years earlier in the violent convulsions of the Yamasee War, and the society he sought to plant in that charred soil was in many ways the offspring of the same fires. Historians have known since Verner Crane's day that the establishment of Georgia represented the culmination of imperial considerations rooted in the post–Yamasee War strategies of John Barnwell and other Carolinians, but the extent to which the Trustees' philanthropic endeavor was shaped by Carolina's experience has never been acknowledged. The essential ligaments of the Georgia experiment, however, had emerged in a recognizable form within the first year of the war, certainly by 1717, when South Carolinians sought to reinforce the plantation regime by regulating the colony's racial composition and creating zones of majority white settlement along the frontiers. Those zones were intended, as was Georgia, to act as a bulwark against external as well as internal enemies, and the mode of attracting white settlers to such defensive zones had been established by 1717 as well: relief from creditors.

The very need to create a racially cohesive defensive zone signaled one of the most telling outcomes of the Yamasee War: the abrupt emergence of a consensus fear that the white minority was imperiled by nonwhite enemies inside as well as outside the colony. As is evident in Commons House legislation as early as 1716, Carolinians became increasingly concerned with regulating and defending the racial landscape of the colony. They sought greater precision in defining racial boundaries, created new methods of segregating problem populations, attempted to manipulate white immigration and settlement patterns, and harnessed the Indian trade wherever possible to serve the interests of the plantation regime.

In The Indian Slave Trade, Alan Gallay argued that the Yamasee War marked "the birth of the Old South," and the evidence presented here supports his contention in several ways. As discussed in earlier chapters, the war served to codify and add persuasive power to the emerging precepts of white racial ideology. But race-based decisions about domestic labor, slave status, and participation in the Indian trade inevitably found expression in economic behavior, and in this respect the wartime and postwar adjustments of South Carolinians offer some much needed perspective on the more familiar historiographical debates concerning the nineteenth-century southern slave system. Was southern slavery, for instance, a capitalist or noncapitalist form of labor? Although these debates have generally been preoccupied with the "antebellum" or pre–Civil War era, there is a colonial aspect to the problem that needs to be added to the discussion.[7]

Based on the evidence presented here, it seems clear that Carolinians sought to regulate economic activity in order to preserve and control the colony's social structure. This impulse was present in prewar efforts to control diplomatic communication with allied Indian nations, but it became explicit in 1716 and 1717 as Carolinians eschewed economic profit in favor of an administered Indian trade capable of securing the frontiers and restraining the slave population. In so doing, they sought to control the subversive influence of market forces on local communities by subduing merchant interests, whose loyalties lay primarily across the Atlantic, and by exerting greater control over the most threatening forms of market conduct: cross-cultural exchange with Native Americans.

If southern planters eventually became adept at managing profits and losses, it should be remembered that this "rational" economic behavior involved a very limited number of transactions, and that many other threatening activities had been radically curtailed or suppressed by the mid-nineteenth century. Perhaps the southern slave economy as it existed prior to the Civil War should be viewed as the result of many years of careful winnowing and regulation, with the Yamasee War as one of the first and greatest of those winnowing events. Additional work will need to be done to determine how far efforts to sublimate the Indian trade to the interests of the plantation regime continued to shape South Carolina's economy and political climate for the rest of the colonial era. If such efforts were indeed a persistent theme, then the Yamasee War may well have functioned as a watershed event in the movement toward a "moral" or political southern economy. What the historian Ulrich B. Phillips euphemistically termed "the central theme of southern History," moreover, will perhaps seem a little more central.[8]

The greater influence wielded by southeastern Indians in the aftermath of the Yamasee War made Carolinians uncomfortable, but it also gave native leaders greater power to control the terms of trade with the English. Especially during the first year of the Cherokee alliance, Carolinians made concession after concession in order to preserve diplomatic ties to the Cherokees at the expense of a profitable trade. As a result, Cherokee headmen shaped the relationship to their own taste and spurred several new developments that became hallmarks of Anglo-Indian trade for the rest of the eighteenth century; they negotiated the first set-price schedules, spurred the conversion from native burdeners to packhorses, and forced Carolinians to participate in gift exchange. As the Creeks negotiated a peace settlement with South Carolina in 1717 and

1718, moreover, they brought traditional ideals of alliance to bear on novel diplomatic challenges. While engaging in new forms of multilateral diplomacy with French, Spanish, and English delegates, the Creeks nevertheless appear to have insisted with new vigor that time-honored values linking trade and alliance be respected by their European neighbors. Their refusal to commit to binding alliances after the Yamasee War, I argue, followed from that insistence on traditional ideals rather than from a new policy of neutrality.

At about the same time, of course, Chicacha Outlacta of the Choctaws was carrying his brother's pro-English head to Mobile in order to renew the Choctaw-French alliance. That distant contest over diplomacy probably involved an extra dimension. If ethnohistorian Greg O'Brien is correct, that the Choctaws in the eighteenth century were reconsidering traditional ideas about the sources and nature of chiefly power, then the duel between pro-English and pro-French leaders during the Yamasee War must surely have intensified that process. The deceased chief, Conchak Emiko, may have been one of the last to rely primarily on spiritual power as an agent of change. Choctaw leaders in the decades following the Yamasee War increasingly wielded a new sort of power, based first on the ability to procure advantageous trade relations and secondarily on the spiritual prestige that followed control of the trade.

Few studies to date have attempted to understand Muscogee conceptions of chiefly power during this epoch, but Tomochichi's rise to prominence raises a number of related questions. Having retired "poor and helpless" to Yamacraw Bluff, he had clearly been judged unfit for positions of influence within Creek society by all the standards that Creek leaders considered valid at the time. And yet the fortuitous arrival of Oglethorpe and the Georgia settlers restored a measure of his prestige by means that lay largely outside the Creek political system. What impact did this new dynamic have on Creek ideas about leadership, trade, and diplomacy? Can they be compared with the transformation of Choctaw ideas in relations with the French? And are there comparisons to be made with studies of Creek spiritual and political ideas at later periods, such as Joel Martin's *Sacred Revolt* and Claudio Saunt's *"A New Order of Things"*?

The portrait of Anglo-Indian trade presented here suggests that the Yamasee War initiated a new era of exchange in which Native American consumers enjoyed greater leverage in shaping the relationship to their own tastes, but the process of dependency continued even as they sought through set-price schedules and treaty agreements to control the uncertainties of market involvement. In this respect, too, the war poses a number of challenges to future scholars of the eighteenth-century South. At what point did southeastern Indians become so reliant on European manufactured goods that they could no longer determine the terms of the exchange relationship on an equal footing? Did the terms of trade begin to deteriorate for Native Americans in the 1750s, as Joshua Piker has argued, or should the end of the Great War for Empire in 1763 be regarded as the fulcrum for such a transition?

Perhaps the greatest challenge remains the quest for a more unified southern historiography, a narrative that carries the ash of all its earlier incinerations with it into the antebellum era and beyond. Tomochichi's handshake with Oglethorpe at Yamacraw Bluff offers one such bridge between seemingly distinct epochs, but surely there are others that can be woven not merely into the scholarly literature but into living memory as well. Tomochichi was searching for the bones of his ancestors, and those bones were still there as the cotton South spread inland. Perhaps this study has contributed in some small way to such an evolving narrative. The author, however, must echo Tomochichi's hope, expressed during his visit with the Georgia Trustees in 1734, that "wiser men may come."

Appendix
The Huspah King's Letter to Charles Craven

The Yamasee message to Governor Charles Craven had been a tantalizing legend in South Carolina history for three centuries, reported in several period documents and noted in early histories of the colony. Yet no text from the letter was found in the records until June 10, 2000, when I stumbled upon it while doing research at the North Carolina State Archives in Raleigh. I was using the British Records Calendar there to identify ships that had put in at Charles Town harbor during 1715 and 1716; my hope was that their captains had included information about the Yamasee War in reports to Admiralty officers.

Captain Jonathan St. Lo's letter was remarkable in itself in this regard. His was the first ship to arrive at Charles Town following the outbreak of hostilities, and the governor was so happy to see it that he rowed out himself rather than wait for St. Lo to anchor and come ashore. While on board, Governor Craven related everything that had happened during April of 1715 and gave an account of the Yamasee letter, dictated by the Yamasees to a captured English boy who mixed gunpowder and water to make ink.

Toward the end of his report, Captain St. Lo indicated that he was enclosing a copy of the Yamasee letter. I immediately leafed forward to see if the enclosure was still present, anticipating disappointment. I still have a vivid mental image of the letter as I first saw it, with the Huspah king's name at the bottom. At that point I had spent nearly a decade of my life on the project and had begun to exhaust my hopes for any further breakthroughs. For some time I sat listening to the air hum through the air conditioner vent before I mustered courage to begin reading the letter. I believe it is a transcription rather than the original letter itself, since it appears to be written in Captain St. Lo's hand. The full text is published here for the first time:

> Mr. Wright said that the white men would come and [fetch] [illegible] the Yamasees in one night, and that they would hang four of their head men and take all the rest of them for Slaves, and that he would send them all off the Country, for he said that the men of the Yamasees were like women, and shew'd his hands one to the other, and what he said vex'd the great Warrier's, and this made them begin the war, and the Indians have kill'd forty or fifty white persons, and the Indians are all comeing to take all the Country, they are three hundd. that are goeing to watch to take the Fort at Capt. Woodwards and that at Well Town for in short all the Indians upon the main are comeing and they say that the white People will not be a handful for them for they say they will fight Six year's but they will take the Country
>
> Charles Craven may goe off himself, for the Indians love him, and they say that he and they are like Brothers.
>
> The Indians say that they that will not fight of the White men, they will save alive, but they that do fight, they will kill, as for the Women and Children them they will save alive, this is all from the
>
> Huspaw King
>
> To Charles Craven King
> att Charles Town

Notes

ABBREVIATIONS

JCHA   Journals of the Commons House of Assembly of South
                Carolina, 1706–1721, William S. Green Transcripts, micro-
                film, South Carolina Department of Archives and History,
                Columbia.
MPA:FD   *Mississippi Provincial Archives: French Dominion*, 3 vols., ed.
                and trans. Dunbar Rowland and Albert Godfrey Sanders
                (Jackson: University of Mississippi Press, 1932).
NCSAR   North Carolina State Archives, Raleigh.
RBPRO   *Records in the British Public Record Office Relating to South
                Carolina*, ed. A. S. Salley; vols. 1–5, Columbia: Histori-
                cal Commission of South Carolina, 1947; vols. 6–9, micro-
                film, South Carolina Department of Archives and History,
                Columbia.
SCDAH   South Carolina Department of Archives and History,
                Columbia.
SPG   Society for the Propagation of the Gospel in Foreign Parts,
                Selected Pages Relating to South Carolina from Library of
                Congress Transcripts of the Papers of the Society for the
                Propagation of the Gospel in Foreign Parts, Series A and
                B; microfilm, South Carolina Department of Archives and
                History, Columbia.
WIMR   Wills, Inventories, & Miscellaneous Records, 1722–1724,
                vol. 58; 1722–1726, vol. 59; 1724–1725, vol. 60; 1726–1727,
                vols. 61A, 61B; microfilm, South Carolina Department of
                Archives and History, Columbia.

INTRODUCTION

1. "Letter of Charles Rodd to His Employer in London," May 8, 1715, in *Calendar of State Papers, Colonial Office Series: America and West Indies, August 1714–December 1715*, 28:167–68.

2. Francis LeJau to the Secretary, May 21, 1715, in LeJau, *The Carolina Chronicle of Dr. Francis LeJau, 1706–1717*, ed. Frank J. Klingberg, 158.

3. For Gary Nash's assessment of the war, see Nash, *Red, White, and Black*, 123. For the war's diplomatic repercussions, and tribal migrations, as well as the collapse of the colony's proprietary government, see Crane, *Southern Frontier*, 137–68.

4. Crane, *Southern Frontier*, 162–67. Milling, *Red Carolinians*, 134–64. Swanton, *Early History of the Creek Indians*, 97. For a modern example of this line of thinking, see Reid, *A Better Kind of Hatchet*, 52–55.

5. May 4, 1714–May 7, 1714, in McDowell, ed., *Colonial Records of South Carolina: Journals of the Commissioners of the Indian Trade*, 53–56 (hereinafter cited as *Journals of the Commissioners*). Longe, "Small Postscript," 3.

6. Some of the most rewarding efforts to gain perspective on intercultural exchange have thus far been produced by scholars of the northern fur trade. See, for instance, Arthur J. Ray and Donald B. Freeman, *"Give Us Good Measure": An Economic Analysis of Relations between the Indians and the Hudson's Bay Company before 1763*. Perhaps the best general introduction to the substantivist position is Marshall Sahlins's *Stone Age Economics*; also see Abraham Rotstein, "Karl Polanyi's Concept of Non-Market Trade." Richard White, *The Middle Ground: Indians, Empires, and Republics in the Great Lakes Region, 1650–1815*, 50.

7. White, *Middle Ground*, x, 52. For excellent discussions of the historiographical implications of the Middle Ground metaphor, see Herman, "Romance on the Middle Ground"; Morgan, "Encounters between British and 'Indigenous' Peoples, c. 1500–1800"; Deloria, "What Is the Middle Ground, Anyway?"; and Desbarats, "Following the Middle Ground."

8. Merrell, *Into the American Woods*, 34, 37, 39.

9. Merrell, *The Indians' New World: Catawbas and Their Neighbors from European Contact through the Era of Removal*; Hatley, *The Dividing Paths: Chero-*

kees and South Carolinians through the Revolutionary Era; Gallay, The Indian Slave Trade: The Rise of the English Empire in the American South, 1680–1717; Oatis, A Colonial Complex: South Carolina's Frontiers in the Era of the Yamasee War, 1680–1730; Hahn, The Invention of the Creek Nation, 1670–1763.

10. Deloria, "What is the Middle Ground, Anyway?" 11–15.

11. Usner, Indians, Settlers, and Slaves in a Frontier Exchange Economy: The Lower Mississippi Valley before 1783.

1. CAROLINIANS IN INDIAN COUNTRY

1. For an environmental approach, see Haan, "The 'Trade Do's Not Flourish as Formerly.'" For James Merrell's discussion of Catawba motives, see Merrell, Indians' New World, 68–75.

2. For efforts to explain the origins of the Yamasee War in terms of dependency theory, see Merrell, "'Our Bond of Peace': Patterns of Intercultural Exchange in the Carolina Piedmont, 1650–1750," 207; and Nash, Red, White, and Black, 124–26. For a concise summation of Richard White's ideas about dependency theory, see White, The Roots of Dependency: Subsistence, Environment, and Social Change among the Choctaws, Pawnees, and Navajos, xiii–xix.

3. Partisan rhetoric among traders became a conspicuous problem in 1712, when Thomas Nairne returned to South Carolina. The names involved in such complaints overwhelmingly belonged to two different camps, one supporting Thomas Nairne, the other John Wright. Compare, for instance, the following entries with the Nairne/Wright partisan struggles in the Court of Common Pleas and the Commons House of Assembly discussed later: McDowell, Journals of the Commissioners, 23, 24, 27, 28, 44. Even the frequently cited Yamasee fear that Thomas Nairne would take their lands away was reported not by the Yamasees but by John Wright's cronies, George Wright and Cornelius McCarty. See McDowell, Journals of the Commissioners, 27–28. For one of the first efforts to untangle this factionalism, see Gallay, Indian Slave Trade, 315–34. My survey of the Journals of the Commissioners of the Indian Trade counted only those cases between 1710 and 1715 where a clear complainant and defendant(s) could be identified. Only

two involved an unidentified complainant or defendant. I have also followed the threads of each case through the *Journals* in order to avoid counting the same case multiple times, since the commissioners often resumed deliberations after lengthy recesses. For the first identifying references to the thirty-two cases involving complaints lodged by English traders against other English traders, see McDowell, *Journals of the Commissioners*, 5–6, 11–13, 17–18, 20–23, 25, 27–28, 38, 41–43, 46–47, 57–58; for the first identifying references to the thirty cases involving complaints lodged by Native Americans against English traders, see 3–5, 9, 11, 18–19, 23, 26, 37–38, 42–43, 49–50, 52–53, 57, 59–60.

4. For complaints against Alexander Nicholas, see Oct. 25, 1712, McDowell, *Journals of the Commissioners*, 37. For complaints against Philip Gilliard and Jess Crossley (identified elsewhere as Joseph Crossley), see Sept. 21, 1710, p. 4. For other cases of beatings, see pp. 50, 52.

5. Longe, "Small Postscript," 30. Admittedly, not all southeastern nations held women in such high esteem. The Chickasaws and Catawbas, for instance, exhibited pronounced patriarchal traits. Indeed, the Chickasaws occasionally mocked the "Ochesees" or Lower Creeks for being so obedient to their womenfolk. Significantly, however, these nations were also relatively content with English trade relations. For Chickasaw opinions of Lower Creek gender relations, see Nairne, *Muskhogean Journals*, 48.

6. Perdue, *Cherokee Women*, 45–46; also see Fox, *Kinship and Marriage*, 97–121, and Wright, *Creeks and Seminoles*, 19.

7. Mr. Osborne to the Secretary, March 1, 1714/15, microfilm frame 93, reel PR0085, Society for the Propagation of the Gospel in Foreign Parts, Selected Pages Relating to South Carolina from Library of Congress Transcripts of the Papers of the Society for the Propagation of the Gospel in Foreign Parts, Series A, Contemporary copies of letters received, vols. 7–17, 1712–1723, South Carolina Department of Archives and History, Columbia (hereinafter cited as SCDAH). See also Mr. Treadway Bull to the Secretary, Jan. 20, 1714/15, microfilm frame 91, reel PR0085, SCDAH.

8. For the diplomatic function of Euro-Indian marriages in the northern

fur trade, see Van Kirk, *Many Tender Ties*, 4, 9–121. For a discussion of Creek-European intermarriage with respect to trade relations, see Piker, *Okfuskee*, 162–76. See also Martin, *Sacred Revolt*, 76–79. For the incident between Musgrove, Stead, and the Tuckesaw King, see Salley, ed., *Journal of the Commons House of Assembly of South Carolina, March 6, 1705/6–April 9, 1706*, 22.

9. Longe, "Small Postscript," 33.

10. For the empowering aspects of women's involvement in the northern fur trade, see Van Kirk, *Many Tender Ties*, 4–6, 9–121. For similar processes in the southern trade, see Piker, *Okfuskee*, 166–67, and Braund, *Deerskins and Duffels*, 84–85. For the connection between women's declining status as a result of their exclusion from the trade, see Perdue, *Cherokee Women*, 76–94; and Saunt, "A New Order of Things," 139–63; see also Nancy Shoemaker, "Introduction," in Shoemaker, ed., *Negotiators of Change*, 10–12.

11. Altamaha was one of the principal Lower Yamasee towns; Salley, ed., *Journals of the Commons House of Assembly for 1702*, 21.

12. For complaints about "taking away" lodged by Native Americans against English traders, see McDowell, *Journals of the Commissioners*, 11 (two accounts), 13, 38, 42, 43, 50, 52. Salley, *Journals of the Commons House of Assembly for 1702*, 21. For Cornelius Meckarty's case, see Nov. 24, 1713, McDowell, *Journals of the Commissioners*, 52.

13. For Cornelius Meckarty's case, see Nov. 24, 1713, McDowell, *Journals of the Commissioners*, 52. For William Ford's case, see June 27, 1712, p. 28.

14. Nairne, *Muskhogean Journals*, 34–35.

15. For James Moore, see *Journal of the Commons House of Assembly for 1702*, 26. For credit-related complications, see May 20, 1714, McDowell, *Journals of the Commissioners*, 57.

16. For early concerns about "relations' debts," see Aug. 3, 1711, McDowell, *Journals of the Commissioners*, 15. For Tuskenehau's case, see June 12, 1712, p. 26. For official instructions on the matter, see July 10, 1712, p. 36.

17. Louis R. Smith Jr., "British-Indian Trade in Alabama, 1670–1756," 71; Braund, *Deerskins and Duffels*, 62. The connection between the credit

cycle and the outbreak of the war was not lost on South Carolina officials seeking to reform the Indian trade. In 1716, they moved to correct the problem by advising the Cherokee factor, Theophilus Hastings, that he was "not on any pretense whatsoever to give any credit or trust any Indians whatsoever, even for the value of one single skin." See McDowell, *Journals of the Commissioners*, 86.

18. For Yamasee trade debts, see Crane, *Southern Frontier*, 167. For an environmental perspective on the topic, see Haan, "The 'Trade Do's Not Flourish.'" For a discussion of late eighteenth-century deer populations, see Waselkov, "The Eighteenth-Century Anglo-Indian Trade," 203–5. The exchange rate in terms of pounds Carolina currency per 100 pounds sterling jumped from 150 in 1712 to 300 in 1714. See McCusker, *Money and Exchange*, 222. A discussion of changing market demands and viable commodities appears in chapter 3 of the present volume. July 27, 1711, McDowell, *Journals of the Commissioners*, 11.

19. For complaints of Indian creditors, see McDowell, *Journals of the Commissioners*, 19, 42, 53, 57.

20. Instruction to the Indian Agent, August 3, 1711, McDowell, *Journals of the Commissioners*, 16. For John Locke's thinking in this area, see Locke, *Second Treatise of Government*, 16.

21. July 10, 1712, McDowell, *Journals of the Commissioners*, 35.

22. August 3, 1711, McDowell, *Journals of the Commissioners*, 16. Traditional forms of slavery among Native Americans differed from European forms in that they were less rigid, were rarely perpetual, and often had as their ultimate aim the assimilation of the slave on a basis of equality. For an excellent discussion of the issue, see Perdue, *Slavery and the Evolution of Cherokee Society*. Also see Hatley, *Dividing Paths*, 57. For the Cherokees, a three-day moratorium on slave trading might still have forced them into premature action, since returning warriors and their captives could require as much as four days for ritual purification. See Longe, "Small Postscript," 45–46.

23. August 3, 1711, McDowell, *Journals of the Commissioners*, 16.

24. April 17, 1712, McDowell, *Journals of the Commissioners*, 23; May 16, 1712, p. 25.

25. Savana or Savano Town was located on the east bank of the Savannah River near present-day Augusta, Georgia.

26. September 20, 1710, McDowell, *Journals of the Commissioners*, 3; October 28, 1710, p. 5; May 15, 1712, p. 24.
27. For demands for additional proof, see September 21, 1710, McDowell, *Journals of the Commissioners*, 3–4.
28. November 12, 1714, McDowell, *Journals of the Commissioners*, 60.
29. A letter from James Lucas was sent from the Lower Creek town of Ocmulgee in 1710. See McDowell, *Journals of the Commissioners*, 6.
30. Salley, ed., *Journal of the Commons House of Assembly, November 20, 1706–February 8, 1706/7*, 32. The Ilcombees rarely appear in English records as anything but victims. Their identity remains very much a mystery. John R. Swanton identified them as one of the ten Yamasee towns, but he was almost certainly mistaken. His suggestion that they may have been associated with the Apalachees who were forcibly relocated to the Savannah River, based on their previous location in northern Florida on the Popple map, seems more reasonable. A location somewhere near the other Apalachee towns near Savano Town would have made them accessible targets for the Pight-Lucas-Probert partnership, probably located on the Ocmulgee River. See Swanton, *Early History of the Creek Indians*, 97, 11–12, and plate 4; also see Verner Crane's discussion of Ilcombee in Crane, *Southern Frontier*, 164n.
31. Salley, ed., *Journal of the Commons House of Assembly, November 20, 1706–February 8, 1706/7*, 33–34.
32. Salley, *Journal . . . 1706/7*, 33.
33. Salley, *Journal . . . 1706/7*, 34; for Pight's involvement in the trade, see June 12, 1714, microfilm frame 4 (1712–1716): 285, Journals of the Commons House of Assembly of South Carolina, 1706–1721, William S. Green Transcripts, South Carolina Department of Archives and History (hereinafter cited as JCHA Green Transcripts, SCDAH). For Probert's continuing ill behavior, see McDowell, *Journals of the Commissioners*, 57.
34. I have found no reference to the Ilcombees dating later than 1710, and that reference concerns a single Ilcombee man taken as a slave. See McDowell, *Journals of the Commissioners*, 3–4.
35. Salley, *Journal . . . 1706/7*, 33–34.
36. June 12, 1712, McDowell, *Journals of the Commissioners*, 26–27.

37. April 18, 1712, McDowell, *Journals of the Commissioners*, 23.

38. For excellent accounts of the English-Indian attacks on the Spanish missions, see Hoffman, *Florida's Frontiers*, 174–82, and Bushnell, *Situado and Sabana*, 193–95. For a speculative discussion of the diplomatic repercussions of the collapse of the Spanish mission system from a Yamasee perspective, see Schrager, "Yamasee Indians and the Challenge of Spanish and English Colonialism," 167–230.

2. INDIAN SLAVES IN THE CAROLINA LOW COUNTRY

1. Greene, ed., *Selling a New World*, 132.

2. In 1972, William Robert Snell produced a study of Indian slavery in colonial South Carolina, but his work was flawed by faulty methodologies and occasional ethnographic misinformation. See Snell, "Indian Slavery in Colonial South Carolina, 1671–1795." For the latest attempt to generate reliable demographic statistics for Indian slavery, see Ramsey, "'All & Singular the Slaves.'"

3. See South Carolina Will Transcripts, Wills of Charleston County, vol. 1, 1671–1724, microfilm, in the South Carolina State Department of Archives and History, Columbia (hereinafter cited as Will Transcripts, SCDAH). This record series contains only seven surviving wills from the two decades following the colony's establishment. Records for the 1690s are more copious but still fall well short of being a reliable sample. As such, they should be regarded only as a rough index to demographic trends.

4. These figures indicate the percentage of households owning slaves of a particular type, "Indian," "Negro," or "mustee." The figures were obtained by dividing the number of estates listing each type of slave by the total number of estates probated per five-year period.

5. Approximately 52 percent of all inventoried estates reported owning some number of African slaves, while only 11 percent reported Indian slaves. Records of the Secretary of the Province, 1692–1700, Manuscripts, South Carolina Department of Archives and History, Columbia. These numbers suggest that prior to 1700 South Carolina was a "society of slaves" rather than a "slave society."

6. May 4, 1714, McDowell, *Journals of the Commissioners*, 53; Braund, *Deerskins and Duffels*, 70–71. Gallay, *Indian Slave Trade*. For the views of Thomas Nairne, see Memorial to the Earl of Sunderland, July 10, 1708, in Nairne, *Muskhogean Journals*, 75.

7. Governour and Councill, September 17, 1708, in Salley, ed., *Records in the British Public Record Office Relating to South Carolina, 1701–1710*, 5:203–10 (hereinafter cited as RBPRO). Only twenty-eight wills survive for the years between 1700 and 1710. For the five-year period 1700 through 1704, available records suggest that the number of households owning Indian slaves increased to 14 percent. For the five-year period 1705 through 1709, however, the figures are clearly an aberration, indicating a rate of ownership in excess of 40 percent. There are forty-six wills for the period between 1710 and 1714. The precise peak of Indian slavery cannot be determined. It occurred at some point between 1705 and 1715, probably between 1708 and 1713. The trend may have crested before 1715, in 1711 or 1712, perhaps as a result of an influx of slaves taken during the Tuscarora War. The forces led by John Barnwell against the Tuscaroras consisted primarily of South Carolina's Indian allies, who hoped to profit from the venture by taking as many slaves as possible. Probate records place the crest of the curve around 1708, but there are only fourteen wills between 1705 and 1709. With such a small number of documents, a single household could skew the figure as much as 7 percent upward or downward, resulting in a 14 percent aberration. Will Transcripts, SCDAH, vol. 1.

8. Lauber, *Indian Slavery in Colonial Times*, 244–45. Greene, *Selling a New World*, 132. For specialized occupations, see Miscellaneous Records, SCDAH, vol. 56 (1714–1717): 269–71, cited in Snell, "Indian Slavery," 155. In addition, a "Mahaw boy slave" (possibly an abbreviation of Altamaha, a Yamasee town) owned by Joseph Atwell, may have taken his name, Boatswain, from his occupation. See the Will of Joseph Atwell, January 13, 1722/3, Will Transcripts, SCDAH, vol. 1, Will Book 1722–1724, p. 26. Of the slave names listed in the Will Transcripts for Indian women between 1690 and 1740, Nanny occurs more often than any other name. Approximately 11 percent of female Indian

slaves referred to by name in South Carolina wills, most of whom probably worked within the household, were named Nanny. Will Transcripts, SCDAH,vols. 1–4.

9. Between about 15 and 20 percent of Carolina slave names were of African origin during the Colonial period, but these became less common over time. By contrast, the use of biblical names increased steadily during the course of the nineteenth century. See Inscoe, "Carolina Slave Names," 532, 535, 542. Other discussions of African names may be found in Puckett, *Black Names in America*, and Turner, *Africanisms in the Gullah Dialect*. Also see Wood, *Black Majority*, 181–86, and De-Camp, "African Day-Names in Jamaica."

10. About 16 percent of Indian slave names derived from classical sources; Will Transcripts, SCDAH, vols. 1–4. By comparison, John Inscoe arrived at a figure of about 21 percent for African slaves during roughly the same period; Inscoe, "Carolina Slave Names," 542. For postmortem inventories in the 1720s, see Wills, Inventories, & Miscellaneous Records, 1722–1724, vol. 58; 1722–1726, vol. 59; 1724–1725, vol. 60; 1726–1727, vols. 61A, 61B, microfilm, South Carolina Department of Archives and History, Columbia (hereinafter cited as WIMR, SCDAH).

11. For African and Native American naming practices, see Wright, *Creeks and Seminoles*, 29–30; Hudson, *Southeastern Indians*, 325; also see Swanton, "Social Organization and Social Usages of the Indians of the Creek Confederacy," 276–307. Inscoe, "Carolina Slave Names," 532.

12. Although the term *mustee* carried different meanings in different parts of the empire, it was used in South Carolina to refer either to Indian-African or Indian-European offspring. The former, however, were probably much more common. See Wood, *Black Majority*, 99; also see Littlefield, *Rice and Slaves*, 171. Will of Robert Seabrooke, September 22, 1720, Will Transcripts, SCDAH, vol. 1, Will Book 1720–1721, 44–47. Seabrooke's plantation is also revealing where questions of gender are concerned. Although Indian slaves comprised 35 percent of the enslaved labor force there, Indian women outnumbered men by five to one. Meanwhile, African men outnumbered African women by seven

to three. As a result, Indian and African responses to slavery on the Seabrooke plantation, considered separately, may have been very strongly influenced by gender differences. In the same Will Book the will of John Goodby, October 18, 1720, 39, indicates that on Goodby's plantation, there were two Indian women and two Indian men, but once again African men outnumbered African women by nine to four. See also Will of William Skipper, January 2, 1724/5, vol. 2, Will Book 1724–1725, 79; Will of John Whitmarsh, June 1, 1718, vol. 1, Will Book 1720–1721, 12–13; and Will of John Whitmarsh, May 20, 1723, vol. 2, Will Book 1722–1724, 40–41, all in Will Transcripts, SCDAH.

13. Will of John Royer, December 13, 1721, Will Transcripts, SCDAH, vol. 1, Will Book 1721–1722, 32–33. Will of Charles Colleton, October 27, 1727, Will Transcripts, SCDAH, vol. 2, Will Book 1727–1729, 15–20. Inventory of the estate of James Stanyarne, 1723, WIMR, 1722–1724, vol. 58, SCDAH; and Inventory of the estate of Nancy Gilbertson, August, 1726, WIMR, 1726–1727, vol. 61A. I am indebted to Alan Gallay for his insightful comments on the process of acculturation at work here.

14. The quote is taken from the title of Kathryn Holland Braund's "Guardians of Tradition and Handmaidens to Change: Women's Roles in Creek Economic and Social Life during the Eighteenth Century," 239–58; see also Braund, *Deerskins and Duffels*, 130–32. For archaeological perspectives on native women and tradition, see Mason, "Eighteenth-Century Culture Change among the Lower Creeks," 68–69, 73–74; see also Fairbanks, "Excavations at Horseshoe Bend, Alabama." Ferguson, *Uncommon Ground*, 82–84.

15. Will of James Lawson, February 4, 1715/16, Will Transcripts, SCDAH, vol. 1, Will Book 1711–1718, 82–83. Population figures are based on the census recorded in 1708, Governor and Council of Carolina to the Council of Trade and Plantations, September 17, 1708, RBPRO, 5:203–10. The majority of recorded instances of mothers fostering mustee children involved native women. There is only one clear instance in which a mustee child belonged to an African mother: see the Will of Thomas Ellis, December 27, 1722, Will Transcripts, SCDAH,

vol. 2, Will Book 1722–1724, 23. For the ratio of mustees to mulattos, see Littlefield, *Rice and Slaves*, 144, 169–71. For the declining rate of household ownership of mustee slaves, see Will Transcripts, SCDAH, vols. 1–4.

16. Will of Richard Prize, May 19, 1707, Will Transcripts, SCDAH, vol. 1, Will Book 1687–1710, 52. Will of Robert Johnson, April 5, 1725, Will Transcripts, SCDAH, vol. 3, Will Book 1732–1737, 249. Governor Robert Johnson mentioned his eldest son Robert in his own will ten years later but made no reference to his wife; see Will of Robert Johnson, Governor, December 21, 1734, Will Transcripts, SCDAH, vol. 3, Will Book 1732–1737, 191; the man who designed to marry Catherina in 1725 is probably the son rather than the governor himself, since the elder Johnson was, by all accounts, resident in England between 1723 and 1730, when he returned to South Carolina as its first Royal Governor; see Sherman, *Robert Johnson*, 59, 74.

17. The single most significant factor in most cases of African slave manumissions in colonial South Carolina appears to have been miscegenation, as suggested by the overwhelming prevalence in the records of women and mulatto children. See, Wood, *Black Majority*, 100. In spite of the prevalence of miscegenation, African slave manumissions appear to have manifested a wider variety of motives than Indian slave manumissions. In 1694, for instance, Humphrey Primat, moved by "love and affection," made arrangements to free "his negroe man Jack." See Miscellaneous Records, SCDAH, vol. 54 (1694–1704): 452. In another instance, an African slave woman named Susanah managed to save up twenty pounds Carolina currency in 1716 and attained her freedom "as a matter of hir own purchas"; see Miscellaneous Records, SCDAH, vol. 56 (1714–1717): 419. Remarkably, there are to date no known examples of Indian male slaves receiving their freedom via private legal actions. Will of John Burick, April 26, 1714, Will Transcripts, SCDAH, vol. 2, Will Book 1724–25, 2. Will of Abraham Fleur de la Plaine, August 2, 1721, Will Transcripts, SCDAH, vol. 1, Will Book 1721–1722, 24–26. As already noted, the term *mustee* was used in South Carolina to designate the mixed-race offspring of Indian and African parents. If de la Plaine's promise of freedom to

Diana grew out of a personal involvement between the two, her son's status as a mustee may have been very significant. For a discussion of the term *mustee*, see Wood, *Black Majority*, 99. Also see Jordan, *White over Black*, 168–69.

18. The closest parallel to this pattern of government-level manumission may be the range of official actions taken by British and American forces during the American Revolution. See Berlin, "The Revolution in Black Life," 349–82; and Frey, *Water from the Rock*.

19. April, 1703, Salley, ed., *Journals of the Commons House of Assembly of South Carolina, 1703*, 75–76.

20. Moore's own estimate of the number of Tuscarora slaves taken during a single attack in March 1713 was 392. This was in addition to 166 "kill'd or taken . . . on ye scout." Letter of James Moore, March 27, 1713, in Saunders, ed., *Colonial Records of North Carolina, 1713–1728*, 2:27. For Anethae's capture and release, see Council Journal, January 9, 1712/13, and Letter of Thomas Pollock, March 6, 1712/13, in Saunders, *Colonial Records*, 2:2, 2:24.

21. Council Journal, January 9, 1712/13, and Letter of Thomas Pollock, March 6, 1712/13, in Saunders, *Colonial Records*, 2:2, 2:24.

22. Miscellaneous Records, SCDAH, vol. 56 (1714–1717): 211–13.

23. Salley, ed., *Journal of the Commons House of Assembly of South Carolina, June 5, 1707–July 19, 1707*, 63. For John Jackson's complaint, see June 9, 1714, JCHA Green Transcripts, SCDAH, microfilm frame 4 (1712–1716): 277.

24. August 12, 1715, JCHA Green Transcripts, SCDAH, microfilm frame 4 (1712–1716): 434.

25. August 12, 1715, JCHA Green Transcripts; Miscellaneous Records, SCDAH, vol. 56 (1714–1717): 169. Green, "The Search for Altamaha," 24–25. Verner Crane, probably incorrectly, placed "Yoa" (a variant of Euhaw) among the Upper Yamasee towns. See Crane, *Southern Frontier*, 164.

26. Wood, *Black Majority*, 182. See also Inscoe, "Carolina Slave Names," 533. Ramsey, "'All & Singular the Slaves.'"

27. August 12, 1715, JCHA Green Transcripts, SCDAH, microfilm frame 4 (1712–1716): 434. Miscellaneous Records, SCDAH, vol. 56 (1714–

1717): 169. For native American naming patterns, see Wright, *Creeks and Seminoles*, 29–30; also see Swanton, "Social Organization and Social Usages of the Indians of the Creek Confederacy," 276–307; and Hudson, *Southeastern Indians*, 325.

28. April 12, 1715, McDowell, *Journals of the Commissioners*, 65. August 12, 1715, JCHA Green Transcripts, SCDAH, microfilm frame 4 (1712–1716): 434; Crane, *Southern Frontier*, 168.

29. April 12, 1715, McDowell, *Journals of the Commissioners*, 65.

30. For a discussion of marriages between English traders and Indian women, see Braund, *Deerskins and Duffels*, 83. Also see Perdue, *Cherokee Women*.

31. December 20, 1716, Miscellaneous Records, SCDAH, vol. 56 (1714–1717): 169. There is no indication as to whether Phillis was Indian or African. August 12, 1715, JCHA Green Transcripts, SCDAH, microfilm frame 4 (1712–1716): 434.

32. December 20, 1716, Miscellaneous Records, SCDAH, vol. 56 (1714–1717): 169. August 12, 1715, JCHA Green Transcripts, SCDAH, microfilm frame 4 (1712–1716): 434.

33. For a discussion of "slave-owning" societies and "slave-societies," see Morgan, "British Encounters with Africans and African-Americans," 163–64. Also see Berlin, *Many Thousands Gone*, 7–9.

34. Menard and Schwartz, "Why African Slavery?" 104.

35. Schwartz, "Indian Labor and New World Plantations." Also see Monteiro, "From Indian to Slave." For local versus transatlantic slave trades, see Menard and Schwartz, "Why African Slavery?" 89–114.

3. MARKET INFLUENCE

1. White, *Middle Ground*, 75, 50–93. The general utility of White's model for other regions and epochs remains a point of controversy. Scholars of the colonial South have been especially suspicious of the "Middle Ground," preferring to emphasize local accommodation and variation over the development of a shared trade culture. For insightful discussions of intercultural exchange, see Cayton and Teute, "Introduction: On the Connection of Frontiers"; and Thompson and Lamar, "Con-

temporary Frontier History"; see also Nobles, "Breaking into the Backcountry."

2. For Cherokeeleechee's recollections, see Patrick Mackay to James Oglethorpe, March 29, 1735, in Lane, ed., *General Oglethorpe's Georgia*, 1:152. For Malatchi's comments, see Speech by Malatchi Opiya Mico to Alexander Heron, Dec. 7, 1747 (microfilm frame 316, reel 12), Colonial Records of the State of Georgia, Original Manuscript Books, vol. 36, Georgia Department of Archives and History, Atlanta. For the Cherokee assessment of English traders, see "Journal of the March of the Carolinians," 335.

3. For seventeenth-century Spanish-Indian trade, see Waselkov, "Seventeenth-Century Trade in the Colonial Southeast." For the classic statement on the acceleration of trade in the first decade of the eighteenth century, see Clowse, *Economic Beginnings*, 162–66. For the Cherokee observation on English trade behavior, see "Journal of the March of the Carolinians," 335.

4. Bienville to Pontchartrain, Sept. 1, 1715, in Rowland and Sanders, eds., *Mississippi Provincial Archives: French Dominion*, 3:187 (hereinafter cited as MPA:FD). Price differences probably had much to do with Louisiana's marginal position in the French empire. In regions where distributional problems were not as severe, Native American consumers in the early eighteenth century often preferred French goods. See Eccles, "A Belated Review of Harold Adams Innis, *The Fur Trade in Canada*"; Dorn, *Competition for Empire*, 254. Bienville to Maurepas, April 20, 1734, in MPA:FD, 3:670–71. For Louisiana and the frontier exchange economy, see Usner, *Indians, Settlers, and Slaves*, 277, 8, 26–27.

5. Bienville to Pontchartrain, Oct. 27, 1711, in MPA:FD, 3:160.

6. For South Carolina's economic development, see Clowse, *Economic Beginnings*, 165; see also Menard, "Financing the Lowcountry Export Boom"; Coclanis, "The Hydra Head of Merchant Capital"; and Nash, "South Carolina and the Atlantic Economy." Cornelius Jaenen explored the long-standing presumption that French attitudes toward Native Americans were inherently more beneficent than those of the English in Jaenen, "French Attitudes towards Native Society."

7. For fur trade export totals, see Colonial Office, America and the West Indies, Virginia: Original Correspondence, Board of Trade, 1715–1717, 5/1317, p. 178, British Public Record Office, Kew, United Kingdom; also available in photocopy in British Records Calendar, 1712–1716, X77.594, pp. 1–2, North Carolina State Archives, Raleigh (hereinafter cited as NCSAR).

8. For Thomas Nairne's observations, see Nairne, *Muskhogean Journals*, 47, 50–51.

9. The Earl of Bellomont to the Lords of Trade, November 28, 1700, in O'Callaghan, ed., *Documents Relative to the Colonial History of New York*, 4:789.

10. "Conference with the Iroquois," July 19, 1701, in O'Callaghan, *Documents Relative to the Colonial History of New York*, 4:905.

11. For the relationship between the beaver market and the English hat industry, see Norton, *The Fur Trade in Colonial New York*, 102; see also Rich, "Russia and the Colonial Fur Trade." For increasing deerskin exports from South Carolina, see Colonial Office, America and the West Indies, Virginia: Original Correspondence, Board of Trade, 1715–1717, 5/1317, p. 178, British Public Record Office, Kew; photocopy in British Records Calendar, 1712–1716, X77.594, pp. 1–2, NCSAR.

12. Bellomont to the Lords of Trade, November 28, 1700, in O'Callaghan, ed., *Documents Relative to the Colonial History of New York*, 4:789; Rich, "Russia and the Colonial Fur Trade," 307–28, esp. 327.

13. "An Accompt Shewing the Quantity of Skins and Furrs Imported Annually into this Kingdom from Carolina from Christmas 1695 to Christmas 1715," in Salley, ed., *Records in the British Public Record Office Relating to South Carolina*, vol. 6 (microfilm frame 6:136), South Carolina State Department of Archives and History, Columbia.

14. For excellent studies of colonial shipping and of South Carolina's role in the Atlantic economy, see Walton, "New Evidence on Colonial Commerce"; Nash, "South Carolina and the Atlantic Economy"; Clark, "War Trade and Trade War." For a draft proposal of the Board of Trade's convoy system, see W. Popple to Josiah Burchet, December 15, 1703, in *Calendar of State Papers, Colonial Series: America and West Indies, 1702–1703*, 876. For the impact of the first convoy season on Virginia's

economy, see Col. Quarry to the Council of Trade and Plantations, May 30, 1704, in *Calendar of State Papers, Colonial Series: America and West Indies, 1704–1705*, 142.

15. For the Dutch trade prohibition, see Clark, "War Trade and Trade War," 271. For the enumeration of rice and its consequences, see Clowse, *Economic Beginnings*, 139; see also Nash, "The Organization of Trade and Finance in the Atlantic Economy," 77; Hardy, "Colonial South Carolina's Rice Industry and the Atlantic Economy," 115; Egnal, *New World Economies*, 100; and Coclanis, "Bitter Harvest."

16. For the failure of the Canadian trade, see Miquelon, *New France, 1701–1744*, 55–76; Eccles, "A Belated Review," 422–23; Eccles, *Frontenac*, 285–94. For an effort to gain perspective on the issue of "treaty trade" in light of more dominant market features, see Ray and Freeman, "*Give Us Good Measure*," 2–9, 231–45. Early efforts to apply the theoretical framework of treaty trade to the northern fur trade may be found in Rich, *The History of Hudson's Bay Company*, and Rich, "Trade Habits and Economic Motivation among the Indians of North America."

17. Bienville to Pontchartrain, February 20, 1707, in MPA:FD, 3:37–38.

18. For Pight, Probert, and Lucas's troubles, see Salley, ed., *Journal of the Commons House of Assembly of South Carolina, November 20, 1706–February 8, 1706/7*, 34. For the traders' credit problems in Charles Town, see William Smith v. Anthony Probert, Nov. 12, 1706, box 2A (microfilm frames 731–32, reel 1705–1707), South Carolina Court of Common Pleas, Judgement Rolls, South Carolina Department of Archives and History, Columbia (hereinafter cited as Judgement Rolls). Peter Mailhett v. John Pight, Jan. 17, 1706/7, box 2A, Judgement Rolls, microfilm frame 803, reel 1705–1707.

Also in the Judgement Rolls, see John Buckley v. Joseph Brynon, October 23, 1706, box 2A, microfilm frame 758, reel 1705–1707; Richard Beresford v. Phillip Gilliard, 1710, box 2C, frame 143, reel 1710–1711; John Buckley v. Shippy Allen, August 2, 1712, box 2D, frame 2, reel 1711–1712; Isaac Mazyck v. Shippy Allen and Alexander Nicholas, August 2, 1712, box 2D, frame 15, reel 1711–1712; Richard Beresford v. Richard Gower, June 22, 1711, box 3A, frame 206, reel 1711–1712; John Wright v. Samuel Hilden and John Cocket, August 13, 1712, box 2D, frame 81, reel 1711–1712; and William Smith v. John Wright, November 4, 1706, box 2A, frame 752, reel 1705–1707.

19. See John Buckley v. Joseph Brynon, October 23, 1706, box 2A, Judgement Rolls, microfilm frame 758, reel 1705–1707; Richard Beresford v. Phillip Gilliard, 1710, box 2C, frame 143, reel 1710–1711; John Buckley v. Shippy Allen, August 2, 1712, box 2D, frame 2, reel 1711–1712; Isaac Mazyck v. Shippy Allen and Alexander Nicholas, August 2, 1712, box 2D, frame 15, reel 1711–1712; Richard Beresford v. Richard Gower, June 22, 1711, box 3A, frame 206, reel 1711–1712; John Wright v. Samuel Hilden and John Cocket, August 13, 1712, box 2D, frame 81, reel 1711–1712; and William Smith v. John Wright, November 4, 1706, box 2A, frame 752, reel 1705–1707.

20. Waselkov, Cottier, and Sheldon, Archaeological Excavations at the Early Historic Creek Indian Town of Fusihatchee; Wesson, "Households and Hegemony"; Waselkov and Smith, "Upper Creek Archaeology," 247; Worth, "The Lower Creeks: Origins and Early History." For Creek town life and spatial organization, though at a later period, see Piker, Okfuskee, 1–12, 111–34. Preferred names are Muskhogee for the language and Muscogee for the people and culture.

21. For Carolina exports to Great Britain, see Colonial Office, American and West Indies, Virginia: Original Correspondence, Board of Trade, 1715–1717, 5/1317, p. 178, (British Public Record Office, Kew); photo copy in British Records Calendar, 1712–1716, X77.594, pp. 1–2, NCSAR. The exchange rate in terms of pounds Carolina currency per 100 pounds sterling jumped from 150 in 1712 to 300 in 1714. See McCusker, Money and Exchange, 222. For Kathryn E. Holland Braund's discussion, see Braund, Deerskins and Duffels, 69.

22. For Parliamentary legislation relating to the dressing of hides and skins, see "Reasons Humbly offer'd for Putting Hides and Skins Curied upon the Same Foot upon Exportation, as Hides or Skins that are Rough and Undrest," 1711, in Eighteenth-Century, British Library, London; also available in microfilm, Tulane University Archives, New Orleans, reel 260, item number 32. For South Carolina's efforts to legislate against the dressing of deerskins, see May 13, 1714, JCHA Green Transcripts, SCDAH, microfilm frame 4:258.

23. Evidence of the intense interest displayed by English leather workers may be found in "Reasons Humbly Offer'd for Putting Hides and Skins Curried upon the Same Foot upon Exportation as Hides and Skins that are Rough and Undrest," 1711, in *Eighteenth-Century*, microfilm reel 260, no. 32; "The Leather Sellers and Leather-Dressers Case, Humbly Offer'd to the Consideration of the Honourable the Knights, Citizens, and Burghesses of Great Britain in Parliament Assembled," 1711, *Eighteenth-Century*, reel 260, no. 30; the quoted material may be found in "The Case of the Dressers & Dealers in Leather, Humbly Offer'd to the Consideration of the Honourable the Knights, Citizens, and Burghesses of Great Britain in Parliament Assembled," 1711, *Eighteenth-Century*, reel 260, no. 31.

24. The Spanish province of Apalachee was located in northern central Florida, centering on present day Tallahassee, while Guale was located along the coast of Georgia.

25. For Thomas Nairne's observations, see Memorial to the Earl of Sunderland, July 10, 1708, in Nairne, *Muskhogean Journals*, 75. For Richard Haan's environmental/demographic argument, see Haan, "The 'Trade Do's Not Flourish.'" For the slaving activities of western Indians, see Memorial, in Nairne, *Muskhogean Journals*, 75. This is not to suggest, however, that western allies of South Carolina were not active in the slave trade earlier. By 1702, the French estimated that about five hundred Choctaws had already been enslaved by Chickasaw raiding parties in league with the English. See Iberville, "Journal Du Sieur D'Iberville," 4:517.

26. "An Act Prohibiting the Importation or Bringing in into this Colony any Indian Servants or Slaves," in Hoadly, ed., *The Public Records of the Colony of Connecticut*, 5:534; the Connecticut Act, passed in 1715, was a transcript of the 1712 Massachusetts Act.

27. *The Statutes at Large of Pennsylvania* (Philadelphia, 1896), 2:433, and *Records of the Colony of Rhode Island and Providence Plantations in New England* (Providence, 1856–1865), 4:134, both cited in Lauber, *Indian Slavery in Colonial Times*, 235–36. Batchellor, ed., *Laws of New Hampshire*, 53; Allinson, ed., *Acts of the General Assembly of the Province of New Jersey*, 31, cited in Lauber, *Indian Slavery in Colonial Times*, 236.

28. For a discussion of South Carolina's experiments with paper currency and the 1712 Bank Act, see Clowse, *Economic Beginnings*, 148–52; McCusker, *Money and Exchange*, 222.

29. Martinez to the King, July 5, 1715, Archivo General de Indias, Audiencia de Santo Domingo 843 (microfilm reel 15), John B. Stetson Collection, P. K. Yonge Library of Florida History, University of Florida, Gainesville (hereinafter cited as Stetson Collection, Gainesville).

30. The unfortunate phrase "forest proletariat" was coined by Harold Hickerson in "Fur Trade Colonialism and the North American Indians," 39. For a characteristic discussion of the transformation of south eastern Indians into producers for a world economy, see Braund, *Deerskins and Duffels*, 61. For the seventeenth-century Spanish trade with southeastern Indians, see Waselkov, "Seventeenth-Century Trade in the Colonial Southeast."

4. TRADE REGULATION AND THE BREAKDOWN OF DIPLOMACY

1. For quotes and a discussion of trade paths and diplomacy, see Piker, "'White & Clean & Contested,'" 331. For the symbolism of the colors red and white, see Lankford, "Red and White: Some Reflections on Southeastern Symbolism."

2. For the Assembly's position on trader behavior, see December 20, 1706, Salley, ed., *Journal of the Commons House of Assembly, November 20, 1706–February 8, 1706/7*, 36. For the regulatory act, see Cooper and McCord, eds., *Statutes at Large of South Carolina*, 2:309–17.

3. According to Verner Crane, this represented a victory of merchant interests over the prerogatives of the governor and his planter allies in the council; see Crane, *Southern Frontier*, 120. For a political history of the Commons House of Assembly during this period, see Moore, "Carolina Whigs," and Moore, "Royalizing South Carolina." For Converse D. Clowse's opinion, see Clowse, *Economic Beginnings*, 165.

4. December 20, 1706, Salley, *Journal . . . 1706/7*, 36.

5. For the power struggle between the Assembly and the governor, see January 31, 1706/7, Salley, Journal . . . 1706/7, 39–42. For the constitutional context surrounding the regulatory act, see Moore, "Royalizing South Carolina," 258–67; see also Sirmans, Colonial South Carolina, 91–92. For the imperial implications of the act, see Hewitt, "The State in the Planters' Service," 53–55.

6. May 4, 1714–May 7, 1714, McDowell, Journals of the Commissioners, 51–55.

7. May 5, 1714, McDowell, Journals of the Commissioners, 55.

8. JCHA Green Transcripts, SCDAH, microfilm frame 4:133.

9. May 6, 1714, McDowell, Journals of the Commissioners, 56; May 5, 1714, p. 54.

10. May 15, 1712, JCHA Green Transcripts, SCDAH, microfilm frame 4:29; May 4, 1714–May 5, 1714, McDowell, Journals of the Commissioners, 53–55.

11. For incidents involving both Welch and Dixon, see September 12, 1713, McDowell, Journals of the Commissioners, 50.

12. For the evolution of the Indian slave trade, see Gallay, Indian Slave Trade. For a discussion of war captives who remained in Cherokee territory, see Perdue, Slavery and the Evolution of Cherokee Society, 3–18. For the bipartite nature of the slave trade, see Ramsey, "A Coat for 'Indian Cuffy'"; also see chapter 1 of the present volume.

13. May 5, 1714, McDowell, Journals of the Commissioners, 54–55.

14. The best introduction to the early history of Nairne's problems as agent may be found in Alexander Moore's introduction to Nairne, Muskhogean Journals, 12, 16–17. For examples of Wright's nuisance suits, see the following items in South Carolina Court of Common Pleas, Judgement Rolls, SCDAH: John Wright v. John Cochrane, Jan. 10, 1713/14, box 5A, microfilm frame 268, reel 1714; John Wright v. John Cochrane, April 19, 1714, box 6A, frames 490–94, reel 1714; John Wright v. Alexander Parris, Jan. 16, 1712/13, box 4A, frame 8, reel 1713); John Wright v. John Beauchamp, Oct. 1714, box 5A, frame 310, reel 1714. For an example of a copy-cat suit, see Edmund Ellis v. Alexander Parris, Sept. 21, 1714, box 6A, frame 498, reel 1715.

15. JCHA Green Transcripts, SCDAH, microfilm frame 4:272, 285). For

a common example of the coordination which appears to have existed
between Messrs. Wright and Pight, see frame 4:289. For information
on Pight's time at the Wright plantation, see Gregorie, ed., *Records of
the Court of Chancery of South Carolina, 1671–1779*, in *American Legal Records*, 6:189.

16. Aug. 31, 1714, McDowell, *Journals of the Commissioners*, 59.

17. JCHA Green Transcripts, SCDAH, microfilm frame 4:289ff. For the
complete preoccupation of Nairne and the commissioners, see Mc-
Dowell, *Journals of the Commissioners*, 60–65.

18. "Journal of the March of the Carolinians," 334–35.

19. Ivers, "Scouting the Inland Passage," 125. For Yamasee diplomatic
activities among neighboring Indian nations, see Governor Francisco
de Corcoles y Martinez to King Philip V, July 5, 1715, Archivo General
de Indias, Audiencia de Santo Domingo 843 (microfilm reel 15),
Stetson Collection, Gainesville.

20. April 12, 1715, McDowell, *Journals of the Commissioners*, 65.

21. "Letter of Charles Rodd to His Employer in London," May 8, 1715, in
*Calendar of State Papers, Colonial Series: America and West Indies, August
1714–December 1715*, 28:167–68; also see Verner Crane's account of
the incident in Crane, *Southern Frontier*, 168–69. The only version of
these events to depart from Crane's original portrait is Oatis, *Colonial
Complex*, 124–28. Oatis was the first scholar to question the assumption
of predetermined action and to propose that the Yamasees were engaged in legitimate debate over the issue of war or peace while Nairne
slept. He argued that they ultimately experienced a crisis of faith in
the promises of English officials. For the standard account, see Crane,
Southern Frontier, 168.

22. Letter of Capt. Jonathan St. Lo to Burchett and Enclosure, July 12,
1715, British Public Record Office, Admiralty Office, 1:2451; photocopy
in British Records Calendar, 1712–1716, 72.1409: pp. 1–4, NCSAR.

23. Letter of Capt. St. Lo and Enclosure, July 12, 1715, pp. 1–4.

24. Martinez to the King, July 5, 1715, Archivo General de Indias, Audiencia de Santo Domingo 843 (microfilm reel 15), Stetson Collection, Gainesville. Francis LeJau reported in May 1715 that as many

as twenty-five Yamasee peace advocates had been killed; see LeJau to
the Secretary, May 14, 1715, in LeJau, *Carolina Chronicle*, 156.

25. Oatis, *Colonial Complex*, 112–39.

5. THE HEART OF THE ALLIANCE

1. Letter of Captain Jonathan St. Lo to Burchett with Enclosure, July 12,
   1715, British Public Record Office, Admiralty Office, 1:2451; photocopy in British Records Calendar, 1712–1716, 72.1409: pp. 1–4,
   NCSAR. Governor Francisco de Corcoles y Martinez to the King, July
   5, 1715, Archivo General de Indias, Audiencia de Santo Domingo
   843 (microfilm reel 36), 58-1-30/42, Stetson Collection, Gainesville.
   For excellent discussions of the Lower Creek/Yamasee diplomatic
   mission to St. Augustine, see Hahn, *Invention of the Creek Nation*, 83–83,
   and Oatis, *Colonial Complex*, 113.

2. Robert Johnson to the Board of Trade, January 12, 1719/20, RBPRO,
   microfilm frame 7:233–50, SCDAH. These claims of universal support came from a very select group of voices: almost exclusively
   Yamasee. The nationality of the Huspah king, the author of the legendary Yamasee letter, should be self-evident, but two official members
   of the May 27 visitation to St. Augustine were also Yamasees. The other
   members of the delegation identified themselves as Lower (or Ocheese)
   Creek or as Apalachicolas (the Spanish designation for Lower Creeks).
   One of the latter, moreover, was almost certainly a Yamasee headman
   seeking to redefine himself as a Creek leader. The documents contain
   no known examples of any similar claims about the initial extent of
   the alliance made by any other nation in the Southeast. In fact, the
   Lower Creek delegates who visited the Spanish that spring may not
   have claimed 161 allies either, since the deerskin strands were presented
   and explained to Governor Martinez by one of the Yamasee emissaries. See Martinez to the King, July 5, 1715, Archivo General de Indias,
   Audiencia de Santo Domingo 843 (microfilm reel 36), Stetson Collection, Gainesville. Also see Hahn, *Invention of the Creek Nation*, 84.

3. "Letter of Charles Rodd to His Employer in London," May 8, 1715, in

Calendar of State Papers, Colonial Office Series: America and West Indies, August
1714–December 1715, 28:167.

4. Crane, Southern Frontier, 164; Gallay, The Formation of a Planter Elite,
11–12; the lower towns consisted of Altamaha, Okete (Eketee), Chechesee, and Euhaw, while the upper towns included Pocotaligo, Huspah, Saupalau, Sadketche, Pocosabo, and Tomatley. See Green, "The
Search for Altamaha," 24–25. For a discussion of these ethnic movements and affinities, see Hall, "Making an Indian People."

5. For De Soto's encounter with central Georgia chiefdoms, see "The
Relation of Ranjel," in Narratives of the Career of Hernando de Soto, 87–91.
For the location of the Yamasee town of Tuscagy, see Stanyarne Land
Plat, February 14, 1700/01, 0275.00, Pringle-Garden Family Papers,
South Carolina Historical Society Archives, Charleston. The first
Yamasee town to move into South Carolina appears to have been
Altamaha, which, following a disagreement with the Spanish, re-
treated first from the Georgia coast into interior Georgia and then
to St. Helena, South Carolina, in 1684; see Covington, "Stuart's Town,"
9. For Yamasee settlement among the Cowetas and Kasitas of the
Lower Creeks, see Letter of Caleb Westbrooke, February 21, 1684/5,
RBPRO, 2:8–9.

6. For examples of English usage, see March 25, 1713, McDowell, Journals
of the Commissioners, 42; Nairne, Muskhogean Journals, 44; and Crane,
"The Origin of the Name of the Creek Indians." For the peoples settled
on the river, see Marvin Smith, Archaeology of Aboriginal Culture Change,
136–37; Juricek, "The Westo Indians," 138. For many years, archaeolo-
gists were at loggerheads regarding the cultural affiliations of the
historic period occupation of Ocmulgee, defined as the Ocmulgee
Fields Culture; see Russell, "Lamar and the Creeks." More recently,
excavations in the Chattahoochee River Valley have provided better
evidence for speculations about the origins of the Ocmulgee Fields
Culture; see Knight, "Ocmulgee Fields Culture and the Historical
Development of Creek Ceramics." For the presence of Apalachee
families, see "Governor and Council to the Lords Proprietors," September 17, 1708, RBPRO, 5:208.

7. Ocheese was a Hitchiti word applied to Muscogee speakers. It meant

simply "people of foreign speech." See Swanton, *Early History of the Creek Indians*, 148. Hudson, Smith, and DePratter, "Hernando De Soto Expedition." For the location of Ocmulgee town, see Hudson et al., "Hernando De Soto Expedition," 70. For the persistence of Ocheesehatche, see Benjamin Hawkins, "A Sketch of the Creek Country in the Years 1798 and 1799," in *Collections of the Georgia Historical Society*, vol. 3, pt. 1, p. 83.

8. Swanton, *Early History of the Creek Indians*, 176. In 1922 Swanton identified the occupants of the mound site as Hitchiti Town, based mainly on cartographic evidence from the 1755 Mitchell map in Cummings, ed., *The Southeast in Early Maps*, pl. 59. Alternatively, Verner W. Crane identified the town as Ocmulgee on the basis of William Bartram's mid-eighteenth-century reference to the site as the "Oakmulgee fields"; see Crane, *Southern Frontier*, 133. For evidence that supports Crane's thesis, see Mason, "Archaeology of Ocmulgee Old Fields," 224–30. Benjamin Hawkins also believed Ocmulgee to have resided at the mound site; see "Letters of Benjamin Hawkins," in *Collections of the Georgia Historical Society* (1916), 9:173. Archaeologist Gregory A. Waselkov has recently suggested that the site may even have been occupied by several towns clustered closely together; see Waselkov, "The Macon Trading House and Early European-Indian Contact," 192. For information on the temple mounds and historic period settlements among them, see Mason, "Archaeology of Ocmulgee Old Fields," 53, 71–75, 62, 69, fig. 2-3, 236; and Williams, "The Origins of the Macon Plateau Site," 130. Archaeologist A. R. Kelly excavated the trading house in the 1930s and '40s; see Kelly, "The Macon Trading Post," and Kelly, *A Preliminary Report on Archeological Explorations at Macon, Georgia*.

9. For the early history of the Apalachicolas on the Chattahoochee, see Bolton, "Spanish Resistance," 119, 121, and Sturtevant, "Spanish-Indian Relations in Southeastern North America," 71. For archaeological work at Palachacola Town, see Caldwell, "Palachacolas Town." For the quote about significance of the site as a fording place and trail nexus, see "An Act for the Better Strengthening and Securing the Frontiers...," ratified February 23, 1722, in Trott, *Laws of the Province of South Carolina*, item no. 484, microfilm frame 399, reel GR 032,

SCDAH (item number refers to Trott's own designation for the entry); and Myer, "The Trail System of the Southeastern United States in the Colonial Period," fold-out map; Ivers, *Colonial Forts*, 69. For the role of Palachacola as a servicing point for the trade, see "Governor & Councill to the Lords Proprietors," September 17, 1708, RBPRO, 5:207–8.

10. For documentary evidence of Oconee Town's presence on the Chattahoochee, see Bolton, "Spanish Resistance," 121n; additional insight into the archaeology of Oconee Town was provided by Mark Williams, Department of Anthropology, University of Georgia, personal communication, 1996. Also see Smith, *Archaeology of Aboriginal Culture Change*, 80. For the Mississippian period legacy of the Oconees, see Williams, "Growth and Decline of the Oconee Province." For the linguistic and cultural history of the Oconees, see Milanich, "The Western Tumuccua," 60–61, 71–72. The name Oconee itself appears to be a Hitchiti term, meaning "place of the skunk"; Mark Williams, personal communication.

11. "Governor and Council to the Lords Proprietors," September 17, 1708, RBPRO, 5:208; for Apalachee and Euchee population figures and quotes on burdeners, see "Exact account," RBPRO, microfilm frame 7:238, SCDAH. Nairne, *Muskhogean Journals*, 51.

12. "Governor & Council to the Lords Proprietors," September 17, 1708, RBPRO, 5:208. "Thomas Nairne to the Reverend Edward Marston," August 20, 1705, cited in Klingberg, "Early Attempts at Indian Education in South Carolina: A Documentary," 2. For the invasion of Apalachee, see James Moore, "An Account of what the Army did Under the Command of Col. Moore, in His Expedition Last Winter, Against the Spaniards and Spanish Indians," in Carroll, ed., *Historical Collections of South Carolina*, 2:575; Hann, *Apalachee: The Land between the Rivers*, 294–95; and Gallay, *Indian Slave Trade*, 144–49, 148.

13. June 12, 1707, Salley, ed., *Journals of the Commons House, June 5, 1707–July 19, 1707*, 27–28. May 15, 1712, JCHA Green Transcripts, SCDAH, microfilm frame 4:29, and June 3, 1712, microfilm frame 4:65.

14. For the beginnings of trade among these nations, see Milling, *Red Carolinians*, 84–85; *Letter of Caleb Westbrooke*, Feb. 21, 1684/5, RBPRO, 2:8–9; Covington, "Stuart's Town," 9–10; Bolton, "Spanish Re-

sistance," 115–30; McDowell, *Journals of the Commissioners*, 3–65. For a narrative discussion of the Yamasee War, see Crane, *Southern Frontier*, 162–86.

15. "Letter of Charles Rodd to His Employer in London," May 8, 1715, in *Calendar of State Papers, Colonial Office Series: America and West Indies, August 1714–December 1715*, 28:166–69 (hereinafter cited as *Calendar of State Papers*).

16. For cattle ranching in Colleton County, see Rowland, Moore, and Rogers, *History of Beaufort County*, 85–88; and Otto, "The Origins of Cattle Ranching in Colonial South Carolina, 1670–1715," 121–22. For Lower Creek involvement in the livestock trade, see Diego Pena to Don Juan de Ayala Escobar, Governor of Florida, September 20, 1717, in Boyd, ed., "Documents Describing the Second and Third Expeditions of Lieutenant Diego Pena," 116, 126. For the Carolinian perspective, see Jno. Tate to Sir John Duddleston, September 16, 1715, *Calendar of State Papers*, 28:351.

17. Crane, *Southern Frontier*, 169. Oatis, *Colonial Complex*, 126. William Osborne to the Secretary, May 28, 1715, microfilm frame 99, reel PR0085, Society for the Propagation of the Gospel in Foreign Parts, Selected Pages Relating to South Carolina from Library of Congress Transcripts of the Papers of the Society for the Propagation of the Gospel in Foreign Parts, Series A, Contemporary Copies of Letters Received, vols. 7–17, 1712–1723, SCDAH (hereinafter cited as SPG transcripts).

18. Letter of Capt. St. Lo with Enclosure, July 12, 1715, photocopy in British Records Calendar, 1712–1716, 72.1409: pp. 1–4, NCSAR. For the locations of the sites, see Ivers, *Colonial Forts*, 8, 75–76.

19. Letter of Capt. St. Lo with Enclosure, July 12, 1715, pp. 1–4. Letter of Charles Rodd, May 8, 1715, *Calendar of State Papers*, 28:168. Milling, *Red Carolinians*, 154.

20. For the battle of the Combahee and patterns of retreat, see Governor Craven to Lord Townshend, May 23, 1715, *Calendar of State Papers*, 28:228; Letter of Charles Rodd, May 8, 1715, *Calendar of State Papers*, 28:168–69; June 13, 1715, *Boston Newsletter*; Crane, *Southern Frontier*, 171; and Oatis, *Colonial Complex*, 144.

21. Juan de Ayala y Escobar to the King, April 18, 1717, Archivo General de Indias, Audiencia de Santo Domingo 843, microfilm, Stetson Collection, Gainesville. For an excellent analysis of the Escobar census and others following the Yamasee War, see Hann, "St. Augustine's Fallout."

22. Juan de Ayala y Escobar to the King, April 18, 1717. Hann, "St. Augustine's Fallout." For the English census, see Johnson to the Board of Trade, January 12, 1719/20, RBPRO, microfilm frame 7:238–39, SCDAH.

23. May 7, 1715, JCHA Green Transcripts, SCDAH, microfilm frame 4:395; see also Commissioners Appointed by the Commons House of Assembly of South Carolina to Correspond with Jos. Boon and Richard Beresford, August 25, 1715, Calendar of State Papers, 28:301. Diego Pena to Don Juan de Ayala Escobar, September 20, 1717, in Boyd, "Documents Describing the Second and Third Expeditions of Lieutenant Diego Pena," 123.

24. Samuel Eveleigh to Messrs. Boone and Berresford, October 7, 1715, Calendar of State Papers, 28:296–97. September 26, 1715, Boston Newsletter. For the "Daufuskie Fight," see also Ivers, "Scouting the Inland Passage," 117–29, and Oatis, Colonial Complex, 145. The location of the ambush may be "Bloody Point" on the southern tip of Daufuskie Island. The name derives from a Yamasee attack on an English scout boat crew stationed there in 1728, but the geography of the site matches the description in the Eveleigh letter. Rowland, Moore, and Rogers, History of Beaufort County, 98, 106–7, consider "Bloody Point" to be the site of the "Dawfuskie Fight" of 1715. For the location of Jackson's Bridge, see Crane, Southern Frontier, 171–72, and Ivers, Colonial Forts, 8.

25. The quote is from Oatis, Colonial Complex, 145.

26. Eveleigh to Boon and Berresford, October 7, 1715, Calendar of State Papers, 28:296–97; Commissioners of the Commons House to Jos. Boon and Richard Berresford, August 25, 1715, Calendar of State Papers, 28:299–301; August 15, 1715, Boston Newsletter. LeJau, Carolina Chronicle, 161. Combined Lower Creek and Yamasee forces were still attacking this target, Pon Pon, as late as 1727. See Salley, ed., Journal of Colonel 21.

27. Eveleigh to Boon and Berresford, October 7, 1715, *Calendar of State Papers*, 28:296–97; Commissioners of the Commons House to Jos. Boon and Richard Berresford, August 25, 1715, *Calendar of State Papers*, 28:299–301.

28. LeJau, *Carolina Chronicle*, 161. Samuel Eveleigh referred to them as "the Apalatchee and other Southern Indians." See Eveleigh to Boon and Berresford, July 19, 1715, *Calendar of State Papers*, 28:299.

29. William Treadway Bull to the Secretary, August 10, 1715 SPG transcripts, SCDAH, Series A, vols. 7–17, 1712–1723, microfilm frame 49, reel PR0085. John Yahola, Muskhogee Red Stick Society, personal communication, November 2004.

30. William Bartram, "Travels Through North and South Carolina, East and West Florida, the Cherokee Country, the Extensive Territories of the Muscogulges, or Creek Confederacy, and the Country of the Chactaws; Containing an Account of the Soil and Natural Productions of Those Regions, Together with Observations on the Manners of the Indians," in Waselkov and Braund, eds., *William Bartram on the Southeastern Indians*, 91n. For Emperor Brims's views as filtered through an English lens, see May 24, 1717, JCHA Green Transcripts, SCDAH, microfilm frame 4:269–91. For Cherokeeleechee's recollections, see Patrick Mackay to James Oglethorpe, March 29, 1735, in Lane, ed., *General Oglethorpe's Georgia*, 1:152. See also Oatis, *Colonial Complex*, 127–8; and Hahn, *Invention of the Creek Nation*, 84. For the presence of "malcontents" among the Lower Creeks, see Boyd, ed., "Diego Pena's Expedition to Apalachee and Apalachicolo in 1716," 26.

31. Corkran, *The Creek Frontier*; Oatis, *Colonial Complex*, 202–5.

32. May 25, 1722, Journals of the Upper House of Assembly, 1721–1726, microfilm reel St 0698, frame 7, SCDAH. "Tobias Fitch's Journal to the Creeks," in Mereness, ed., *Travels in the American Colonies*, 182.

6. AUXILIARY CONFEDERATES

1. For a typical reference to the "confederate" nations, see May 10, 1715, JCHA Green Transcripts, SCDAH, microfilm frame 4:407).

2. For the origins of trade, see Crane, *Southern Frontier*, 45; Pryce Hughes

to the Duchess of Ormond, 1713, in Five Pryce Hughes Autograph Letters, Proposing a Welsh Colony, 1713, MS, South Caroliniana Library, University of South Carolina, Columbia; La Harpe, *Historical Journal of the Establishment of the French in Louisiana*, 89.

3. For the positive benefits of trade competition among the Catawbas, see Merrell, *Indians' New World*, 68. For a discussion of the same process in the Mississippi Valley, see Usner, "Economic Relations in the Southeast until 1783." For Cherokee access to alternative trade, see Hatley, *Dividing Paths*, 22. Evidence of Virginia's continuing interest in fur trade commodities may be found in Colonial Office, America and the West Indies, Virginia: Original Correspondence, Board of Trade, 1715–1717, 5/1317, p. 178, British Public Record Office, Kew; photocopy in British Records Calendar, 1712–1716, X77.594, pp. 1–2, NCSAR.

4. Merrell, *Indians' New World*, 68. For Virginia exports, see Colonial Office, 5/1317, p. 178.

5. Merrell, *Indians' New World*, 69–70; Merrell, "'Our Bond of Peace,'" 209. Some South Carolinians suspected that Virginia might even have encouraged the Yamasee War as a way of defeating their Charles Town trade rivals. See, for instance, Abel Kettleby and Other Merchants and Planters Trading to Carolina," 1715, *Calendar of State Papers*, 28:236.

6. The Waxhaws were often referred to as Flatheads because many of them still practiced the ancient custom of head deformation among infants. The Iroquois may have been using the term indiscriminately to designate Indians in the vicinity of the Waxhaws. "Account of a Conference with the Iroquois," Colonial Office, America and West Indies, New York: Original Correspondence, Board of Trade, 1710–1715, 5/1050, p. 640; photocopy in British Records Calendar, 1712–1716, X77.572, pp. 1–5, NCSAR.

7. John Evans, "Journal of a Virginia Indian Trader in North and South Carolina," in the South Caroliniana Library, University of South Carolina, Columbia. For James Merrell's discussion of the Evans journal, see Merrell, *Indians' New World*, 69–74.

8. Governor Spotswood to Coll. Hunter, March 2, 1715/16, in Palmer, ed., *Calendar of Virginia State Papers and Other Manuscripts*, 1:178.

9. Hatley, *Dividing Paths*, 22–23.
10. "Journal of the March of the Carolinians." May 11, 1715, JCHA Green Transcripts, SCDAH microfilm frame 4:409–10, and May 10, 1715, microfilm frame 4:407).
11. Crane, *Southern Frontier*, 172. "Journal of the March of the Carolinians." Samuel Eveleigh to Messrs. Boone and Beresford, July 19, 1715, *Calendar of State Papers*, 28:297–98.
12. "Journal of the March of the Carolinians," 334–35.
13. August 18, 1713, McDowell, *Journals of the Commissioners*, 49.
14. "Report on Plantations in America and French Settlements and Encroachments with a Proposal for a Colonial Organization," September 8, 1721, Cholmondeley Manuscripts, papers 84, item 11, Cambridge University Archives, Cambridge, United Kingdom.
15. Giraud, "France and Louisiana in the Early Eighteenth Century," 657, 668; also see Allain, *Not Worth a Straw*.
16. Giraud, *History of French Louisiana*, 1:204–5.
17. Giraud, *History of French Louisiana*, 1:206–7.
18. Giraud, *History of French Louisiana*, 1:206–7.
19. Usner, *Indians, Settlers, and Slaves*, 27; Surrey, *Commerce of Louisiana*, 342.
20. Brown, "Early Indian Trade in the Development of South Carolina," 124; Surrey, *Commerce of Louisiana*, 344.
21. Brasseaux, "Cadillac-Duclos Affair," 257–69.
22. Brasseaux, "Cadillac-Duclos Affair," 264, 266, 270.
23. Brasseaux, "Cadillac-Duclos Affair," 266–67.
24. Woods, *French-Indian Relations*, 33–34.
25. Woods, *French-Indian Relations*, 34.
26. Brasseaux, "Cadillac-Duclos Affair," 269–70.
27. Bienville to Pontchartrain, June 15, 1715, in Rowland and Sanders, eds., *Mississippi Provincial Archives: French Dominion* (MPA:FD), 3:183; La Harpe, *Historical Journal*, 89. For Conchak Emiko's pro-English activism, see Beaudouin to Salmon, November 23, 1732, MPA:FD 1:156–58. The English mockery of Cadillac reads "ces Anglais repondirent qu'ils se mocquaient du gouverneur de la Louisiane et de 40 ou 50 coquins qui y etaient." See "Disposition des Savauges de la Louisiane

et des anglais de Caroline," April 29, 1716, in General Correpondence of Louisiana, Ministry of the Colonies, Series C 13, Archives Nationale. Aix en Provence, France; also available in microfilm, Tulane University Archives, New Orleans.

28. La Harpe, *Historical Journal*, 91.

29. McWilliams, ed. and trans., *Fleur de Lys and Calumet*, 162.

30. This incident was clearly behind Bienville's decision to establish New Orleans in 1718. Hughes himself predicted that "the french when sensible of our designs will probably send some settlers to our neighborhood from Moville [*sic*]." See Five Pryce Hughes Autograph Letters, Proposing a Welsh colony, 1713, MS, South Caroliniana Library. "Bienville to Pontchartrain," June 15, 1715, MPA:FD, 3:182.

31. Pryce Hughes Letters, South Caroliniana Library.

32. November 21, 1713, McDowell, *Journals of the Commissioners*, 52.

33. November 21, 1713, McDowell, *Journals of the Commissioners*, 52.

34. For more on Pryce Hughes, see Barker, "Pryce Hughes, Colony Planner."

35. Bienville to Pontchartrain, June 15, 1715, MPA:FD, 3:182.

36. Bienville to Pontchartrain, June 15 1715, MPA:FD, 3:181.

37. Bienville to Pontchartrain, June 15 1715, MPA:FD, 3:181.

38. Bienville to Pontchartrain, June 15 1715, MPA:FD, 3:183.

39. Bienville to Pontchartrain, September 1, 1715, MPA:FD, 3:186.

40. French documents are consistently vague about the exact identity of the Indians involved in Bienville's gambit, but they must certainly have been predominantly Choctaw and Upper Creek, especially Alabamas. According to David Corkran, Bienville "operated through the Alabamas to work up Creek determination to take arms against the trading tyrants." See Corkran, *The Creek Frontier*, 58. For Bienville's Mobile hoax, see Bienville to Pontchartrain, September 1, 1715, MPA:FD, 3:186–87.

41. For the Alabama trade, see Bienville to Pontchartrain, June 15, 1715, MPA:FD, 3:183; for the Mobile conference (and Bienville's first clear reference to the Yamasee War), see Bienville to Pontchartrain, September 1, 1715, MPA:FD, 3:186–87. David Corkran regarded Bienville's actions as one of the prime causes of the Yamasee War. See Corkran, *The Creek Frontier*, 57.

42. "Disposition des Sauvages de la Louisiane et des Anglais de la Caroline," April 29, 1716, Series C, General Correspondence, Archives des Colonies, Archives Nationale, Aix en Provence, France; also available in microfilm at Tulane University Rare Books and Manuscripts, New Orleans.

43. Bienville was clearly aware of these three divisions as early as 1702. See Iberville, *Iberville's Gulf Journals*, 174. For the structure of the Choctaw Confederacy, see O'Brien, *Choctaws in a Revolutionary Age*, 13–14. Also see Galloway, "Choctaw Factionalism and Civil War, 1746–1750," 123–25; Galloway, *Choctaw Genesis, 1500–1700*, 1–4, 193–99, 312–15; Galloway, "Formation of Historic Tribes and the French Colonial Period," 58; Galloway, "Confederacy as a Solution to Chiefdom Dissolution," 408–9; White, *Roots of Dependency*, 37.

44. La Harpe, *Historical Journal*, 89. Beaudouin to Salmon, November 23, 1732, MPA:FD, 1:156–58. Richard White argues that Chicacha Outlacta was not necessarily Conchak Emiko's immediate brother but merely a close relative from the same "Iksa" or lineage. See White, *Roots of Dependency*, 48.

45. O'Brien, *Choctaws in a Revolutionary Age*, 1–8. For the environmental and market aspects of this transformation, see White, *Roots of Dependency*, 97–111.

46. For Upper Creek and Chickasaw slave raids against the Choctaws, see Nairne, *Muskhogean Journals*. By 1702, the French estimated that slave raids by the Chickasaws alone had carried away 500 Choctaw prisoners and left 1,800 dead. See Iberville, *Iberville's Gulf Journals*, 172. In 1706, the Chickasaws took 300 Choctaw prisoners for sale as slaves. See La Harpe, *Historical Journal*, 73. Also see White, *Roots of Dependency*, 35; and Gallay, *Indian Slave Trade*, 131–32, 142–43, 185, 288–92, 297–98.

47. McWilliams, *Fleur de Lys and Calumet*, 163.

48. For the political significance of trade among southeastern Indians, see Martin, "Southeastern Indians and the English Trade in Skins and Slaves," 308.

49. For a typically hasty generalization concerning Chickasaw loyalties, see Ramsey, "'Something Cloudy in Their Looks,'" 73. For Alan Gallay's

insightful discussion of Chickasaw involvement in the Yamasee War, see Gallay, *Indian Slave Trade*, 334–35. For Thomas Nairne's comments, see Nairne, *Muskhogean Journals*, 50. For Chickasaw allegations against Lower Creek warriors, see "Journal of the March of the Carolinians," 335.

50. For French relations with the Chickasaws and Choctaws, see Usner, *Indians, Settlers, and Slaves*, 26. For the Chickasaw delegation to Charles Town, see December 17, 1714, JCHA Green Transcripts, SCDAH, microfilm frame 4:334.

51. For the testimony of captured native prisoners, see William Guy to the Society, September 20, 1715, SPG transcripts, SCDAH, Series B, vol. 4, microfilm pt. 1, frame 25. For a Carolinian perspective on this growing factionalism, see Robert Maule to the Society, February 18, 1715/16, SPG transcripts, SCDAH, Series B, vol. 4, microfilm pt. 1, frames 202–5.

52. For Catawba setbacks, see Merrell, *Indians' New World*, 76–77. For Iroquois involvement, see Governor Hunter to the Council of Trade and Plantations, July 25, 1715, *Calendar of State Papers*, 28:243; Merrell, *Indians' New World*, 78. For Catawba overtures to Alexander Spotswood, see Merrell, *Indians' New World*, 77–79.

53. For a discussion of Catawba involvement in the Yamasee War, see Merrell, *Indians' New World*, 76–77. For French and Spanish supplies, see Committee of the Assembly of South Carolina to Messrs. Boone and Beresford, August 6, 1716, *Calendar of State Papers, Colonial Office Series: America and West Indies, January 1716–July 1717*, 29:219–20. For the growing use of bows and arrows, see LeJau to John Chamberlain, August 22, 1715, in LeJau, *Carolina Chronicle*, 162.

54. Jno. Tate to Sir John Duddleston, September 16, 1715, *Calendar of State Papers, 1714–1715*, 28:351.

55. LeJau to the Secretary, October 3, 1715, in LeJau, *Carolina Chronicle*, 167.

56. LeJau to the Secretary, October 3, 1715, and November 28, 1715; LeJau to John Robinson, Bishop of London, December 1, 1715, all in LeJau, *Carolina Chronicle*, 167–71. For initial English jubilation over this turn of events, see LeJau to the Secretary, November 28, 1715, 169. Hatley, *Dividing Paths*, 24.

57. "Journal of the March of the Carolinians," 324–52.
58. "Journal of the March of the Carolinians," 324–52; Crane, *Southern Frontier,* 182–86.
59. LeJau to the Secretary, March 19, 1716, in LeJau, *Carolina Chronicle,* 175. For continuing Lower Creek resentment, see "Tobias Fitch's Journal to the Creeks," in Mereness, *Travels in the American Colonies,* 182.
60. October 24, 1717, McDowell, *Journals of the Commissioners,* 222. Hatley, *Dividing Paths,* 26–28.
61. The French text reads: "Chalakis . . . etaient venus les trouver de la part du Governeur de la Caroline pour les engager a recevoir les anglais dans leur village." The French description of the Illinois response reads: "Les Illinois ont tue aussi trois Chalakis et en jirent bruler deux vivents." See "Disposition des Sauvages de la Louisiane et des Anglais de la Caroline," April 29, 1716, Series C, General Correspondence, Archives des Colonies, Archives Nationale, Paris, France; also available in microfilm at Tulane University Rare Books and Manuscripts, New Orleans). The French text for the attack on Kaskaskia reads "un gros party de la Nation Charaquia a ete en guerre aux Cascasquia Village Illinois qui en ont tue et faits prissonnier quantite et dix ou douze Francois des habitants"; see "Bienville to the Navy Council," January 20, 1716, Ministry of the Colonies, Series C, c. 13, General Correspondence of Louisiana, Archives Nationale, Aix en Provence. An English translation of this letter is listed as "Bienville to Raudot," January 20, 1716, in MPA:FD, 3:197–200.
62. The French text reads "depuis que Mr. de la Mothe a passé ches eux en moutant le descendent du voyage qu'il fait aux Islinoi sur lequel leur avoit refuse les calumet de paix qu'ils [illegible] luy chanter, ce qui [illegible] tres gros insulte [illegible] touttes les nations sauvage [illegible] surtout du grand chef des Francois," and "il semble que Mr. de la Mothe ait inspire la guerre a toutes les nations etablier sure le fleuve Saint Louis." "Bienville to the Navy Council (or Pontchartrain)," January 20, 1716, Ministry of the Colonies, Series C, c. 13, General Correspondence of Louisiana, Archives Nationale, Aix en Provence; also available in "Bienville to Raudot," January 20, 1716, MPA:FD, 3:198. For a perspective on the calumet faux pas from one of Ca-

dillac's most bitter adversaries, see "Duclos to Pontchartrain," June 7, 1716, MPA:FD, 3:208–9. These incidents have been discussed in several secondary works, but no scholar has yet considered them in the context of the Yamasee War. See for instance Usner, *Indians, Settlers, and Slaves*, 29; Giraud, *History of French Louisiana*, 2:78; and Woods, "The French and the Natchez Indians in Louisiana."

63. Duclos to Pontchartrain, June 7, 1716, MPA:FD, 3:204–5.
64. Duclos to Pontchartrain, June 7, 1716, MPA:FD, 3:204–5.

7. MONSTERS AND MEN

1. August 1715, JCHA Green Transcripts, SCDAH, microfilm frame 4 (1712–1716): 389–95.
2. Abel Kettleby and Other Planters and Merchants trading to Carolina to the Council of Trade and Plantations, July 18, 1715, *Calendar of State Papers*, 28:236. Letter of Capt. Jonathan St. Lo to Burchett with Enclosure, July 12, 1715, British Public Record Office, Admiralty Office 1:2451; photocopy in British Records Calendar, 1712–1716, 72.1409: pp. 1–4, NCSAR. John Squyre to the Presbytery, September 18, 1715, 1/2/35, folios 193–94, General Assembly Papers, 1715, Church of Scotland, Scottish Record Office, Edinburgh, Scotland; also available on microfilm in British Records Calendar, 1712–1716, microfilm reel 2.5.278, NCSAR.
3. Edmund Morgan's discussion of Anglo-Powhatan relations during this period, and especially of the social consequences of the 1622 attack, remains informative. See Morgan, *American Slavery*. For an innovative perspective on Anglo-Powatan relations, see Gleach, *Powhatan's World and Colonial Virginia*. For English justifications of the violence of the Pequot War, see Karr, "'Why should you be so Furious?'" For a discourse study of King Philip's War, see Lepore, *The Name of War*.
4. For discussions of Carolina's coastal nations, see Crane, *Southern Frontier*, 3–21; and Merrell, *Indians' New World*. For the participation of "settlement" Indians, see William Treadway Bull to the Secretary, August 15, 1715, SPG transcripts, SCDAH, Series A, vols. 7–17, micro-

film frame 49; and Governor Craven to Lord Townshend, May 23, 1715, *Calendar of State Papers*, 28:228.

5. William Treadway Bull to the Secretary, August 15, 1715, SPG transcripts, SCDAH, Series A, vols. 7–17, microfilm frame 49. Letter of Capt. Jonathan St. Lo to Burchett with Enclosure, July 12, 1715, British Public Record Office, Admiralty Office, 1:2451, photocopy in British Records Calendar, 1712–1716, 72. 1409: pp. 1–4, NCSAR.

6. For early measures, see "An Act to Confirm and Justify the Proceedings of the Right Honourable the Governor, the Honourable the Deputy Governor, and the rest of the Members of the Council, in their acting for the Service of his Majesty and the Lords Proprietors, in Defence of this Province," in Trott, *Laws of the Province of South Carolina*, microfilm frames 290–91, reel GR 032, SCDAH; "An Act to impower the Right Honourable Charles Craven Esq, Governour Captain General, etc. with the Consent of his Council, to raise Forces to carry on the War against the Indian Enemies, & their Confederates, and also to establish Martial Law in this Province," May 10, 1715, in Trott, *Laws*, 292; and "An Act to appoint a Press-Master, and lay a Penalty upon any person or persons that shall refuse upon Oath, to appraise such goods and all other Necessaries as Shall be impressed for the service of the Publick," June 30, 1716, in Trott, *Laws*, 206. For African slaves who negotiated with Indian raiding parties, see Landers, "Gracia Real de Santa Teresa de Mose," 17. For later stipulations about "trusty" slaves, see "An Act for Enlisting Such Trusty Slaves as shall be Thought serviceable to the Settlements in time of Alarms," February 13, 1719/20, in Trott, *Laws*, 336. For Governor Craven's expedition, see "Abel Kettleby and Other Planters," July 18, 1715, in *Calendar of State Papers*, 28:236. The best secondary discussion of this aspect of the Yamasee War remains Wood, *Black Majority*, 127–29. For the decision concerning female slaves, see Memorial to the Lords of Trade and Plantations, December 5, 1716, RBPRO, microfilm frame 6:262–63, SCDAH.

7. For the influence of African slaves among the Cherokees, see Chicken, in "Journal of the March of the Carolinians," 344; and Lieutenant Governor Bennett to Mr. Popple, February 16, 1718, in *Calendar of State Papers, Colonial Office Series: America and West Indies, 1717–1718*, 186.

For Spotswood's observations, see Letter of Alexander Spotswood, July 19, 1715, *Calendar of State Papers, 1714–1715*, 28:182.

8. August 20, 1715, JCHA Green Transcripts, SCDAH, microfilm, frame 4:441. For a discussion of the Tuscarora War, see Parramore, "The Tuscarora Ascendancy."

9. For "Tuscuerora Betty," see Mortgage of John Wright, June 15, 1714, Miscellaneous Records, SCDAH, vol. 56 (1714–1717): 42. For demographic estimates of the Indian slave population, see Menard, "The Africanization of the Lowcountry Labor Force"; and Ramsey, "'All & Singular the Slaves,'" 171.

10. Cooper and McCord, *Statutes at Large*, 2:671.

11. For the 1715 statute, see Clark, ed., *The State Records of North Carolina: Laws of North Carolina*, 23:65. For renewed warfare in North Carolina, see Introduction to Higher Court Minutes, in Saunders, ed., *Colonial Records of North Carolina*, 168–70, 200. For continuing violence after the traditional end of the Tuscarora War, see "North Carolina Higher Court Minutes," July 18, 1716, in Price, ed., *Colonial Records of North Carolina*, 5:124. For Kirsten Fischer's discussion of the 1715 North Carolina legislation, see Fischer, *Suspect Relations*, 85–86; also see Kay and Carry, *Slavery in North Carolina, 1748–1775*, 61–69.

12. Willis, "Divide and Rule," 157–76, esp. 160, 176. Wood, *Black Majority*.

13. "Copy of a Proclamation for taking up persons coming out of Carolina without Passports," June 15, 1715, *Calendar of State Papers, 1714–1715*, 28:320. "An Act to encourage the Importation of white Servants into this Province," ratified June 30, 1716, in Trott, *Laws of the Province of Carolina*, microfilm frame 295, reel GR 032, SCDAH. "An Act to appropriate the Yamasee Lands to the Use of such Persons as shall come into and settle themselves in this Province, and to such other Persons qualified as therein mentioned," ratified June 13, or 30, 1716, Trott, *Laws*, microfilm frame 295; "An Act to grant several Privileges, Exemptions, and Encouragements, to such of his Majesty's Protestant Subjects as are desirous to come into and settle this Province," ratified February, 1716/17, in Trott, *Laws*, microfilm frame 295.

14. "An Act for the Better Governing and Regulating white Servants,"

ratified December 11, 1717, in Trott, *Laws*, microfilm frames 312–18, reel GR 032, SCDAH.

15. Wood, *Black Majority*, 99.

16. May 25, 1722, Journals of the Upper House of Assembly, Early State Records, microfilm frames 8–9, reel AI a/1, SCDAH.

17. "An Act for the better Strengthening and Securing the Frontiers of this Province, by continuing the Garrison at Fort Moore, erecting the Garrison at the Pallachicola old Town on the Savanna River, repairing the Fort at Beaufort, and continuing the Two Scout Boats, and limiting the Bounds of the Indians Hunt by the Savanna River," ratified February 23, 1722, in Trott, *Laws*, item no. 484, microfilm frame 399, reel GR 032, SCDAH.

18. "An Act for Preventing the Desertion of Insolvent Debtors, and for the Better Settling the Frontiers of the Province," in Trott, *Laws*, item no. 478, microfilm frames 390–93, reel GR 032, SCDAH.

19. William Robert Snell, in his 1972 dissertation at the University of Alabama, came to a very different conclusion. His unique handling of primary and archival source materials led to questionable population estimates and, most controversial of all, the assertion that Indian slavery did not "dwindle" away following the Yamasee War, as was the general assumption, but that it actually increased. According to Snell, the war "disrupted the flow of black labor," forcing the colony to place "a renewed emphasis upon Indian slaves." Based upon his survey of "the colonial records," he found that the largest number of Indian slaves occurred between 1716 and 1724, when the native population purportedly reached a high of two thousand souls. See Snell, "Indian Slavery," 94–95. Snell's approach to the two record series that generated the bulk of his statistics, the Miscellaneous Records and the South Carolina Will Transcripts, both housed at the South Carolina Department of Archives and History, seems to have been nothing more than a simple running tally. As he read through the documents, he recorded the number of references made to Indian slaves per year and arrived ultimately at a raw total, which he regarded as a ready index to population trends. Observing, rightly, that the largest number of references occurred in the 1720s, he concluded that the use of

Indian slaves must have increased after the Yamasee War, with a peak of activity coming in 1724, when forty-nine Indian slaves appeared in the records, see Snell, "Indian Slavery," 130, appendix 2, table 3. Snell's error lay in his failure to compare his yearly tallies to the total number of documents he consulted from those years. Had the number of extant records been exactly equal for each year between 1670 and 1795, the range of his survey, his method might still have produced some useful information. Of course, they were not. The years for which he found the largest number of references to Indian slaves also happen to have produced the largest number of surviving documents. In fact, for the five-year period between 1720 and 1724, there are over three times as many wills in the Charleston County Will Books as there are for the preceding five-year period. For the five-year period between 1715 and 1719, there are only forty-three surviving wills, while the period from 1720 to 1724 boasts 133. Thus, although records from the latter period contain a larger number of estates that owned Indian slaves, they represent a smaller percentage of the whole sample than for the earlier period. See South Carolina Will Transcripts, Wills of Charleston County, vols. 1–4, microfilm, SCDAH.

20. The real significance of this decline naturally depends on the total number of households that existed in each period. Peter Wood found that the free white population increased from about 4,200 in 1710 to 6,525 in 1720. The resulting increase in households may thus make decline appear more exaggerated than it actually was. But I consider it unlikely. There was after all no such effect on the rate of household ownership of African slaves during the same period. Wood, *Black Majority*, 152.

21. In order to arrive at a figure for the percentage of households that owned Indian slaves during any five-year period between 1690 and 1740, the number of estates that indicated ownership of Indians (regardless of how many individuals were listed for any particular estate) was divided by the total number of estates probated during that five-year period. For instance, between 1735 and 1739, 185 wills were recorded, out of which only seven reflected possession of Indian slaves, indicating that only about 3 percent of all households owned

such slaves during the late 1730s. Estates owning slaves of African descent were recorded as a control. For the same period, 1735–39, about 41 percent of all households owned African slaves. Mustee slaves were recorded separately in order to provide an index to miscegenation. It should be noted that the percentage of households owning Indian or any other type of slaves should not be confused with the percentage of Indian slaves in the total slave population. Many estates, for instance, owned substantially more than one Indian slave, especially in earlier and peak periods. The relationship between the number of households owning Indian slaves and the actual number of Indian slaves held in South Carolina is discussed more fully later in chapter 7.

22. Will Transcripts, SCDAH: Will of Christopher Smyth, July 9, 1706, vol. 1, Will Book 1687–1710, 38–41; Will of Robert Daniell, May 1, 1719, vol. 1, Will Book 1711–1718, 94–97; Will of Henry Bower, July 26, 1724, vol. 2, Will Book 1722–1726, 5–8; Will of Robert Stevens, September 8, 1720, vol. 2, Will Book 1720–1721, 37. Gift patterns in the will transcripts clearly suggest that slaves identified by name were intended for use as personal servants. Between 1690 and 1725, all native female slaves identified as "girls" were bequeathed to a female relative, usually a daughter or granddaughter. The same was true of "Mustee girl" slaves. There was simply no clear instance in which an Indian or Mustee "girl" passed to a male recipient. Adult Indian women slaves appear to have been distributed with less discrimination, but the majority, 60 percent, were also bequeathed to female relatives. Meanwhile, 67 percent of all Indian "boy" slaves passed to male relatives, usually sons or grandsons. Decedents almost never bequeathed adult Indian men by name. For the Crosse and Dalton examples, see Will of Mary Crosse, March 6, 1699/1700, vol. 1, Will Book 1687–1710, 2–4; Will of Thomas Dalton, October 3, 1709, vol. 1, Will Book 1711–1718, 12–13. Likewise, in 1709 Thomas Hubbard gave his "two Indian girles Inotly and Nanny" to his two grandchildren, Ann and Dorothe; see the Will of Thomas Hubbard, August 26, 1709, vol. 1, Will Book 1687–1710, 51ff.

23. Will Transcripts, SCDAH, vols. 1–2. For a fuller exposition of this argument, see Ramsey, "'All & Singular the Slaves,'" 174–77.

24. Postmortem inventories are not available for the first and final years of the 1720s, but a survey of 169 inventories from 1722 to 1727 indicates that Indian slaves comprised only 7 to 8 percent of the total labor force. Between 1722 and 1727, Indian slaves numbered 121 out of a total number of 1,696 slaves listed in postmortem inventories; WIMR, vols. 58–61A, SCDAH. Postmortem inventories between 1722 and 1727 indicate that the population of native slaves had declined in absolute terms by about 300 persons from its prewar level of 1,400. Yet it seems to have reached a plateau by the middle of the decade. The ratio of Indians to Africans remained fairly constant, as did the rate of household ownership; WIMR, vols. 58–61A, SCDAH. I have assumed a rough population figure of 16,000 for the total number of slaves at work in South Carolina during the mid-1720s, based on population estimates in Peter Wood's Black Majority, 146–50. Between 1722 and 1726, African men were worth on average about eighty pounds more per person than Indian men, and African women were worth about sixty pounds more than Indian women. Indeed, African women were on average appraised at about thirty pounds more than Indian men. Unfortunately, there are not enough inventories from the first and second decades of the eighteenth century to make a reliable comparison with slave prices prior to the Yamasee War. See WIMR, vols. 58–61MB, SCDAH. No adult Indian men at all appear in the Will Transcripts, vols. 1–2, prior to 1715. Nevertheless, a 1708 census indicated that males comprised fully 33 percent of the total population of enslaved Indians, and they appear at a rate of 31 percent in postmortem inventories between 1722 and 1727.

25. Jordan, White over Black, 90; several other authors have also produced insightful identity studies that complement Jordan's arguments, including Berkhofer, The White Man's Indian; Pearce, The Savages of America; and Sheehan, Savagism and Civility. More recently, Jill Lepore has made use of the argument to elucidate Puritan motivations during King Philip's War; see Lepore, The Name of War. For collusion between enslaved and free Indians, see Salley, ed., Commissions and Instructions from the Lords Proprietors of South Carolina to the Public Officials of South Carolina, 1685–1715, 144.

26. The average price for an Indian child in South Carolina during the 1720s was 75 pounds, while the average price for an adult male Indian was 129 pounds. For a survey of both African and Indian slave prices, see Ramsey, "'All & Singular the Slaves.'" For the case involving the two children, see January 28, 1706/7, Salley, ed., *Journal of the Commons House of Assembly of South Carolina, November 15, 1726–March 11, 1726/7,* 90.

27. January 28, 1726/7, Salley, *Journal . . . 1726/7,* 90. Ramsey, "'All & Singular the Slaves,'" 171.

28. McDowell, *Journals of the Commissioners,* 86, 138.

29. Council Journal, July 8, 1715, in Hoadly, ed., *Public Records of the Colony of Connecticut,* 5:516.

30. May 20, 1714, McDowell, *Journals of the Commissioners,* 57. June 13, 1715, *Boston News Letter.*

31. Littlefield, "The Slave Trade to Colonial South Carolina," 71.

8. NEW PATTERNS OF EXCHANGE AND DIPLOMACY

1. Gideon Johnston to the Secretary, January 27, 1715/16, SPG transcripts, SCDAH, Series B, vols. 1–4 (1715–16), microfilm frame 6, reel PR0086.

2. Address to the Lords Proprietors, January 26, 1716/17, RBPRO, microfilm frame 7:3–4, SCDAH.

3. For Carolina's perspective on peace with the Catawbas and other "Northern Indians," see Committee of the Assembly of Carolina to Messrs. Boone and Beresford, August 6, 1716, *Calendar of State Papers,* 29:219. For Creek-English debates over the location of peace talks, see May 31, 1717, JCHA Green Transcripts, SCDAH microfilm, frame 5:295–96.

4. The best discussion of the factory system remains Verner Crane, *Southern Frontier,* 187–205.

5. July 14, 1716, McDowell, *Journals of the Commissioners,* 79; see also July 31, 1716, p. 95.

6. July 16, 1716, McDowell, *Journals of the Commissioners,* 80; August 15, 1716, p. 105.

7. July 28, 1716, McDowell, *Journals of the Commissioners*, 92–93; July 30, 1716, p. 93.

8. June 12, 1718, McDowell, *Journals of the Commissioners*, 287. Cooper and McCord, *Statutes at Large of South Carolina*, 3:332. Wood, *Black Majority*, 115–16.

9. Willis, "Divide and Rule," 175. Gary L. Hewitt makes this argument in Hewitt, "The State in the Planter's Service," 49–73. See also Hewitt, "Expansion and Improvement," 25–71. And see Crane, *Southern Frontier*, 198; and Sirmans, *Colonial South Carolina*, 116.

10. July 12, 1716, McDowell, *Journals of the Commissioners*, 77; July 14, 1716, p. 79; February 23, 1716/17, p. 166; August 7, 1717, p. 202.

11. July 12, 1716, McDowell, *Journals of the Commissioners*, 77; July 24, 1716, p. 84. For a fascinating glimpse into the complex agreements worked out between factors and burdeners, see Vassar, ed., "Some Short Remarkes," 412–13.

12. September 20, 1717, McDowell, *Journals of the Commissioners*, 211.

13. Vassar, "Some Short Remarkes," 406, 409.

14. For the persistence of these patterns after the Yamasee War, see Vassar, "Some Short Remarkes," 411–17.

15. For the ticketing scheme, see November 23, 1716, McDowell, *Journals of the Commissioners*, 130; September 20, 1717, p. 211. Some contemporary observers attributed such failures to the ignorance of the government with respect to native wishes; see Vassar, "Some Short Remarkes," 405.

16. October 24, 1717, McDowell, *Journals of the Commissioners*, 221–22. For the death of the Conjuror, see Vassar, "Some Short Remarkes," 419. November 23, 1717, McDowell, *Journals of the Commissioners*, 231; May 8, 1718, p. 272.

17. Crane, *Southern Frontier*, 127–28. Braund, *Deerskins and Duffels*, 90.

18. This history underscores the need to be aware of the materialist tendencies of dependency theory. See Richard White's comments in this regard in White, *Roots of Dependency*, xix.

19. For the Cherokee agreement, see July 23, 1716, McDowell, *Journals of the Commissioners*, 89. For Cherokee influence over the prices, see November 1, 1716, p. 120. For bargaining behavior prior to set price

schedules, see August 3, 1711, p. 15. For the Creek agreement, see June 3, 1718, pp. 281–82.

20. Arthur Ray and Donald Freeman argue that fixed exchange rates in New France were circumvented in a similar manner by both Europeans and Indians. See Ray and Freeman, "*Give Us Good Measure*," 234. For one of the earliest Cherokee complaints about fraudulent measuring, see January 29, 1716/17, McDowell, *Journals of the Commissioners*, 155. For Cherokee manipulations of the price agreements, see Vassar, "Some Short Remarkes," 408.

21. For fears of a Cherokee invasion, see chapter 7. For anti-English sentiment in Cherokee country, see December 2, 1717, McDowell, *Journals of the Commissioners*, 236. Vassar, "Some Short Remarkes," 408.

22. "Articles of Friendship and Commerce . . .," in Easterby, ed., *The Colonial Records of South Carolina*, 108–11. Piker, *Okfuskee*, 21, 213 (footnote 10). For discussions of the neutrality policy in the context of Creek factionalism, see Green, *The Politics of Indian Removal*, 22–23; and Braund, *Deerskins and Duffels*, 22. Hahn, *Invention of the Creek Nation*, 110–20. See also Corkran, *The Creek Frontier*, 61.

23. Piker, *Okfuskee*, 21. There are numerous references in the *Journals of the Commons House of Assembly* to the treaty of peace worked out between Creek emissaries and Carolina officials in Charles Town between November 7 and November 16, 1717; see JCHA Green Transcripts, SCDAH, microfilm frame 5:355–71. See also Crane, *Southern Frontier*, 259.

24. Extract of a Letter from South Carolina to Joseph Boone, June 8, 1717, *Calendar of State Papers*, 29:324–25. See also Hahn, *Invention of the Creek Nation*, 102. For a discussion of women as frequent targets of war parties, see Perdue, *Cherokee Women*.

25. June 14, 1717, JCHA Green Transcripts, SCDAH, microfilm frame 5:319, and June 27, 1717, microfilm frame 5:329.

26. Thomas Bosomworth discussed some elements of the 1717 articles of peace in 1717, though he was not personally present at the negotiations. August 4, 1752, in McDowell, ed., *Colonial Records of South Carolina: Documents Relating to Indian Affairs, 1750–1754*, 274. Hahn, *Invention of the Creek Nation*, 108.

27. Diego Pena to Don Juan de Ayala Escobar, September 20, 1717, in Boyd, "Documents Describing the Second and Third Expeditions of Lieutenant Diego Pena," 117, 115, 118. Hahn, *Invention of the Creek Nation*, 104–5. November 15, 1717, JCHA Green Transcripts, SCDAH, microfilm, frame 5:370.

28. Diego Pena to Don Juan de Ayala Escobar, September 20, 1717, in Boyd, "Documents Describing the Second and Third Expeditions of Lieutenant Diego Pena," 115–26. Hahn, *Invention of the Creek Nation*, 104–5. This state of affairs was a far cry from the Creek-Spanish understandings of 1715 and 1716.

29. Barcia, *Barcia's Chronological History of the Continent of Florida*, 361–62. Steven Hahn argues that Chipacasi's meeting with Don Juan was primarily an effort to clarify his status within Creek society. See Hahn, *Invention of the Creek Nation*, 115–19.

30. November 13, 1717, JCHA Green Transcripts, SCDAH, microfilm frame 5:363. Account of Juan Ayala Escobar's Meeting with the Uchise Chiefs, April 4, 1717, Archivo General de las Indias, Audiencia de Santo Domningo 843, John Worth Manuscripts Collection (microfilm reel 4, frame 24–31), Pineland Research Center, Pineland, Florida, cited in Hahn, *Invention of the Creek Nation*, 97–98. White, *Middle Ground*, 50–93, 456. Jane Merritt found a very similar process of cultural borrowing at work in negotiations on the Pennsylvania frontier. See Merritt, *At the Crossroads*, 213.

31. Extract of a letter from South Carolina to Joseph Boone, June 8, 1717, *Calendar of State Papers*, 29:324. Crane, *Southern Frontier*, 257. For Iroquois approaches to neutrality, see Wallace, "The Origins of Iroquois Neutrality"; Richter, *The Ordeal of the Longhouse*, 190–235; and Haan, "Covenant and Consensus: Iroquois and English, 1676–1760," 53. Hahn, *Invention of the Creek Nation*, 117.

32. The Alabamas may have invited the French to locate a fort in their territory as early as the fall of 1715. See Andre Penicaut's narrative in McWilliams, *Fleur de Lys and Calumet*, 165; see also Bienville to Pontchartrain, September 1, 1715, MPA:FD, 3:188; and Bienville to the Regency Council, May 10, 1717, 3:221. Crane, *Southern Frontier*, 256–57. Thomas, *Fort Toulouse*, 6–24, 42–52. Journal of the Proceedings of the

Governor and Council, March 8, 1759–December 31, 1762, in Candler, *The Colonial Records of the State of Georgia, 1759–1762*, 8:529.

33. Piker, *Okfuskee*, 21–28, 215–16, n. 21. Piker, "'White & Clean & Contested.'"

34. Piker, *Okfuskee*, 21. Crane, *Southern Frontier*, 191. For seminal viewpoints on factionalism and neutrality, see Green, *The Politics of Indian Removal*, 22–23; Braund, *Deerskins and Duffels*, 22. Corkran, *The Creek Frontier*, 61.

35. Barcia, *Chronological History*, 362–66. Jose Primo de Rivera to the Governor, April 28, 1718, Archivo General de Indias, Audiencia de Santo Domingo 843, AI 58-1-30 (microfilm reel 37), Stetson Collection, Gainesville; cited as De Ribera to Escobar, April 18, 1718, in Hahn, *Invention of the Creek Nation*, 117. (The letter is incorrectly dated April 18 in Hahn's book, but Dr. Hahn was kind enough to confirm by personal communication that the actual date of the document as it appears in the Stetson collection is April 28. So I believe we are talking about the same letter. The author's signature appears to be "Rivera" rather than "Ribera.") Hahn's discussion of the Coweta Resolution may be found in Hahn, *Invention of the Creek Nation*, 110–18.

36. November 15, 1717, JCHA Green Transcripts, SCDAH, microfilm frame 5:368. Barcia, *Chronological History*, 363.

37. Barcia, *Chronological History*, 365.

38. Barcia, *Chronological History*, 362–64.

39. Barcia, *Chronological History*, 364.

40. Barcia, *Chronological History*, 364.

41. Barcia, *Chronological History*, 366.

42. I was unable to locate a specific phrase that corresponded with Hahn's translation, but the Stetson Collection microfilm copy of this letter is in very poor condition and much of it is illegible. So the error may well be mine. I have thus tried to convey what I take to be the sense of the exchange rather than the specific language. Rivera to the Governor, April 28, 1718, Stetson Collection.

43. Crane, *Southern Frontier*, 250–51. Hahn, *Invention of the Creek Nation*, 142–44.

44. April 25, 1728, *Boston Newsletter*. Crane, *Southern Frontier*, 249–50.

45. "Journal of Charlesworth Glover," RBPRO, microfilm frame 13:152–61, SCDAH.

CONCLUSION

1. For an account of the Yamasee Indians who camped at Yamacraw Bluff briefly en route to Port Royal in 1685, see Letter of Caleb Westbrooke, February 21, 1684/5, RBPRO 2:8–9. For the first encounter between the Georgians and the Yamacraws, see Thomas Causton to His Wife, March 12, 1733, in Lane, ed., *General Oglethorpe's Georgia*, 1:9.

2. The imperial priorities leading to the establishment of Georgia were first elucidated in Crane, *Southern Frontier*, 281–325. Tomochichi's decision to settle at Yamacraw Bluff was probably related to the presence of a small trading post there. See "Proceedings of the President & Assistants in Council Assembled for the Colony of Georgia Commencing 24 day of July 1749," in Peter Force Papers, Series 7E, microfilm roll 10, Library of Congress, Washington DC. Also see Sweet, *Negotiating for Georgia*, 1–39.

3. Scholars remain divided over the cause and chronology of Tomochichi's banishment. David Corkran, for instance, suggests that the rupture occurred around 1728. See Corkran, *The Creek Frontier*, 82–83; also see Spalding, *Oglethorpe in America*, 78; and Sweet, *Negotiating for Georgia*, 21. For the best contemporary treatment of Tomochichi's history, see Hahn, *Invention of the Creek Nation*, 152–55. For Yahou-Lakee's comments and Tomochichi's early talks with Oglethorpe, see *South Carolina Gazette*, June 2, 1733. For Tomochichi's speech to the king, see *The Gentleman's Magazine, or Monthly Intelligencer* (August 1734), 448–49.

4. Hudson, "The Genesis of Georgia's Indians," 25. "Cpt. Glover's Account of Indian Tribes," *South Carolina Historical and Genealogical Magazine* 32 (July 1931): 241–42.

5. Salley, ed., *Journal of the Commons House of Assembly, November 20, 1706–February 8, 1706/7*, 28. For Tomochichi's meeting with the Georgia Trustees, see "Journal of the Trustees for Establishing the Colony of Georgia

in America," July 3, 1734, in Candler, ed., *The Colonial Records of the State of Georgia*, 1:178.

6. *Gentleman's Magazine* 3 (July 1733): 384.

7. Gallay, *Indian Slave Trade*, 338; Eugene Genovese framed the debate over the precapitalist nature of the southern slave economy in several early works. See Genovese, *The World the Slaveholders Made*, and Genovese, *The Political Economy of Slavery*.

8. For an excellent overview of some of the historiographical points at stake, see Fogel, *The Slavery Debates*. Phillips, "The Central Theme of Southern History."

Bibliography

UNPUBLISHED PRIMARY SOURCES

Admiralty Office, Public Record Office, United Kingdom.

Archivo General de Indias, Audiencia de Santo Domingo. John B. Stetson Collection, P. K. Yonge Library of Florida History, University of Florida, Gainesville.

British Records Calendar, 1712–1716. North Carolina State Archives, Raleigh.

Cholmondeley Manuscripts. Cambridge University Archives, Cambridge, United Kingdom.

Colonial Office, America and the West Indies, New York: Original Correspondence, Board of Trade, 1710–1715, series 5. Public Record Office, Kew, United Kingdom.

Colonial Office, America and the West Indies, Virginia: Original Correspondence, Board of Trade, 1715–1717, series 5. Public Record Office, Kew, United Kingdom.

Colonial Records of the State of Georgia: Original Manuscript Books, vol. 36, microfilm reel 12. Georgia Department of Archives and History, Atlanta.

Evans, John. "Journal of a Virginia Indian Trader in North and South Carolina." South Caroliniana Library, University of South Carolina, Columbia.

General Assembly Papers, 1715, Church of Scotland. Scottish Record Office, Edinburgh, United Kingdom.

General Correspondence of Louisiana, Ministry of the Colonies, Series C 13, Archives Nationale. Aix en Provence, France. Microfilm, Tulane University Archives, New Orleans.

Journals of the Commons House of Assembly of South Carolina, 1706–1721, William S. Green Transcripts. Microfilm, South Carolina Department of Archives and History, Columbia.

Journals of the Upper House of Assembly, 1721–1726. Microfilm, South Carolina Department of Archives and History, Columbia.

Pringle-Garden Family Papers. South Carolina Historical Society Archives, Charleston.

Pryce Hughes Letters, Proposing a Welsh Colony. South Caroliniana Library, University of South Carolina, Columbia.

Records of the Secretary of the Province, 1692–1700. Manuscripts, South Carolina Department of Archives and History, Columbia.

Salley, A. S., ed. *Records in the British Public Record Office Relating to South Carolina*, vols. 6–9. Microfilm, South Carolina Department of Archives and History, Columbia.

Society for the Propagation of the Gospel in Foreign Parts. Selected Pages Relating to South Carolina from Library of Congress Transcripts of the Papers of the Society for the Propagation of the Gospel in Foreign Parts. Series A, Contemporary Copies of Letters Received, vols. 7–17, 1712–1723. Series B, Original Letters Received, vols. 1–4, 1715–1716, 1715–1735. Microfilm, South Carolina Department of Archives and History, Columbia.

South Carolina Court of Common Pleas, Judgment Rolls. Microfilm, South Carolina Department of Archives and History, Columbia.

South Carolina Will Transcripts, Wills of Charleston County, vols. 1–4. Microfilm, South Carolina Department of Archives and History, Columbia.

Wills, Inventories, & Miscellaneous Records, 1722–1724, vol. 58; 1722–1726, vol. 59; 1724–1725, vol. 60; 1726–1727, vols. 61A, 61B. Microfilm, South Carolina Department of Archives and History, Columbia.

PUBLISHED SOURCES

Allain, Mathe. *Not Worth a Straw: French Colonial Policy and the Early Years of Louisiana*. Lafayette: Center for Louisiana Studies, University of Southwestern Louisiana, 1988.

Allinson, Samuel, ed. *Acts of the General Assembly of the Province of New Jersey*. Burlington NJ, 1776.

Barcia, Andres Gonsales de. *Barcia's Chronological History of the Continent of Florida*, trans. Anthony Kerrigan. Gainesville: University of Florida Press, 1951.

Barker, Eirlys M. "Pryce Hughes, Colony Planner, of Charles Town and Wales." *South Carolina Historical Magazine* 95 (1994): 302–13.

Batchellor, Albert Stillman, ed., *Laws of New Hampshire*. Manchester NH, 1904.

Berkhofer, Robert F., Jr. *The White Man's Indian: Images of the American Indian from Columbus to the Present*. New York: Alfred A. Knopf, 1978.

Berlin, Ira. *Many Thousands Gone: The First Two Centuries of Slavery in North America*. Cambridge MA: Belknap Press, 1998.

———. "The Revolution in Black Life." In *The American Revolution: Explorations in the History of American Radicalism*, ed. Alfred F. Young. Dekalb: Northern Illinois University Press, 1976. 349–82.

Bolton, Herbert E. "Spanish Resistance to the Carolina Traders in Western Georgia (1680–1704)." *Georgia Historical Quarterly* 9 (June 1925): 115–30.

Boston Newsletter.

Boyd, Mark F., ed. "Diego Pena's Expedition to Apalachee and Apalachicolo in 1716: A Journal Translated and With an Introduction." *Florida Historical Quarterly* 28 (1949): 1–27.

———. "Documents Describing the Second and Third Expeditions of Lieutenant Diego Pena to Apalachee and Apalachicola in 1717 and 1718." *Florida Historical Quarterly* 31 (October 1952): 109–39.

Brasseaux, Carl A. "The Cadillac-Duclos Affair: Private Enterprise versus Mercantilism in Colonial Mobile." *Alabama Review* 37 (1984): 257–70.

Braund, Kathryn E. Holland. *Deerskins and Duffels: Creek Indian Trade with Anglo-America, 1685–1815*. Lincoln: University of Nebraska Press, 1993.

———. "Guardians of Tradition and Handmaidens to Change: Women's Roles in Creek Economic and Social Life during the Eighteenth Century." *American Indian Quarterly* 14 (Summer 1990): 239–58.

Brown, Philip M. "Early Indian Trade in the Development of South Carolina: Politics, Economics, and Social Mobility during the Proprietary Period, 1670–1719." *South Carolina Historical Magazine* 76 (July 1975): 118–28.

Bushnell, Amy Turner. *Situado and Sabana: Spain's Support System for the*

Presidio and Mission Provinces of Florida. Anthropological Papers of the American Museum of Natural History, 74. 1994.

Caldwell, Joseph R. "Palachacolas Town, Hampton County, South Carolina." *Journal of the Washington Academy of Sciences* 38 (October 15, 1948): 321–24.

Calendar of State Papers, Colonial Series: America and West Indies, 1702–1703, ed. Cecil Headlam. London: His Majesty's Stationery Office, 1913.

Calendar of State Papers, Colonial Series: America and West Indies, 1704–1705, ed. Cecil Headlam. London: His Majesty's Stationery Office, 1916.

Calendar of State Papers, Colonial Office Series: America and West Indies, August 1714–December 1715. Vol. 28. London: His Majesty's Stationery Office, 1928.

Calendar of State Papers, Colonial Office Series: America and West Indies, January 1716–July 1717, ed. Cecil Headlam. Vol. 29. London: Her Majesty's Stationery Office, 1929.

Calendar of State Papers, Colonial Office Series: America and West Indies, August 1717–December 1718, ed. Cecil Headlam. London: Her Majesty's Stationery Office, 1930.

Candler, Allen D., ed. *The Colonial Records of the State of Georgia*. 28 vols. Atlanta: Franklin Printing and Publishing Company, 1904–1916.

Carroll, B. R., ed. *Historical Collections of South Carolina*, 2 vols. New York: Harper and Brothers, 1836.

Cayton, Andrew R. L., and Fredericka J. Teute. "Introduction: On the Connection of Frontiers." In *Contact Points: American Frontiers from the Mohawk Valley to the Mississippi, 1750–1830*, ed. Andrew R. L. Cayton and Fredericka J. Teute. Chapel Hill: University of North Carolina Press, 1998. 1–15.

Clark, G. N. "War Trade and Trade War, 1701–1713." *Economic History Review* 1 (January 1928): 262–80.

Clark, Walter, ed. *The State Records of North Carolina: Laws of North Carolina*, 23 vols. Winston: State of North Carolina, 1895–1906.

Clowse, Converse D. *Economic Beginnings in Colonial South Carolina, 1670–1730*. Columbia: University of South Carolina Press, 1971.

Coclanis, Peter A. "Bitter Harvest: The South Carolina Low Country in Historical Perspective." *Journal of Economic History* 45 (June 1985): 254–55.

———. "The Hydra Head of Merchant Capital: Markets and Merchants in Early South Carolina." In *The Meaning of South Carolina History: Essays in Honor of George C. Rogers, Jr.*, ed. David R. Chesnutt and Clyde N. Wilson. Columbia: University of South Carolina Press, 1991. 1–18.

Cooper, Thomas, and David J. McCord, eds. *The Statutes at Large of South Carolina*. 2 vols. Columbia: A. S. Johnson, 1837.

Corkran, David H. *The Creek Frontier: 1540–1783*. Norman: University of Oklahoma Press, 1967.

Covington, James W. "Stuart's Town, the Yamasee Indians and Spanish Florida." *Florida Anthropologist* 21 (March 1968): 8–13.

Crane, Verner W. "The Origin of the Name of the Creek Indians." *Mississippi Valley Historical Review* 5 (December 1918): 339–42.

———. *The Southern Frontier, 1670–1732*. New York: W. W. Norton, 1981.

Cummings, William P., ed. *The Southeast in Early Maps*. Princeton: Princeton University Press, 1958.

DeCamp, David. "African Day-Names in Jamaica." *Language* 63 (March 1967): 139–49.

Deloria, Philip J. "What Is the Middle Ground, Anyway?" *William and Mary Quarterly* 63 (January 2006): 11–22.

Desbarats, Catherine. "Following the Middle Ground." *William and Mary Quarterly* 63 (January 2006): 81–96.

Dorn, Walter L. *Competition for Empire*. New York: Harper and Brothers, 1940.

Easterby, J. H., ed. *The Colonial Records of South Carolina: The Journal of the Commons House of Assembly, November 10, 1736–June 7, 1739*. Columbia: Historical Commission of South Carolina, 1951.

Eccles, W. J. "A Belated Review of Harold Adams Innis, *The Fur Trade in Canada*." *Canadian Historical Review* 60 (December 1979): 430–31.

———. *Frontenac: The Courtier Governor*. Toronto: University of Toronto Press, 1959.

Egnal, Marc. *New World Economies: The Growth of the Thirteen Colonies and Early Canada*. New York: Oxford University Press, 1998.

Eighteenth Century. British Library, London. Eighteenth Century Microfilm Collection, Reels 1–5355, call no. PR 1134–E3, Tulane University, New Orleans, Louisiana.

Fairbanks, Charles. "Excavations at Horseshoe Bend, Alabama." *Florida Anthropologist* 25 (1962): 41–56.

Ferguson, Leland. *Uncommon Ground: Archaeology and Early African America, 1650–1800.* Washington DC: Smithsonian Institution Press, 1992.

Fischer, Kirsten. *Suspect Relations: Sex, Race, and Resistance in Colonial North Carolina.* Ithaca NY: Cornell University Press, 2002.

Fogel, Robert William. *The Slavery Debates.* Baton Rouge: Louisiana State University Press, 2003.

Fox, Robin. *Kinship and Marriage: An Anthropological Perspective.* Baltimore, 1967.

Frey, Sylvia R. *Water from the Rock: Black Resistance in a Revolutionary Age.* Princeton NJ: Princeton University Press, 1991.

Gallay, Alan. *The Formation of a Planter Elite: Jonathan Bryan and the Southern Colonial Frontier.* Athens: University of Georgia Press, 1989.

———. *The Indian Slave Trade: The Rise of the English Empire in the American South, 1670–1717.* New Haven CT: Yale University Press, 2002.

Galloway, Patricia. "Choctaw Factionalism and Civil War, 1746–1750." In *The Choctaw before Removal,* ed. Carolyn Keller Reeves. Jackson: University Press of Mississippi, 1985. 120–56.

———. *Choctaw Genesis, 1500–1700.* Lincoln: University of Nebraska Press, 1995.

———. "Confederacy as a Solution to Chiefdom Dissolution." In *The Forgotten Centuries: Indians and Europeans in the American South,* ed. Charles Hudson and Carmen Chaves Tesser. Athens: University of Georgia Press, 1994. 393–420.

———. "Formation of Historic Tribes and the French Colonial Period." In *Native, European, and African Cultures in Mississippi, 1500–1800,* ed. Patricia Galloway. Jackson: University Press of Mississippi, 1991. 57–75.

Genovese, Eugene D. *The Political Economy of Slavery: Studies in the Economy and Society of the Slave South.* New York: Pantheon Books, 1965.

———. *The World the Slaveholders Made: Two Essays in Interpretation.* New York: Pantheon Press, 1969.

The Gentleman's Magazine, or Monthly Intelligencer.

Giraud, Marcel. "France and Louisiana in the Early Eighteenth Century." *Mississippi Valley Historical Review* 36 (1949–50): 657–80.

———. *A History of French Louisiana*, vol. 1: *The Reign of Louis XIV, 1698–1715*, trans. Joseph C. Lambert. Baton Rouge: Louisiana State University Press, 1974.

———. *A History of French Louisiana*, vol. 2: *Years of Transition, 1715–1717*, trans. Brian Pearce. Baton Rouge: Louisiana State University Press, 1993.

Gleach, Frederic W. *Powhatan's World and Colonial Virginia: A Conflict of Cultures*. Lincoln: University of Nebraska Press, 2000.

Glover, Charlesworth. "Cpt. Glover's Account of Indian Tribes." *South Carolina Historical and Genealogical Magazine* 32 (July 1931): 241–42.

Green, Michael D. *The Politics of Indian Removal: Creek Government and Society in Crisis*. Lincoln: University of Nebraska Press, 1982.

Green, William. "The Search for Altamaha: The Archaeology of an Early Eighteenth-Century Yamasee Town." Master's thesis, University of South Carolina, 1991.

Greene, Jack P., ed. *Selling a New World: Two Colonial South Carolina Promotional Pamphlets*. Columbia: University of South Carolina Press, 1989.

Gregorie, Anne King, ed., *Records of the Court of Chancery of South Carolina, 1671–1779*. In *American Legal Records*, vol. 6. Washington DC, 1950.

Haan, Richard L. "Covenant and Consensus: Iroquois and English, 1676–1760." In *Beyond the Covenant Chain: The Iroquois and Their Neighbors in Indian North America, 1600–1800*, ed. Daniel K. Richter and James H. Merrell. Syracuse NY: Syracuse University Press, 1987. 41–57.

———. "The 'Trade Do's Not Flourish as Formerly': The Ecological Origins of the Yamassee War of 1715." *Ethnohistory* 28 (Fall 1981): 341–58.

Hahn, Steven C. *The Invention of the Creek Nation, 1670–1763*. Lincoln: University of Nebraska Press, 2004.

Hall, Joseph M. "Making an Indian People: Creek Formation in the Colonial Southeast, 1590–1735." PhD diss., University of Wisconsin–Madison, 2001.

Hann, John H. *Apalachee: The Land between the Rivers*. Gainesville: University Press of Florida, 1988.

———. "St. Augustine's Fallout from the Yamasee War." *Florida Historical Quarterly* 68 (October 1989): 180–200.

Hardy, Stephen G. "Colonial South Carolina's Rice Industry and the Atlantic Economy." In *Money, Trade, and Power: The Evolution of Colonial South Carolina's Plantation Society*, ed. Jack P. Greene, Rosemary Brana-Shute, and Randy J. Sparks. Columbia: University of South Carolina Press, 2001. 108–41.

Hatley, Tom. *The Dividing Paths: Cherokees and South Carolinians through the Revolutionary Era*. New York: Oxford University Press, 1995.

Hawkins, Benjamin. "Letters of Benjamin Hawkins, 1796–1806." In *Collections of the Georgia Historical Society*, vol. 9. Savannah: Georgia Historical Society, 1916.

———. "A Sketch of the Creek Country in the Years 1798 and 1799." In *Collections of the Georgia Historical Society*, vol. 3. Savannah: Georgia Historical Society, 1848.

Hickerson, Harold. "Fur Trade Colonialism and the North American Indians." *Journal of Ethnic Studies* 1 (Summer 1973): 15–44.

Herman, Daniel J. "Romance on the Middle Ground." *Journal of the Early Republic* 19 (1999): 279–91.

Hewitt, Gary L. "Expansion and Improvement: Land, People, and Politics in South Carolina and Georgia, 1690–1745." PhD diss., Princeton University, 1996.

———. "The State in the Planters' Service: Politics and the Emergence of a Plantation Economy in South Carolina." In *Money, Trade, and Power: The Evolution of Colonial South Carolina's Plantation Society*, ed. Jack P. Greene, Rosemary Brana-Shute, and Randy J. Sparks. Columbia: University of South Carolina Press, 2001. 49–73.

Hoadly, Charles J., ed. *The Public Records of the Colony of Connecticut*. 15 vols. Reprint, New York: AMS Press, 1968.

Hoffman, Paul E. *Florida's Frontiers*. Bloomington: University of Indiana Press, 2002.

Hudson, Charles. "The Genesis of Georgia's Indians." In *Forty Years of Diversity: Essays on Colonial Georgia*, ed. Harvey H. Jackson and Phinizy Spalding. Athens: University of Georgia Press, 1984. 25–45.

———. *Southeastern Indians*. N.p.: University of Tennessee Press, 1982.

Hudson, Charles, Marvin T. Smith, and Chester B. DePratter. "The Hernando De Soto Expedition: From Apalachee to Chiaha." *Southeastern Archaeology* 3 (Summer 1984): 68–70.

Iberville, Pierre LeMoyne de. *Iberville's Gulf Journals*, ed. and trans. Richebourg Gaillard McWilliams. Tuscaloosa: University of Alabama Press, 1991.

———. "Journal Du Sieur D'Iberville." In *Decouvertes et Etablissements des Francais dans l'Oest et dans le Sud de l'Amerique Septentrionale*. Paris: Maisonneuve et c'ie, 1881.

Inscoe, John C. "Carolina Slave Names: An Index to Acculturation." *Journal of Southern History* 49 (November 1983): 527–54.

Ivers, Larry E. *Colonial Forts of South Carolina, 1670–1775*. Columbia: University of South Carolina Press, 1970.

———. "Scouting the Inland Passage, 1685–1787." *South Carolina Historical Magazine* 73 (April 1972): 117–29.

Jaenen, Cornelius. "French Attitudes towards Native Society." In *Old Trails and New Directions: Papers of the Third North American Fur Trade Conference*, ed. Carol M. Judd and Arthur J. Ray. Toronto: University of Toronto Press, 1980. 59–72.

Jordan, Winthrop D. *White over Black: American Attitudes toward the Negro, 1550–1812*. Baltimore: Penguin Books, 1969.

"Journal of the March of the Carolinians into the Cherokee Mountains." In *City of Charleston Year-book, 1894*, ed. Langdon Cheves. Charleston SC: Walker, Evans, and Cogwell Company, 1894. 324–52.

Juricek, John T. "The Westo Indians," *Ethnohistory* 11 (Spring 1964): 134–73.

Karr, Ronald Dale. "'Why Should You Be So Furious?': The Violence of the Pequot War." *Journal of American History* 85 (December 1998): 876–909.

Kay, Marvin L. Michael, and Lorin Lee Carry. *Slavery in North Carolina, 1748–1775*. Chapel Hill: University of North Carolina Press, 1995.

Kelly, Arthur R. "The Macon Trading Post: An Historical Foundling." *American Antiquity* 4 (1939): 328–33.

———. *A Preliminary Report on Archeological Explorations at Macon, Georgia*. Smithsonian Institution, Bureau of American Ethnology Bulletin 119. Washington DC, 1938.

Klingberg, Frank J. "Early Attempts at Indian Education in South Carolina: A Documentary." *South Carolina Historical Magazine* 61 (January 1960): 1–10.

Knight, Vernon James, Jr. "Ocmulgee Fields Culture and the Historical Development of Creek Ceramics." In *Ocmulgee Archaeology, 1936–1986*, ed. David J. Hally. Athens: University of Georgia Press, 1994. 181–89.

La Harpe, Jean-Baptiste Bernard de. *Historical Journal of the Establishment of the French in Louisiana*. Ed. and trans. Glenn R. Conrad, Virginia Koenig, and Joan Cain. Lafayette: University of Southwest Louisiana Press, 1971.

Landers, Jane. "Gracia Real de Santa Teresa de Mose: A Free Black Town in Spanish Colonial Florida." *American Historical Review* 95 (February 1990): 9–30.

Lane, Mills, ed. *General Oglethorpe's Georgia: Colonial Letters, 1733–1743*, 2 vols. Savannah: Beehive Press, 1975.

Lankford, George E. "Red and White: Some Reflections on Southeastern Symbolism." *Southern Folklore* 50 (1993): 53–80.

Lauber, Almon Wheeler. *Indian Slavery in Colonial Times within the Present Limits of the United States*. Studies in History, Economics, and Public Law, vol. 54, no. 3. New York: Columbia University, 1913.

LeJau, Francis. *The Carolina Chronicle of Dr. Francis Lejau, 1706–1717*. Ed. Frank J. Klingberg. Berkeley: University of California Press, 1956.

Lepore, Jill. *The Name of War: King Philip's War and the Origins of American Identity*. New York: Alfred A. Knopf, 1999.

Littlefield, Daniel C. *Rice and Slaves: Ethnicity and the Slave Trade in Colonial South Carolina*. Baton Rouge: Louisiana State University Press, 1981.

———. "The Slave Trade to Colonial South Carolina: A Profile." *South Carolina Historical Magazine* 91 (April 1990): 68–99.

Locke, John. *Second Treatise of Government*. Indianapolis: Bobbs-Merrill Company, 1952.

Longe, Alexander. "A Small Postscript on the Ways and Manners of the Indians Called Cherokees." Ed. David Corkran. *Southern Indian Studies* 21 (1969): 1–49.

Martin, Joel. *Sacred Revolt: The Muskhogees' Struggle for a New World*. Boston: Beacon Press, 1991.

———. "Southeastern Indians and the English Trade in Skins and Slaves." In *The Forgotten Centuries: Indians and Europeans in the American South, 1521–1704*, ed. Charles Hudson and Carmen Chaves Tesser. Athens: University of Georgia Press, 1994. 304–24.

Mason, Carol I. "The Archaeology of Ocmulgee Old Fields, Macon, Georgia." PhD diss., University of Michigan, Ann Arbor, 1963. University Microfilms.

———. "Eighteenth-Century Culture Change among the Lower Creeks." *Florida Anthropologist* 16 (September 1963): 65–80.

McCusker, John J. *Money and Exchange in Europe and America, 1600–1775: A Handbook.* Chapel Hill: University of North Carolina Press, 1978.

McDowell, William L., Jr., ed. *Colonial Records of South Carolina: Documents Relating to Indian Affairs, 1750–1754.* Columbia: South Carolina Department of Archives and History, 1992.

———. *Colonial Records of South Carolina: Journals of the Commissioners of the Indian Trade, September 20, 1710–August 29, 1718.* Columbia: South Carolina Department of Archives and History, 1992.

McWilliams, Richebourg Gaillard, ed. and trans. *Fleur de Lys and Calumet: Being the Penicaut Narrative of French Adventure in Louisiana.* Baton Rouge: Louisiana State University Press, 1953.

Menard, Russell R. "The Africanization of the Lowcountry Labor Force, 1670–1730." In *Race and Family in the Colonial South*, ed. Winthrop D. Jordan and Sheila L. Skemp. Jackson: University Press of Mississippi, 1987. 81–108.

———. "Financing the Lowcountry Export Boom: Capital and Growth in Early Carolina." *William and Mary Quarterly* 51 (October 1994): 659–76.

Menard, Russell R., and Stuart B. Schwartz, "Why African Slavery? Labor Force Transitions in Brazil, Mexico, and the Carolina Lowcountry." In *Slavery in the Americas*, ed. Wolfgang Binder. Würzburg: Konigshausen and Neumann, 1993. 89–114.

Mereness, Newton D., ed. *Travels in the American Colonies.* New York: Antiquarian Press, 1961.

Merrell, James H. *The Indians' New World: Catawbas and Their Neighbors from European Contact through the Era of Removal.* New York: W. W. Norton, 1991.

———. *Into the American Woods: Negotiators on the Pennsylvania Frontier.* New York: W. W. Norton, 1999.

———. "'Our Bond of Peace': Patterns of Intercultural Exchange in the

Carolina Piedmont, 1650–1750." In *Powhatan's Mantle: Indians in the Colonial Southeast*, ed. Peter H. Wood, Gregory A. Waselkov, and M. Thomas Hatley. Lincoln: University of Nebraska Press, 1989. 196–222.

Merritt, Jane T. *At the Crossroads: Indians and Empires on a Mid-Atlantic Frontier, 1700–1763*. Chapel Hill: University of North Carolina Press, 2003.

Milanich, Jerald T. "The Western Tumuccua: Patterns of Acculturation and Change." In *Tacachale: Essays on the Indians of Florida and Southeastern Georgia during the Historic Period*, ed. Jerald T. Milanich and Samuel Proctor. Gainesville: University Press of Florida, 1978. 59–88.

Milling, Chapman J. *Red Carolinians*. Chapel Hill: University of North Carolina Press, 1940.

Miquelon, Dale. *New France, 1701–1744: "A Supplement to Europe."* Toronto: University of Toronto Press, 1987.

Monteiro, John M. "From Indian to Slave: Forced Native Labour and Colonial Society in Sao Paulo during the Seventeenth Century." *Slavery and Abolition* 9 (September 1988): 105–27.

Moore, Alexander. "Carolina Whigs: Colleton County Members of the South Carolina Commons House of Assembly, 1692–1720." Master's thesis, University of South Carolina, 1981.

———. "Royalizing South Carolina: The Revolution of 1719 and the Transformation of Early South Carolina Government." PhD diss., University of South Carolina, 1991.

Morgan, Edmund. *American Slavery—American Freedom: The Ordeal of Colonial Virginia*. New York: W. W. Norton, 1975.

Morgan, Philip D. "British Encounters with Africans and African-Americans, circa 1600–1780." In *Strangers within the Realm: Cultural Margins of the First British Empire*, ed. Bernard Bailyn and Philip D. Morgan. Chapel Hill: University of North Carolina Press, 1991. 157–219.

———. "Encounters between British and 'Indigenous' Peoples, c. 1500–1800." In *Empire and Others: British Encounters with Indigenous Peoples, 1600–1850*, ed. Martin Daunton and Rick Halpern. Philadelphia: University of Pennsylvania Press, 1999. 42–78.

Myer, William E. "The Trail System of the Southeastern United States in the Colonial Period," fold-out map. In *Forty-Second Annual Report of the Bureau of American Ethnology*. Washington DC, 1928.

Nairne, Thomas. *Nairne's Muskhogean Journals: The 1708 Expedition to the Mississippi River.* Ed. Alexander Moore. Jackson: University of Mississippi Press, 1988.

Narratives of the Career of Hernando de Soto. New York: A. S. Barnes and Company, 1904.

Nash, Gary B. *Red, White, and Black: The Peoples of Early North America.* Englewood Cliffs NJ: Prentice Hall, 2000.

Nash, R. C. "The Organization of Trade and Finance in the Atlantic Economy: Britain and South Carolina, 1670–1775." In *Money, Trade, and Power: The Evolution of Colonial South Carolina's Plantation Society,* ed. Jack P. Greene, Rosemary Brana-Shute, and Randy J. Sparks. Columbia: University of South Carolina Press, 2001. 74–107.

———. "South Carolina and the Atlantic Economy in the Late Seventeenth and Eighteenth Centuries." *Economic History Review* 45 (November 1992): 677–702.

Nobles, Gregory H. "Breaking into the Backcountry: New Approaches to the Early American Frontier, 1750–1800." *William and Mary Quarterly* 46 (October 1989): 641–70.

Norton, Thomas Elliot. *The Fur Trade in Colonial New York, 1686–1776.* Madison: University of Wisconsin Press, 1974.

Oatis, Steven James. *A Colonial Complex: South Carolina's Frontiers in the Era of the Yamasee War, 1680–1730.* Lincoln: University of Nebraska Press, 2004.

O'Brien, Greg. *Choctaws in a Revolutionary Age, 1750–1830.* Lincoln: University of Nebraska Press, 2003.

O'Callaghan, E. B., ed. *Documents Relative to the Colonial History of New York.* 15 vols. Albany NY: Weed, Parsons, and Company, 1894.

Otto, John S. "The Origins of Cattle Ranching in Colonial South Carolina, 1670–1715." *South Carolina Historical Magazine* 87 (July 1986): 117–24.

Palmer, William P., MD, ed. *Calendar of Virginia State Papers and Other Manuscripts, 1652–1781, Preserved in the Capitol at Richmond.* 11 vols. Richmond: R. F. Walker, Superintendent of Public Printing, 1875–93.

Parramore, Thomas C. "The Tuscarora Ascendancy." *North Carolina Historical Review* 59 (October 1982): 310–26.

Pearce, Roy H. *The Savages of America: A Study of the Indian and the Idea of Civilization.* Baltimore: Johns Hopkins University Press, 1953.

Perdue, Theda. *Cherokee Women: Gender and Culture Change, 1700–1835.* Lincoln: University of Nebraska Press, 1998.

———. *Slavery and the Evolution of Cherokee Society, 1540–1866.* Knoxville: University of Tennessee Press, 1979.

Phillips, U. B. "The Central Theme of Southern History." *American Historical Review* 34 (October 1928): 30–43.

Piker, Joshua. *Okfuskee: A Creek Indian Town in Colonial America.* Cambridge MA: Harvard University Press, 2004.

———. "'White & Clean & Contested': Creek Towns and Trading Paths in the Aftermath of the Seven Years' War." *Ethnohistory* 50 (Spring 2003): 315–47.

Price, William S., Jr. *Colonial Records of North Carolina.* Raleigh: Division of Archives and History, 1977.

Puckett, Newbell N. *Black Names in America: Origins and Usage.* Boston: G. K. Hall, 1975.

Ramsey, William L. "'All & Singular the Slaves': A Demographic Profile of Indian Slavery in Colonial South Carolina." In *Money, Trade, and Power: The Evolution of a Planter Society in Colonial South Carolina,* ed. Jack P. Greene, Rosemary Brana-Shute, and Randy Sparks. Columbia: University of South Carolina Press, 2001. 170–90.

———. "A Coat for 'Indian Cuffy': Mapping the Boundary between Freedom and Slavery in Colonial South Carolina." *South Carolina Historical Magazine* 103 (January 2002): 48–66.

———. "'Something Cloudy in Their Looks': The Origins of the Yamasee War Reconsidered." *Journal of American History* 90 (June 2003): 44–75.

Ray, Arthur J., and Donald B. Freeman, *"Give Us Good Measure": An Economic Analysis of Relations between the Indians and the Hudson's Bay Company before 1763.* Toronto: University of Toronto Press, 1978.

Reid, John Philip. *A Better Kind of Hatchet: Law, Trade, and Diplomacy in the Cherokee Nation during the Early Years of European Contact.* University Park: Pennsylvania State University Press, 1976.

Rich, E. E. *The History of Hudson's Bay Company, 1670–1870,* 2 vols. London: Hudson's Bay Record Society, 1958–59.

———. "Russia and the Colonial Fur Trade." *Economic History Review* 7 (April 1955): 307–37.

———. "Trade Habits and Economic Motivation among the Indians of North America." *Canadian Journal of Economics and Political Science* 27 (1960): 35–53.

Richter, Daniel. *The Ordeal of the Longhouse: The Peoples of the Iroquois League in the Era of European Colonization.* Chapel Hill: University of North Carolina Press, 1992.

Rotstein, Abraham. "Karl Polanyi's Concept of Non-Market Trade." *Journal of Economic History* 30 (March 1970): 117–26.

Rowland, Dunbar, and Albert Godfrey Sanders, eds. and trans. *Mississippi Provincial Archives: French Dominion,* 3 vols. Jackson: University of Mississippi Press, 1932.

Rowland, Lawrence S., Alexander Moore, and George C. Rogers Jr. *The History of Beaufort County, South Carolina,* vol. 1: 1514–1861. Columbia: University of South Carolina Press, 1996.

Russell, Margaret Clayton. "Lamar and the Creeks: An Old Controversy Revisited." *Early Georgia* 3, no. 1: 53–67.

Sahlins, Marshall. *Stone Age Economics.* New York: Aldine Publishing Company, 1972.

Salley, A. S., Jr., ed. *Commissions and Instructions from the Lords Proprietors of South Carolina to the Public Officials of South Carolina, 1685–1715.* Columbia: Historical Commission of South Carolina, 1916.

———. *Journal of Colonel John Herbert, Commissioner of Indian Affairs for the Province of South Carolina, October 17, 1727, to March 19, 1727/8.* Columbia: Historical Commission of South Carolina, 1936.

———. *Journals of the Commons House of Assembly for 1702.* Columbia: Historical Commission of South Carolina, 1932.

———. *Journals of the Commons House of Assembly of South Carolina, 1703.* Columbia: Historical Commission of South Carolina, 1934.

———. *Journal of the Commons House of Assembly of South Carolina, March 6, 1705/6–April 9, 1706.* Columbia: Historical Commission of South Carolina, 1937.

———. *Journal of the Commons House of Assembly, November 20, 1706–February 8, 1706/7.* Columbia: Historical Commission of South Carolina, 1939.

———. *Journal of the Commons House of Assembly of South Carolina, June 5, 1707–July 19, 1707*. Columbia: Historical Commission of South Carolina, 1940.

———. *Journal of the Commons House of Assembly of South Carolina, November 15, 1726–March 11, 1726/7*. Columbia: Historical Commission of South Carolina, 1946.

———. *Records in the British Public Record Office Relating to South Carolina, 1701–1710*, vols. 1–5. Columbia: Historical Commission of South Carolina, 1947.

———. *Records in the British Public Record Office Relating to South Carolina*, vols. 6–9. Microfilm, South Carolina Department of Archives and History, Columbia.

Saunders, William L., ed. *Colonial Records of North Carolina, 1713–1728*, vol. 2. Wilmington NC: Broadfoot Publishing, 1993.

Saunt, Claudio. *"A New Order of Things": Property, Power, and the Transformation of the Creek Indians, 1733–1816*. Cambridge MA: Cambridge University Press, 1999.

Schrager, Bradley Scott. "Yamasee Indians and the Challenge of Spanish and English Colonialism in the North American Southeast, 1660–1715." PhD diss., Northwestern University, 2001.

Schwartz, Stuart. "Indian Labor and New World Plantations: European Demands and Indian Responses in Northeastern Brazil." *American Historical Review* 83 (February 1978): 43–79.

Sheehan, Bernard W. *Savagism and Civility: Englishmen and Indians in Colonial Virginia*. Cambridge MA: Cambridge University Press, 1980.

Sherman, Richard P. *Robert Johnson: Proprietary and Royal Governor of South Carolina*. Columbia: University of South Carolina Press, 1966.

Shoemaker, Nancy, ed. *Negotiators of Change: Historical Perspectives on Native American Women*. New York: Routledge, 1995.

Sirmans, Marion Eugene. *Colonial South Carolina: A Political History*. Chapel Hill: University of North Carolina Press, 1966.

Smith, Louis R., Jr. "British-Indian Trade in Alabama, 1670–1756." *Alabama Review* 27 (January 1974): 65–75.

Smith, Marvin. *Archaeology of Aboriginal Culture Change in the Interior Southeast: Depopulation during the Early Historic Period*. Gainesville: University Press of Florida, 1987.

Snell, William Robert. "Indian Slavery in Colonial South Carolina, 1671–1795." PhD diss., University of Alabama, 1972.

Spalding, Phinizy. *Oglethorpe in America*. Chicago: University of Chicago Press, 1977.

Sturtevant, William C. "Spanish-Indian Relations in Southeastern North America." *Ethnohistory* 9 (Winter 1962): 41–94.

Surrey, Nancy M. *The Commerce of Louisiana during the French Regime: 1699–1763*. New York: Columbia University, 1916.

Swanton, John R. *The Early History of the Creek Indians and Their Neighbors*. Gainesville: University Press of Florida, 1998.

———. "Social Organization and Social Usages of the Indians of the Creek Confederacy." In *Forty-Second Annual Report of the Bureau of American Ethnology*. Washington DC, 1928.

Sweet, Julie Anne. *Negotiating for Georgia: British-Creek Relations in the Trustee Era, 1733–1752*. Athens: University of Georgia Press, 2005.

Thomas, Daniel H. *Fort Toulouse: The French Outpost at the Alabamas on the Coosa*. Tuscaloosa: University of Alabama Press, 1989.

Thompson, Leonard, and Howard Lamar. "Comparative Frontier History." In *The Frontier in History: North America and Southern Africa Compared*, ed. Leonard Thompson and Howard Lamar. New Haven CT: Yale University Press, 1982. 3–13.

Trott, Nicholas. *Laws of the Province of South Carolina, 1663–1734*. Charles Town: Lewis Timothy, 1736. Microfilm, South Carolina Department of Archives and History, Columbia.

Turner, Lorenzo D. *Africanisms in the Gullah Dialect*. Chicago: University of Chicago Press, 1949.

Usner, Daniel H. Jr. "Economic Relations in the Southeast until 1783." In *Handbook of American Indians: History of Indian-White Relations*, ed. Wilcomb E. Washburn, 17 vols. Washington DC: Smithsonian Institution, 1988. 4:391–5.

———. *Indians, Settlers, and Slaves in a Frontier Exchange Economy: The Lower Mississippi Valley Before 1783*. Chapel Hill: University of North Carolina Press, 1992.

Van Kirk, Sylvia. *Many Tender Ties: Women in Fur Trade Society, 1670–1870*. Norman: University of Oklahoma Press, 1983.

Vassar, Rena, ed. "Some Short Remarkes on the Indian Trade in the Charikees and in Managment thereof since the year 1717." *Ethnohistory* 8 (Fall 1961): 401–23.

Wallace, Anthony F. C. "The Origins of Iroquois Neutrality: The Grand Settlement of 1701." *Pennsylvania History* 24 (July 1957): 223–35.

Walton, Gary. "New Evidence on Colonial Commerce." *Journal of Economic History* 28 (September 1968): 363–89.

Waselkov, Gregory A. "The Eighteenth-Century Anglo-Indian Trade in Southeastern North America." In *New Faces of the Fur Trade: Selected Papers of the Seventh North American Fur Trade Conference, Halifax, Nova Scotia, 1995*, ed. Jo-Anne Fiske, Susan Sleeper Smith, and William Wicken. East Lansing: Michigan State University Press, 1998.

———. "The Macon Trading House and Early European-Indian Contact in the Colonial Southeast." In *Ocmulgee Archaeology*, ed. David Halley. Athens: University of Georgia Press, 1994.

———. "Seventeenth-Century Trade in the Colonial Southeast." *Southeastern Archaeology* 8 (1989): 117–30.

Waselkov, Gregory A., John W. Cottier, and Craig T. Sheldon Jr., *Archaeological Excavations at the Early Historic Creek Indian Town of Fusihatchee (Phase I: 1988–89)*. Washington DC: Smithsonian Institution, 1996.

Waselkov, Gregory, and Kathryn Holland Braund, eds. *William Bartram on the Southeastern Indians*. Lincoln: University of Nebraska Press, 1995.

Waselkov, Gregory A., and Marvin T. Smith. "Upper Creek Archaeology." In *Indians of the Greater Southeast: Historical Archaeology and Ethnohistory*, ed. Bonnie G. McEwan. Gainesville: University Press of Florida, 2000.

Wesson, Cameron. "Households and Hegemony: An Analysis of Historic Creek Culture Change." PhD diss., University of Illinois, Urbana–Champaign, 1997.

White, Richard. *The Middle Ground: Indians, Empires, and Republics in the Great Lakes Region, 1650–1815*. Cambridge MA: Cambridge University Press, 1992.

———. *The Roots of Dependency: Subsistence, Environment, and Social Change among the Choctaws, Pawnees, and Navajos*. Lincoln: University of Nebraska Press, 1983.

Williams, Mark. "Growth and Decline of the Oconee Province." In *The*

Forgotten Centuries: Indians and Europeans in the American South, 1521–1704, ed. Charles Hudson and Carmen Chaves Tesser. Athens: University of Georgia Press, 1994. 179–93.

———. "The Origins of the Macon Plateau Site." In *Ocmulgee Archaeology*, ed. David Halley. Athens: University of Georgia Press, 1994.

Willis, William S. "Divide and Rule: Red, White, and Black in the Southeast." *Journal of Negro History* (July 1963): 157–76.

Wood, Peter H. *Black Majority: Negroes in Colonial South Carolina from 1670 through the Stono Rebellion*. New York: W. W. Norton, 1974.

Woods, Patricia. "The French and the Natchez Indians in Louisiana, 1700–1730," *Louisiana History* 29 (1978): 413–35.

———. *French-Indian Relations on the Southern Frontier, 1699–1762*. Ann Arbor: UMI Research Press, 1980.

Worth, John E. "The Lower Creeks: Origins and Early History." In *Indians of the Greater Southeast: Historical Archaeology and Ethnohistory*, ed. Bonnie G. McEwan. Gainesville: University Press of Florida, 2000. 284–85.

Wright, J. Lietch, Jr. *Creeks and Seminoles: The Destruction and Regeneration of the Muscogulge People*. Lincoln: University of Nebraska Press, 1989.

Index

The Invention of the Creek Nation, 1670–1763
By Steven C. Hahn

Bad Fruits of the Civilized Tree
Alcohol and the Sovereignty of the Cherokee Nation
By Izumi Ishii

Epidemics and Enslavement
Biological Catastrophe in the Native Southeast, 1492–1715
By Paul Kelton

An Assumption of Sovereignty
Social and Political Transformation among the Florida Seminoles, 1953–1979
By Harry A. Kersey Jr.

The Caddo Chiefdoms
Caddo Economics and Politics, 700–1835
By David La Vere

The Moravian Springplace Mission to the Cherokees, Volume 1: 1805–1813
The Moravian Springplace Mission to the Cherokees, Volume 2: 1814–1821
Edited and with an introduction by Rowena McClinton

Keeping the Circle
American Indian Identity in Eastern North Carolina, 1885–2004
By Christopher Arris Oakley

Choctaws in a Revolutionary Age, 1750–1830
By Greg O'Brien

Cherokee Women
Gender and Culture Change, 1700–1835
By Theda Perdue

The Brainerd Journal
A Mission to the Cherokees, 1817–1823
Edited and introduced by Joyce B. Phillips and Paul Gary Phillips

The Yamasee War
A Study of Culture, Economy, and Conflict in the Colonial South
By William L. Ramsey

The Cherokees
A Population History
By Russell Thornton

Buffalo Tiger
A Life in the Everglades
By Buffalo Tiger and Harry A. Kersey Jr.

American Indians in the Lower Mississippi Valley
Social and Economic Histories
By Daniel H. Usner Jr.

Powhatan's Mantle
Indians in the Colonial Southeast
Edited by Peter H. Wood, Gregory A. Waselkov, and M. Thomas
Hatley

Creeks and Seminoles
The Destruction and Regeneration of the Muscogulge People
By J. Leitch Wright Jr.

CPSIA information can be obtained at www.ICGtesting.com
Printed in the USA
LVOW11s0619230415

435721LV00001B/31/P